IN THE BARRIOS

IN THE BARRIOS

Latinos and the Underclass Debate

EDITED BY

Joan Moore
and
Raquel Pinderhughes

RUSSELL SAGE FOUNDATION   NEW YORK

The Russell Sage Foundation

The Russell Sage Foundation, one of the oldest of America's general purpose foundations, was established in 1907 by Mrs. Margaret Olivia Sage for "the improvement of
social and living conditions in the United States." The Foundation seeks to fulfill this
mandate by fostering the development and dissemination of knowledge about the country's political, social, and economic problems. While the Foundation endeavors to assure
the accuracy and objectivity of each book it publishes, the conclusions and interpretations
in Russell Sage Foundation publications are those of the authors and not of the Foundation, its Trustees, or its staff. Publication by Russell Sage, therefore, does not imply
Foundation endorsement

Library of Congress Cataloging-in-Publication Data

In the barrios : Latinos and the underclass debate / Joan Moore and
    Raquel Pinderhughes, editors.
        p.   cm.
    Includes bibliographical references and index.
    ISBN 0-87154-612-4 (hard) — ISBN 0-87154-613-2 (pbk.)
    1. Hispanic Americans—Economic conditions.   2. Hispanic
Americans—Social conditions.   3. Poor—United States.   4. United
States—Economic conditions—1981–   I. Moore, Joan W.
II. Pinderhughes, Raquel.
E184.S7515   1993
305.868–dc20   93-17668
                                                                    CIP

RUSSELL SAGE FOUNDATION
112 East 64th Street, New York, New York 10021

10 9 8 7 6 5 4 3 2 1

CONTENTS

ACKNOWLEDGMENTS

This book has been a cooperative venture throughout. The editors collaborated in the editorial process and in writing the introduction. It gives us particular pleasure to be able to thank the colleagues and friends who supported us in this endeavor. This book would not have been written without the support of Eric Wanner and the Russell Sage Foundation board. Patricia Fernandez-Kelly, Maxine Baca Zinn, and Herbert Gans found time to review an earlier draft of the volume and the book is better as a consequence of their comments. Lisa Nachtigall, publications director at Russell Sage, and Anna Marie Muskelly, managing editor, were helpful throughout. Bradley Javenkoski and Donna Schenstrom of the Cartographic Services Lab at the University of Wisconsin–Milwaukee designed the maps especially for this book. We also thank Jaime Castañenda and Ron Peleck of the SSRC. The contributors shared insights that extended beyond their assigned topics and helped us shape the volume into a coherent whole. Our husbands, Howard Pinderhughes and Burton Moore, were consistently helpful. We extend a special thanks to them for their intellectual contribution, love, and support.

Joan Moore
Raquel Pinderhughes

NOTES ON CONTRIBUTORS

Norma Stoltz Chinchilla is professor of women's studies and sociology and director of women's studies at California State University, Long Beach. She has written articles on women and social movements in Latin America, social and economic change in Central America, and is doing research on Central American immigration to Los Angeles with Nora Hamilton.

Phillip Gonzales is associate professor of sociology at the University of New Mexico. He is co-author of *Sunbelt Working Mothers: Reconciling Family and Factory* (1993). He has written articles and chapters on Latino collective action and ethnopolitical identity and maintains an interest in interactional and historical sociology.

Guillermo J. Grenier is director of the Florida Center for Labor Research and Studies and associate professor and chairman of the department of sociology/anthropology at Florida International University. He is the author of *Inhuman Relations: Quality Circles and Anti-Unionism in American Industry* (1988). Forthcoming books include *Night for Hard Houses: Hurricane Andrew and the Reshaping of Miami* and *Labor, Community and Capital: Immigrants and Economic Restructuring in the United States.*

Nora Hamilton is associate professor of political science at the University of Southern California and author of *The Limits of State Autonomy: Post Revolutionary Mexico* (1982). In addition to her research with Norma Chinchilla, she is working on collaborative research on regional economic cooperation in Central America and Southern Africa and on economic liberalization and political reform in Mexico and South Korea.

James Loucky, associate professor of anthropology at Western Washington University, has conducted research on family relations and social and economic change in highland Guatemala for twenty years. Since the early 1980s, he has worked with Latin American communities in the United States and Canada, concentrating on role shifts associated with immigration, children's learning at home and in school, and identity issues.

Joan Moore is professor of sociology at the University of Wisconsin-Milwaukee. She has been doing research with Chicano gangs in Los Angeles since the mid 1970s: *Homeboys* (1978) and *Going Down to the Barrio* (1991) represent this research. She has also co-edited a volume on *Drugs in Hispanic Communities* (1991). This focus is part of a long-standing concern with poverty.

Felix M. Padilla is professor of sociology and anthropology at Northeastern University. He is founder and editor of the *Latino Studies Journal*, and author of *The Gang as an American Enterprise* and *Outside the Prison: One Woman's Struggle*.

Raquel Pinderhughes is assistant professor of urban studies at San Francisco State University. Her research areas and interests include the social psychological impact of unemployment on U.S. workers, Latino immigration to the United States, the social and economic conditions of Latinos in the United States, and the relationship between race, poverty, and the environment.

Nestor P. Rodriguez is associate professor of sociology at the University of Houston. His research areas and interests include immigration and urban restructuring, relations between established residents and newcomers, and spatial semiotics.

Alex Stepick is director of both the comparative sociology graduate program and the Institute for Immigration and Ethnicity at Florida International University in Miami. He is the co-author of *City on the Edge: The Transformation of Miami* (1993) and *Social Inequality in Oaxaca (Mexico): A History of Resistance and Change* (1991). In 1988, he received the Margaret Mead Award for his work with Haitian refugees.

Mercer Sullivan is senior research associate at the Community Development Research Center of the New School for Social Research where he is directing a major study of the effects of community development on the lives of residents of poor neighborhoods. A social anthropologist, he is the author of *Getting Paid: Youth Crime and Work in the Inner City* (1990) and other ethnographic studies of the relationship between community context and human development.

Avelardo Valdez is associate professor of sociology at the University of Texas at San Antonio and a Fulbright Scholar. He has published extensively in the areas of Chicano social stratification and Chicano-Mexicano relations. His current research focuses on heroin use among Mexican Americans.

Carlos G. Vélez-Ibáñez is director of the Bureau of Applied Research in Anthropology and professor of anthropology at the University of Arizona. His books include *Bonds of Mutual Trust: The Cultural Systems of Rotating Credit Associations Among Urban Mexicans and Chicanos* (1983) and *Rituals of Marginality: Politics, Process, and Cultural Change in Central Urban Mexico* (1983).

James Diego Vigil is professor of anthropology at the University of Southern California. An urban anthropologist, he is author of *Barrio Gangs* (1988) and is presently completing a book on culture and education in the adolescent Mexican American community.

INTRODUCTION

Joan Moore and Raquel Pinderhughes

THIS BOOK began to take shape in 1987, after the publication of *The Truly Disadvantaged*, William Julius Wilson's seminal work on persistent, concentrated poverty in Chicago's black neighborhoods. In that book, Wilson used the term "underclass" to refer to the new face of poverty, and traced its origins to economic restructuring. He emphasized the impact of persistent, concentrated poverty not only on individuals but on communities.

This volume is one response to Wilson's new paradigm. It emerged out of a series of discussions among scholars who have been engaged for many years in in-depth research in poor Latino communities. We were concerned about the applicability of Wilson's framework beyond the Rustbelt black communities that were his particular focus. The authors examine Latino communities in eight cities—New York, Los Angeles, Miami, Houston, Chicago, Albuquerque, Laredo, and Tucson.

The term "Hispanic" is used particularly by state bureaucracies to refer to individuals who reside in the United States who were born in, or trace their ancestry back to, one of twenty-three Spanish-speaking nations. Many of these individuals prefer to use the term "Latino," and in this chapter that term is used.

The Underclass Debate

It is clear that there is as yet no consensus about the term "underclass" or about the concepts behind it. The debate about whether the American urban poor can be characterized as an "underclass" is part of a larger debate about urban poverty in the United States. The terms of that debate have shifted significantly over the past two decades. In the sixties and seventies the debate focused on matters of labor-supply resources, tax rates, and equal opportunity. In the eighties, the emphasis shifted to dependency and joblessness, with emphasis on their radiating consequences (Ellwood 1988). Currently, the debate reflects a deep concern about a group of people who manifest a distinctive set of values, attitudes, beliefs, norms, and behaviors (Ricketts and Sawhill 1988; Morris 1989; Wilson 1987).

The underclass debate can also be seen as an extension of the debate about who is responsible for the condition of the poor—the individual or society? Is persistent poverty caused by behavioral pathology or the economic structure?

Up through the mid-1970s, the rich literature on poverty shows few mentions of the term "underclass".[1] When the term appears, it usually refers to the poorest of the poor. After the mid-1970s scholars began to add residential, ethnic, racial, and behavioral criteria to define this population. At this time the underclass began to be seen as a predominantly urban population, as illustrated by a 1977 article in *Time* magazine (Russell 1977) emphasizing the underclass as a subset of the poor who are overwhelmingly urban. The overall image of the underclass presented in that article was that of an urban group that was prone to crime and welfare, holding values at odds with those of the mainstream (Wilson 1989). That same year Frank Levy, in an unpublished but widely circulated paper (1977), added another element by using the term to describe a subgroup of the poor who remained poor for long periods of time—the chronic, persistently poor. Using data from a panel study of income sources (the PSID), Levy produced estimates of the size of the persistently poor population. He emphasized that it was their inability to escape from poverty that distinguished the underclass from other poor Americans.

The term gained widespread popularity when New York journalist Ken Auletta published three articles in *The New Yorker* magazine and a book entitled *The Underclass* (1982). Auletta was concerned with the increase in socially dysfunctional behaviors among a diverse population living in New York City in the late 1970s: chronically jobless men, welfare mothers, alcoholics, drug dealers, street criminals, and the mentally ill. To describe this very diverse group, Auletta chose the term "underclass", which he described as a group that "feels excluded from society, rejects commonly accepted values, suffers from behavioral as well as income deficiencies. They don't just tend to be poor; to most Americans their behavior seems aberrant" (1982, p. xiii).

Cultural interpretations, like Auletta's, claim that the values, attitudes, and expectations of certain subgroups are outside the mainstream and that these values persist precisely because the group being discussed is socially isolated from the mainstream. They maintain that this explains why an "underclass" subculture can be sustained and transmitted intergenerationally. Morris (1989) points out that in social science discussions of poverty there has been a dramatic decline in the number of listings under "culture" and a dramatic increase in the number under "underclass". But he also recalled Matza's assertion that "shifting terms to designate the same entity is a familiar phenomenon in social science" (Matza 1966, p. 289).

By the late 1980s social scientists and policy makers were using the term "underclass" to describe an even more specific sector of the persistently poor population—that group of able-bodied Americans, young black males in particular, who experienced long-term detachment from the formal labor market. Now it was not long-term poverty that was emphasized, but, rather, long-term detachment from the labor force. This is what separated the "underclass" from other persistently poor people. It was the emphasis on lack of attachment to the labor force and on dependency, the distinction between the non-working poor and the working poor, and the movement away from issues of income that infused discussions of the underclass with heavy moral overtones.

No matter what the details, when one examines the history of the term among sociologists, it is clear that Wilson's 1987 work seriously jolted the somewhat chaotic and unfocused study of poverty in the United States. He described sharply increased rates of what he called "pathology" in Chicago's black ghettos. By this, Wilson referred specifically to female headship, declining marriage rates, illegitimate births, welfare dependency, school dropouts, and youth crime. The changes in the communities he examined were so dramatic that he considered them something quite new.

Two of the causes of this new poverty were particularly important, and his work shifted the terms of the debate in two respects. First, Wilson argued effectively that dramatic increases in joblessness and long-term poverty in the inner city were a result of major economic shifts—economic restructuring. "Restructuring" referred to changes in the global economy that led to deindustrialization, loss and relocation of jobs, and a decline in the number of middle-level jobs—a polarization of the labor market. Second, he further fueled the debate about the causes and consequences of persistent poverty by introducing two neighborhood-level factors into the discussion. He argued that the outmigration of middle- and working-class people from the urban ghetto contributed to the concentration of poverty. These "concentration effects" meant that ghetto neighborhoods showed sharply increased proportions of very poor people. This, in turn, meant that residents in neighborhoods of concentrated poverty were isolated from "mainstream" institutions and role models. As a result, Wilson postulates, the likelihood of their engaging in "underclass behavior" was increased. Thus the social life of poor communities deteriorated because poverty intensified.

By the eighties, both liberals and conservatives agreed that there was indeed a major problem in the increasingly large percentage of young black men who were not employed in the regular economy. But they disagreed about its root causes. Conservatives like Charles Murray and Lawrence Mead argued that welfare and the Great Society programs encouraged blacks to become dependent on public assistance and that chronic poverty was a result of the reluctance of the poor to commit themselves to work. Liberals like Wilson argued that recent structural changes—and most importantly the decline of the industrial sector in the Rustbelt—had a devastating affect on poor blacks. Large-scale social and economic changes in the structure of the urban ghetto had cut these young men off from job networks, making it almost impossible for them to find stable employment.

Conservatives and liberals also disagreed about the larger significance of male joblessness. Conservatives emphasized the negative effects of welfare and government assistance. Because they believed that jobs are available, they argued that these men need to change their attitudes and behaviors and accept low wages in entry-level jobs in order independently to support their families and establish bridges to better jobs. In contrast, liberals emphasized job loss and lack of access to jobs. They argued that inner-city blacks are cut off from job networks and that their attitudes and behaviors are a consequence of long-term joblessness and poverty and can be changed with employment and the alleviation of poverty.

An extraordinary spate of research followed the appearance of *The Truly Disadvantaged*, along with an intense debate among scholars. Some of the so-called underclass debate has been semantic, focusing on whether the term "underclass" is in fact a valid or a useful term. In fact, Wilson in 1990 agreed with his critics that the term itself had distracting connotations, and should be dropped. He substituted the term "the ghetto poor" for "the underclass". Most of the debate, however, has been around the substantive question of whether the nature of American urban poverty really has changed as dramatically as Wilson and others argued. And if so, has it changed evenly, in all regions, for all races and ethnic groups, and for the same causes? Further, what is the value of distinguishing the "ghetto poor" from the totality of all poor people?

It has proved very difficult to test Wilson's specific points— especially with the data that are most readily available, those from the census. For example, Urban Research Institute scholars Erol Ricketts and Isabel Sawhill postulated that in 1980 about 2.5 million persons lived in 880 census tracts that constituted "underclass areas". They defined the underclass as those who engage in "various socially costly behaviors" (1988, p. 321); the behaviors were measured by high school dropouts, males not working regularly, households receiving public assistance, and households with children headed by women. There were a number of criticisms of this and similar measures of the underclass, but to a large extent their shortcomings reflect the difficulties inherent in using census data to measure a complex social reality.

In seeking to explain this complex social reality, Wilson's hypotheses about the neighborhood consequences of economic restructuring generated a new interest in ethnographic research. Elijah Anderson, for example, examined shifting norms and social controls in a poor African American neighborhood. Mercer Sullivan (1989a) compared the resources available to young black, Puerto Rican, and white men making the transition to adulthood. This current volume reflects that regenerated interest in ethnographic research.

Scholars engaged in research on poverty in Latino communities were often critical of Wilson's framework, but intrigued by his analysis. Although he focused exclusively on black poverty, much of what Wilson described at the neighborhood level was familiar to scholars examining poverty in Latino communities—but it needed modification. Moore (1989) summarized the value of certain elements of the analysis and some of the potential modifications in an early overview of existing research evidence. She concluded that economic restructuring was clearly an important factor in understanding Latino poverty. However, since most Latinos are located outside the Rustbelt, analyses of their poverty needed to take into account the diverse forms that economic restructuring has taken in different parts of the United States. Then again, Wilson's emphasis on the importance of migration in contributing to the development of an urban black "underclass" fell short when applied to Latinos. Wilson was concerned with out-migration of middle-class residents from the ghettos: by contrast, any examination of Latino poverty needed to consider how the vast wave of new, poor immigrants affected poor neighborhoods. There was much evidence that immigration is not only important but often critical.

The overview also suggested that by contrast with Wilson's portrayal of the decay of the black family and other institutions, Latino institutions were generally viable. The evidence on familism was skimpy, but there was good reason to believe that in many areas Latino families still operate to support and control their members. The evidence about street problems was very mixed: certainly it is not generally an occasion for despair, bad as it is in some locales.

The authors in this book discuss many of these issues in much greater depth. One by one, they argue that the Latino communities they study are quite different from the black communities studied by Wilson. Some authors document dramatic changes, but others see much less change. They agree, however, that what is happening in these Latino communities warrants special attention. They show especially that the particular sources of change that Wilson identified need extensive rethinking if they are to be applied to poverty among Latinos.

Most of the remainder of this introductory essay focuses on how the studies in this volume alter the way in which we look at Wilson's three major factors: economic restructuring (including the informal economy), immigration, and concentration effects. In addition, we consider two factors that scholars immersed in the underclass debate have generally neglected. These factors are significant not only in the communities our authors profile but in poor communities throughout the nation. First, these studies point out that location in the city plays a role in poverty. Second, they make it clear that the depletion of publicly supported activities has had a baneful influence on life in poor communities.

The underclass debate has been framed largely in terms of African American communities. This is not surprising, because Latinos have generally been poorly understood, and the rich literature on their communities is familiar only to a limited group of scholars. We hope that this volume will change the terms of the debate by including Latinos, but here we must deal with the generally low level of information about the population and its problems. Thus, before we discuss the studies in this volume and how they amplify and broaden the underclass debate, we offer some minimal background on the Latino population and how its poverty has been conceptualized in the past.

The Latino Population—Some Background

American minorities have been incorporated into the general social fabric in a variety of ways. Just as Chicago's black ghettos reflect a history of slavery, Jim Crow legislation, and struggles for civil and economic rights, so the nation's Latino barrios reflect a history of conquest, immigration, and a struggle to maintain cultural identity.

In 1990 there were some 22 million Latinos residing in the United States, approximately 9 percent of the total population. Of these, 61 percent were Mexican in origin, 12 percent Puerto Rican, and 5 percent Cuban. These three groups were the largest, yet 13 percent of Latinos were of Central and South American origin and another 9 percent were classified as "other Hispanic".[2] Latinos were among the fastest-growing segments of the American population, increasing by 7.6 million, or 53 percent, between 1980 and 1990. There are predictions that Latinos will outnumber blacks by the twenty-first century. If Latino immigration and fertility continue at their current rate, there will be over 54 million Latinos in the United States by the year 2020.

This is an old population: as early as the sixteenth century, Spanish explorers settled what is now the American Southwest. In 1848, Spanish and Mexican settlers who lived in that region became United States citizens as a result of the Mexican-American War. Although the aftermath of conquest left a small elite population, the precarious position of the masses combined with the peculiarities of southwestern economic development to lay the foundation for poverty in the current period (see Barrera 1979; Moore and Pachon 1985).

In addition to those Mexicans who were incorporated into the United States after the Treaty of Guadalupe Hidalgo, Mexicans have continually crossed the border into the United States, where they have been used as a source of cheap labor by U.S. employers. The volume of immigration from Mexico has been highly dependent on fluctuations in certain segments of the U.S. economy. This dependence became glaringly obvious earlier in this century. During the Great Depression of the 1930s state and local governments "repatriated" hundreds of thousands of unemployed Mexicans, and just a few years later World War II labor shortages reversed the process as Mexican contract-laborers (*braceros*) were eagerly sought. A little later, in the 1950s, massive deportations recurred when "operation Wetback" repatriated hundreds of thousands of Mexicans. Once again, in the 1980s, hundreds of thousands crossed the border to work in the United States, despite increasingly restrictive legislation.

High levels of immigration and high fertility mean that the Mexican-origin population is quite young—on the average, 9.5 years younger than the non-Latino population—and the typical household is large, with 3.8 persons, as compared with 2.6 persons in non-Latino households (U.S. Bureau of the Census 1991b). Heavy immigration, problems in schooling, and industrial changes in the Southwest combine to constrain advancement. The occupational structure remains relatively steady, and though there is a growing middle class, there is also a growing number of very poor people.

The incorporation of Puerto Ricans into the United States began in 1898, when the United States took possession of Puerto Rico and Cuba during the Spanish-American War. Although Cuba gained its independence in 1902, Puerto Rico became a commonwealth of the United States in 1952. Thus Puerto Rican citizens are also citizens of the United States. The colonial relationship strongly influenced the structure of the Puerto Rican economy and the migration of Puerto Ricans to the mainland. As a result of the U.S. invasion, the island's economy was transformed from a diversified, subsistence economy, which emphasized tobacco, cattle, coffee, and sugar, to a one-crop sugar economy, of which more than 60 percent was controlled by absentee U.S. owners (Steward 1956). The constriction of the sugar economy in the 1920s resulted in high unemployment and widespread poverty, and propelled the first wave of Puerto Rican migration to the United States (C. Rodriguez 1989).

Puerto Rican migration to the mainland took place in roughly three periods (Stevens-Arroyo and Diaz-Ramirez 1974). The first, 1900–1945, was marked by the arrival of rural migrants forced to leave the island to find work after some of these economic transformations. Many migrants directly responded to U.S. companies who valued Puerto Rican citizenship status and experience in agriculture and recruited Puerto Rican laborers for agriculture and industry in the United States (Morales 1986; Maldonado, 1972). Almost all settled in New York City, most working in low-skilled occupations.

The second period, 1946–1964, is known as the "great migration" because it was during this period that the greatest number of Puerto Ricans migrated. This movement reflected factors that included the search for work, artificially low fares between the island and New York arranged by the island government, labor recruitment, and the emergence of Puerto Rican settlements on the mainland. Though Puerto Ricans were still relegated to low-wage jobs, they were employed in large numbers.

The period after 1965 has been characterized by a fluctuating pattern of net migration as well as greater dispersion to parts of the United States away from New York City (C. Rodriguez 1989). It is known as the "revolving-door migration": during most of this period the heavy flow from the island to the mainland was balanced by equally substantial flows in the opposite direction. However, since 1980 the net outflows from Puerto Rico have rivaled those experienced in the 1950s.

Over the past three decades the economic status of Puerto Ricans dropped precipitously. By 1990, 38 percent of all Puerto Rican families were below the poverty line. A growing proportion of these families were concentrated in poor urban neighborhoods located in declining industrial centers in the Northeast and Midwest, which experienced massive economic restructuring and diminished employment opportunities for those with less education and weaker skills. The rising poverty rate has also been linked to a dramatic increase in female-headed households. Recent studies show that the majority of recent migrants were not previously employed on the island. Many were single women who migrated with their young children (Falcon and Gurak 1991). Currently, Puerto Ricans are the most economically disadvantaged group of all Latinos. As a group they are poorer than African Americans.

Unlike other Latino migrants, who entered the United States as subordinate workers and were viewed as sources of cheap labor, the first large waves of Cuban refugees were educated middle- and upper-class professionals. Arriving in large numbers after Castro's 1959 revolution, Cubans were welcomed by the federal government as bona fide political refugees fleeing communism and were assisted in ways that significantly contributed to their economic well-being. Cubans had access to job-training programs and placement services, housing subsidies, English-language programs, and small-business loans. Federal and state assistance contributed to the growth of a vigorous enclave economy (with Cubans owning many of the businesses and hiring fellow Cubans) and also to the emergence of Miami as a center for Latin American trade. Cubans have the highest family income of all Latino groups. Nevertheless, in 1990, 16.9 percent of the Cuban population lived below the poverty line.

In recent years large numbers of Salvadorans and Guatemalans have come to the United States in search of refuge from political repression. But unlike Cubans, few have been recognized by the U.S. government as bona fide refugees. Their settlement and position in the labor market have been influenced by their undocumented (illegal) status. Dominicans have also come in large numbers to East Coast cities, many also arriving as undocumented workers. Working for the lowest wages and minimum job security, undocumented workers are among the poorest in the nation.

Despite their long history and large numbers, Latinos have been an "invisible minority" in the United States. Until recently, few social scientists and policy analysts concerned with understanding stratification and social problems in the United States have noticed them. Because they were almost exclusively concerned with relations between blacks and whites, social scientists were primarily concerned with generating demographic information on the nation's black and white populations, providing almost no information on other groups.[3] Consequently, it has been difficult, sometimes impossible, to obtain accurate data about Latinos.

Latinos began to be considered an important minority group when census figures showed a huge increase in the population. By 1980 there were significant Latino communities in almost every metropolitan area in the nation. As a group, Latinos have low education, low family incomes, and are more clustered in low-paid, less-skilled occupations. Most Latinos live in cities, and poverty has become an increasing problem. On the whole, Latinos are more likely to live in poverty than the general U.S. population: poverty is widespread for all Latino subgroups except Cubans. They were affected by structural factors that influenced the socioeconomic status of all U.S. workers. In 1990, 28 percent were poor as compared with 13 percent of all Americans and 32 percent of African Americans (U.S. Bureau of the Census 1991b). Puerto Ricans were particularly likely to be poor.

Views of Latino Poverty: Earlier Studies of Poor Latino Communities

Not all Latinos are poor, however, and since the earliest settlements in the sixteenth century there has always been considerable class variation. Most studies of Latinos have concentrated on the poor and, during the 1940s, 1950s, and 1960s, primarily on Mexican Americans. After the great migration, mainland Puerto Ricans also began to be studied. Until very recently, Cubans, Dominicans, and Central Americans were not numerous enough to attract wide attention.

There are few forerunners of the underclass debate in the studies of poor Mexican Americans. Many of the early studies focused either on rural communities or on semirural barrios in the Southwest. These have included important exposés of the conditions of migrant workers (McWilliams 1942; Galarza 1965; Taylor 1928, 1930). Castelike conditions, with severe discrimination, were discovered in several towns (Goldschmidt 1947; Taylor 1934).

One of the features that distinguished the early literature on Mexican American poverty was a fascination with the special traits of Mexican American culture. This fascination has several sources. Some of it reflects popular culture: movies and novels tended to romanticize the sturdy, rural Mexican American poor, as images from John Steinbeck's novels shaped the very faint American consciousness of actual conditions. In addition, among the social scientists it was mostly anthropologists who were attracted to southwestern populations, and they were intrigued by what they saw as the tenacity of Mexican culture. The *Manitos* of New Mexico—a people culturally isolated in the upper Rio Grande Valley since the sixteenth century—received particular notice (see Edmundson 1957; Kluckhohn and Strodtbeck 1961; Leonard and Loomis 1938; Sanchez 1940; Saunders 1954). A little later, the culture of rural Texas along the U.S.–Mexico border also drew academic attention (Madsen 1964; Rubel 1966). Some of these studies had direct practical application as resources for health and mental-health-care providers to these rural populations. Although this work enhanced cultural awareness, some of the studies were criticized because they were used to reinforce cultural stereotypes about, for example, the overwhelming importance of fatalism and familistic values as a subcultural complex found among all Mexican Americans, which was viewed as responsible for poverty (Montiel 1970; Romano-V 1968; Vaca 1970). It is dangerous to assume that the values prevalent in isolated New Mexican villages are also common in the barrios of Los Angeles. More generally, it is dangerous to assume that such values lead to poverty. Ironically, in the 1990s the aspect of Mexican American culture that draws the greatest attention is its so-called work ethic, which is—misleadingly—counterposed to what is assumed to be a diminished work ethic among African Americans.

Urban communities were less frequently studied in the early years. A few investigators of urban Latino life were driven by the concerns with culture—especially with beliefs about health and mental health—that inspired so much of the rural research (esp. Clark 1959; Crawford 1961). Only a handful of scholars argued that Mexican American urban poverty was the result of structural factors (McWilliams 1949; Menefee and Cassmore 1940). Social problems and structural conditions were rarely a concern[4] (see Grebler, Moore, and Guzman 1970 for a review of urban studies and for findings of survey studies in Los Angeles and San Antonio.)

By contrast, studies of Puerto Ricans on the mainland emphasized class composition and settlement patterns, predominantly in New York City. This emphasis was evident as early as the 1930s, and persisted throughout the post–World War II period. These studies were largely concerned with the demographic characteristics of Puerto Rican migrants. Contrary to popular belief, which stereotypes the 1940s migrants as unskilled illiterates, a series of early studies (Mills et al. 1950; Senior 1965; Chenault 1938; Gosnell 1949; Handlin 1959) showed that even though the majority of Puerto Rican migrants were employed in working-class occupations, they were well prepared to enter the urban (mainland) work force. Sociologist Clara Rodriguez states that the early Puerto Rican migrants were "superior" (1989, p. 5).

After World War II a significant number of studies on Puerto Ricans in the United States began to anticipate some of the concerns in the underclass literature (Padilla 1958; Rand 1958; Wakefield 1959). These studies examined the post-1950 migrant communities, focusing on problems experienced by Puerto Rican migrants. They characterized "the great migration" population as poorly prepared for the urban work force—younger, unskilled, predominantly rural, with limited work experience outside of agriculture. In addition, in contrast to the 1940s migration, which included large numbers of Puerto Rican women, the 1950s migration brought much larger numbers of men. A heated debate developed in the 1960s focusing on Oscar Lewis' *La Vida, A Puerto Rican Family in the Culture of Poverty*, which argued that Puerto Ricans in a San Juan barrio were living in a culture of poverty that undermined their capacity for upward mobility. Glazer and Moynihan's 1970 study struck another theme, identifying overdependence on the welfare state as the group's major problem on both the island and the mainland. Mainland Puerto Ricans were characterized as politically passive and nonparticipatory as a result of their political dependence on the United States, and it was claimed that they had a "welfare mentality" with regard to government generally. These conclusions were also hotly contested.

Studies examining Puerto Ricans in the 1970s continued to emphasize the socioeconomic problems faced by Puerto Ricans on the mainland. Wagenheim (1975) found unemployment among Puerto Ricans to be almost six times as high as the figure nationwide, and educational levels to be lower than those of black and white Americans. Average income lagged far behind that of other Americans, with no signs of advancement as a consequence of the nation's "War on Poverty". He saw rapidly shrinking job opportunities in urban areas in the Northeast, particularly for unskilled and semiskilled males— a somber predictor of the struggle Puerto Ricans would face in the 1980s.

The Communities in this Volume

The national image of urban poverty has come to be that of the Rustbelt black ghetto. This volume portrays a very different, largely neglected dimension of urban poverty and a variety of economic circumstances. The authors have been studying their communities for many years. Their reports utilize a wide range of research approaches, including long-range participant observation, ethnographic interviewing and analysis, interviews with key informants, systematic surveys, and analysis of statistical and other official data and historical documents.

Although the selection of communities was opportunistic and although the very poorest (like the South Bronx) are not represented, almost all the communities analyzed in this book are poor, with poverty rates hovering around 20 percent or higher. The studies begin with three cities with rapidly growing Latino populations— New York, Los Angeles, and Miami. In a working-class Puerto Rican community in Brooklyn, Mercer Sullivan finds substantial "institutional resiliency", along with a number of problems and a wide diversity of adaptations to the changed economic circumstances. Superficially, the Puerto Rican pattern of high teen pregnancy rates resembles that of blacks, but Sullivan argues that the outcome of these pregnancies is very different. He also suggests that the high frequency of female-headed households among Puerto Ricans may be misleading. Sullivan also discusses the pattern of transition from school to work and characterizes it as one of early school-leaving and labor-force entry. However, he emphasizes that work careers include many spells of joblessness and severe restrictions on job opportunities.

Joan Moore and Diego Vigil portray four Chicano communities that stretch east from downtown Los Angeles. Though there are differences along this urban-rural continuum, all of these long-standing Chicano communities have been particularly affected by economic shifts and by the recent massive immigration of low-wage laborers from Mexico. Schools and other institutions have been seriously strained by this influx, and the strain occurs within the context of a restructured government in which the tradition of community advocacy established during the activist days of the 1960s has all but disappeared. However, immigrants appear to have had a revitalizing effect at the neighborhood level. Street problems have been contained, and community controls appear to be effective.

On the other side of Los Angeles, just west of the central business district, Nora Hamilton and Norma Chinchilla describe a very poor community of Central American immigrants who arrived in large numbers only after the economy had shifted away from its manufacturing base. Community-building efforts face rough going in a neighborhood that is hard-pressed both by wealthy developers and by interethnic strains; many Central Americans were drawn into the protest riots that rocked Los Angeles in the spring of 1992.

New York and Los Angeles Latinos have all been deeply affected by large-scale deindustrialization, but Miami is different. Cubans are generally characterized as the "successful" Latinos. Alex Stepick and Guillermo Grenier argue that this success is due partly to "massive state assistance" and political capital of these refugees from communism, and partly to the economic and social capital they brought to the United States. Miami's thriving enclave economy and intense community solidarity also help reduce poverty, but they conceal the exploitation of the poor, and of women workers in particular.

Houston presents a classic boom-and-bust situation, in what is anything but a traditional Sunbelt city. But Nestor Rodriguez contends that to understand poverty in the city's Latino communities one must go beyond the economy. Recent Mexican and Central American immigrants were deeply affected by the social and cultural organization of the receiving communities, and by the extent to which they were concentrated and culturally isolated: manipulation by real estate interests played a significant role. Rodriguez argues that "concentration effects" have been positive. Poverty has indeed become more compacted, but the concentration of immigrants has also encouraged an ethnic economy and provided a comfortable cultural ambience and access to useful networks.

Felix Padilla analyzes another neighborhood of working-class poor in Chicago—one that Puerto Ricans call "Suburbia" even though it is well within the city's limits. Padilla emphasizes the irony of Puerto Ricans' trying to build their communities just at the time when their chances for economic well-being were so drastically reduced. The informal economy and drug dealing play a significant role in "Suburbia", but there are strong community-based organizations and, as in Houston, a lively ethnic economy despite the many problems.

Albuquerque, Laredo, and Tucson—part of the traditional Mexican American Southwest—have been peripheral to the dramatic economic changes that provide the underpinning for the underclass debate. Therefore, Latino poverty survives in a very different context. In Albuquerque, poverty as Phillip Gonzales analyzes it is found partly in very old, traditionalist "urban villages", now undermined by urban expansion, and partly in newer, less tightly integrated settlements of Chicano in-migrants and Mexican immigrants. History is more important than recent economic restructuring in understanding the social organization of these poor communities.

Avelardo Valdez looks at three barrios in the predominantly Chicano border city of Laredo, one of the poorest communities in the nation. He concentrates on the city's appalling poverty, its deep entanglement with the Mexican economy, and the importance of illicit money-making activities. Though there have been drastic economic shifts, poverty did not change. A generations-old pattern of class relations simply got stronger. However, economic restructuring is not confined simply to Rustbelt-style deindustrialization: the free-trade agreement between Mexico and its northern neighbors will promote a massive restructuring with a particularly strong impact on border communities.

Finally, Carlos Vélez-Ibáñez focuses on the Borderlands context of Mexican American poverty in Tucson, and on the extraordinary functioning of cross-border and cross-class "household clusters" of relatives and nonrelated families. These clusters provide access to practical and emotional resources and to deeply rooted "funds of knowledge". These long-lasting networks play a role in community revitalization, as well.

We are now in a position to advance some generalizations about what these studies add to the underclass debate. We will begin with the first major factor in Wilson's approach—economic restructuring.

The Importance of Economic Restructuring

The meaning of economic restructuring has shaped the debate about the urban underclass, and the studies in this volume suggest that the simpler formulations must be amplified. The earliest evidence of a new and important economic change appeared in the 1970s. Jobs seemed to be relocating: they declined massively in some formerly prosperous parts of the country and grew quickly in other, formerly peripheral regions—especially the South and West (Perry and Watkins 1977). It became obvious that the nation as a whole was losing "good" manufacturing jobs as production became internationalized (AFL-CIO Industrial Union Department 1986; Bluestone and Harrison 1982). In the 1990s, white-collar employment began to be restructured as well.

By the late 1980s there was consensus that the geographical shift in the location of job growth was a manifestation of a second and more important aspect of economic restructuring—the shift from a manufacturing to a service economy, and of the increasing globalization of the economy. This was a major transformation, and it became obvious that traditional manufacturing was not going to revive. Jobs continued to be created in the new service and information economy, but many were disproportionately at either the high or the low end of the wage and salary distributions, and many of the new firms functioned without the internal differentiation that might permit workers to move up within the company.[5]

Rustbelt manufacturing decline and Sunbelt growth have come to epitomize what economic restructuring means. But in reality things are a lot more subtle, a lot more complex, and demand a more elaborate conceptualization, especially as these trends affect Latino poverty. Elements of a more complex model are being developed by a number of researchers, but as of this writing none is yet adequate to understand the shifts that are evident in the cities represented in this volume. Several of these deserve particular emphasis.

First, there is the "Rustbelt in the Sunbelt" phenomenon. Some researchers have argued that deindustrialization has been limited to the Rustbelt, and that the causal chain adduced by Wilson therefore does not apply outside that region. But the fact is that many Sunbelt cities developed manufacturing industries, particularly during and after World War II. Thus Rustbelt-style economic restructuring—deindustrialization, in particular—has also affected them deeply. In the late 1970s and early 1980s cities like Los Angeles experienced a major wave of plant closings that put a fair number of Latinos out of work (Morales 1985; Soja, Morales, and Wolff 1983).

Second, there has been significant reindustrialization and many new jobs in many of these cities, a trend that is easily overlooked. Most of the expanding low-wage service and manufacturing industries, like electronics and garment manufacturing, employ Latinos (McCarthy and Valdez 1986; Muller and Espenshade 1986), and some depend almost completely on immigrant labor working at minimum wage (Fernandez-Kelly and Sassen 1991). In short, neither the Rustbelt nor the Sunbelt has seen uniform economic restructuring.

Third, Latinos are affected by the "global cities" phenomenon, particularly evident in New York and Chicago. This term refers to a particular mix of new jobs and populations and an expansion of both high- and low-paid service jobs (see Sassen-Koob 1984). When large multinational corporations centralize their service functions, upper-level service jobs expand. The growing corporate elite want more restaurants, more entertainment, more clothing, and more care for their homes and children, but these new consumer services usually pay low wages and offer only temporary and part-time work. The new service workers in turn generate their own demand for low-cost goods and services. Many of them are Latino immigrants and they create what Sassen calls a "Third World city . . . located in dense groupings spread all over the city": this new "city" also provides new jobs (1989, p. 70).

Los Angeles, the third global city in this volume, has experienced many of these patterns.[6] The loss of manufacturing jobs has been far less visible than in New York or Chicago, for although traditional manufacturing declined, until the 1990s high-tech manufacturing did not. Moreover, Los Angeles' international financial and trade functions flourished (Soja 1987). The real difference between Los Angeles on the one hand and New York and Chicago on the other was that more poor people in Los Angeles seemed to be working.[7] In all three cities internationalization had similar consequences for the *structure* of jobs for the poor. More of the immigrants pouring into Los Angeles were finding jobs, while the poor residents of New York and Chicago were not.

Fourth, even though the deindustrialization framework remains of overarching importance in understanding variations in the urban context of Latino poverty, we must also understand that economic restructuring shows many different faces. It is different in economically specialized cities. Houston, for example, has been called "the oil capital of the world", and most of the devastating economic shifts in that city were due to "crisis and reorganization in the world oil-gas industry" (Hill and Feagin 1987, p. 174). Miami is another special case. The economic changes that have swept Miami have little to do with deindustrialization, or with Europe or the Pacific Rim, and much to do with the overpowering influence of its Cuban population, its important "enclave economy", and its "Latino Rim" functions (see Portes and Stepick 1993).

Finally, economic change has a different effect in peripheral areas. Both Albuquerque and Tucson are regional centers in an economically peripheral area. Historically, these two cities served the ranches, farms, and mines of their desert hinterlands. Since World War II, both became military centers, with substantial high-tech defense industrialization.[8] Both cities are accustomed to having a large, poor Latino population, whose poverty is rarely viewed as a crisis. In Tucson, for example, unemployment for Mexican Americans has been low, and there is stable year-round income. But both cities remain marginal to the national economy, and this means that the fate of their poor depends more on local factors.

Laredo has many features in common with other cities along the Texas border, with its substantial military installations, and agricultural and tourist functions. All of these cities have been affected by general swings in the American and Texan economy. These border communities have long been the poorest in the nation, and their largely Mexican American populations have suffered even more from recent economic downturns. They are peripheral to the U.S. economy, but the important point is that their economic well-being is intimately tied to the Mexican economy. They were devastated by the collapse of the peso in the 1980s. They are also more involved than most American cities in international trade in illicit goods, and poverty in Laredo has been deeply affected by smuggling. Though Texas has a long history of discrimination against Mexican Americans, race is not an issue within Laredo itself, where most of the population—elite as well as poor—is of Mexican descent. This fact is of particular importance in evaluating the underclass debate.

The Informal and Illicit Economies

The growth of an informal economy is part and parcel of late twentieth-century economic restructuring. Particularly in the global cities, a variety of "informal" economic activities proliferates—activities that are small-scale, informally organized, and largely outside government regulations (cf. Portes, Castells, and Benton 1989). Some low-wage reindustrialization, for example, makes use of new arrangements in well-established industries (like home work in the garment industry, as seamstresses take their work home with them). Small-scale individual activities such as street vending and "handyman" house repairs and alterations affect communities in peripheral as well as global cities. The Los Angeles and Houston chapters in this volume detail what are essentially household expedients among the very poor. These money-generating activities are easily ignored by researchers who rely exclusively on aggregate data sources: they never make their way into the statistics on labor-market participation, because they are "off the books". But they play a significant role in the everyday life of many African American neighborhoods as well as in the barrios.

And, finally, there are illicit activities—most notoriously, a burgeoning drug market. There is not much doubt that the new poverty in the United States has often been accompanied by a resurgence of illicit economic activities (see Fagan, forthcoming, for details on five cities). It is important to note that most of the Latino communities discussed in this volume have been able to contain or encapsulate such activities so that they do not dominate neighborhood life. But in most of them there is also little doubt that illicit economic activities form an "expanded industry". They rarely provide more than a pittance for the average worker: but for a very small fraction of barrio households they are part of the battery of survival strategies.

Researchers often neglect this aspect of the underclass debate because it is regarded as stigmatizing. However, some of the profiles in this volume make it clear that the neglect of significant income-generating activities curtails our understanding of the full range of survival strategies in poor communities. At the worst (as in Laredo) it means that we ignore a significant aspect of community life, including its ramifications in producing yet more overpolicing of the barrios. Even more important, many of these communities have been able to encapsulate illicit economic activities so that they are less disruptive. This capacity warrants further analysis.

Immigration

Immigration—both international and from Puerto Rico—is of major significance for poor Latino communities in almost every city in every region of the country. Further, there is every reason to believe that immigration will continue to be important.[9]

First, it has important economic consequences. Immigration is a central feature of the economic life of global cities: for example, Los Angeles has been called the "capital of the Third World" because of its huge Latino and Asian immigration (Rieff 1991). In our sample, those cities most bound to world trends (New York, Los Angeles, Chicago, Houston, and Miami) experienced massive Latino immigration in the 1980s. In the Los Angeles, Houston, and Miami communities profiled in this volume, immigration is a major factor in the labor market, and the residents of the "second settlement" Puerto Rican communities described in New York and Chicago operate within a context of both racial and ethnic change and of increased Latino immigration. The restructured economy provides marginal jobs for immigrant workers, and wage scales seem to drop for native-born Latinos in areas where immigration is high.[10] This is a more complicated scenario than the simple loss of jobs accompanying Rustbelt deindustrialization. Immigrants are ineligible for most government benefits, are usually highly motivated, and are driven to take even the poorest-paying jobs. They are also more vulnerable to labor-market swings.

These may be construed as rather negative consequences, but in addition, immigrants have been a constructive force in many cities. For example, these authors point to the economic vitality of immigrant-serving businesses. Socially and culturally, there are references in most chapters to the revival of language and of traditional social controls, the strengthening of networks, and the emergence of new community institutions. Recent research in Chicago (van Haitsma 1991) focuses on the "hard work" ethos of many Mexican immigrants and the extensive resource base provided by kinship networks, a pattern that is echoed and amplified in the chapter on Tucson. Most of Tucson's Chicano poor—not just immigrants—are involved in such helping networks.

Though immigrants have been less important in the peripheral cities of Albuquerque, Laredo, and Tucson, each of these cities is special in some way. Albuquerque has attracted few Mexican immigrants, but it draws on a historical Latino labor pool—English-speaking rural *Manitos*—who are as economically exploitable as are Spanish-speaking immigrants from Mexico. Until recently Tucson was also largely bypassed by most Mexican immigrants. Instead, there is an old, relatively self-contained set of cross-border networks, with well-established pathways of family movement and mutual aid. Similar networks also exist in Laredo. Laredo's location on the border means that many of its workers are commuters—people who work in Laredo but live in Mexico.

In recent years, immigration has not been very significant in most

African American communities, and as a consequence it is underemphasized in the underclass debate. It is also often interpreted as wholly negative. This is partly because the positive effects can be understood only by researchers who study immigrant communities themselves, partly because in some places large numbers of immigrants have strained public resources, and partly because immigrants have occasionally become a source of tension among poor minority populations. Though the specific contouring of immigration effects varies from place to place, in each city in this volume immigration is a highly significant dimension of Latino poverty, both at the citywide level and also in the neighborhoods. It is an issue of overriding importance for the understanding of Latino poverty, and thus for the understanding of American urban poverty in general.

Concentration Effects

One of the most important features of Wilson's analysis of black poverty in Chicago is his emphasis on the dramatic increase both in the number of poor neighborhoods between 1970 and 1980 and also in the proportion of poor people in already poor neighborhoods. Poverty became intensely concentrated. Not only did people have more difficulty getting jobs, but also, for the first time, middle- and working-class blacks were able to leave the ghettos and move into housing that was formerly closed to them. In Wilson's analysis, this concentration of poverty meant that achieving role models were gone, the marriage market was weakened, job networks were vitiated, and those remaining in the ghettos were deprived of the support that middle-class residents gave to churches, schools, and other stabilizing institutions.

Generally speaking, poverty did not become as concentrated in Latino neighborhoods during the 1970s as it did in black Chicago. An examination of trends in the sixty largest cities showed that it happened only in a few cities in the Northeast and Midwest (Massey and Eggers 1990). Translated into ethnic terms, this implies that it was primarily in some Puerto Rican communities that concentrated poverty became a serious problem. Most cities with large Mexican American populations did not experience an increased concentration of poverty in the 1970s; the large influx of immigrants in the 1980s may have changed this.

The concentration of poverty comes about not only because of market forces or the departure of the middle classes for better housing; in Houston, Rodriguez shows that restructuring in real estate had the effect of concentrating poverty. Concentrated poverty can also result from government planning. Chicago's decision decades ago to build a concentration of high-rise housing projects right next to one another is a clear case in point. Another is in New York's largely Latino South Bronx, where the city's ten-year-plan created neighborhoods in which the least enterprising of the poor are concentrated, and in which a set of undesirable "Not-In-My-Back-Yard" institutions, such as drug-treatment clinics and permanent shelters for the homeless, were located. These neighborhoods are likely to remain as pockets of unrelieved property for many generations to come (Vergara 1991). It was not industrial decline and the exodus of stable working people that created these pockets: the cities of Chicago and New York chose to segregate their problem populations in permanent buildings in those neighborhoods.

Some of the dynamics that Wilson identified as responsible for the concentration of black poverty are different in Latino neighborhoods. To be sure, they also saw jobs vanish, but two factors in particular tend to distinguish Latino from black communities: continual immigration and a historically lower level of housing discrimination. These two factors mean that there has been a continual traffic—both into and out of—most poor Latino urban communities. Immigrants from rural areas or from outside the United States move into the poorest neighborhoods, and those who can afford it move into somewhat better neighborhoods as the city's Latino *colonia* expands. To a superficial observer, the old neighborhood may look the same, but there is a continual population turnover. In this volume, Moore and Vigil describe some of these patterns in Los Angeles.

Though this kind of population turnover may siphon off some of a neighborhood's achieving residents, this does not mean that cross-class linkages necessarily disappear, or that there is complete social isolation. Vélez-Ibáñez describes cross-class household clusters that transcend neighborhood boundaries and provide extensive resources to the poor. This topic urgently demands further research: many of the black as well as the Latino middle class come from humble roots, and it cannot be taken for granted that they cut themselves off from those roots.[11]

In addition, these studies demonstrate that it is not just poverty that gets concentrated. Most immigrants are poor, and most settle in poor communities, thus further concentrating poverty. But, as Rodriguez shows, immigrant communities may be economically, culturally, and socially vital. Social isolation early in the immigration process, he argues, can strengthen group cohesion and lead to community development, rather than to deterioration. The Los Angeles studies also portray institution-building among immigrants in poor communities, and institutional "resilience" characterizes many of the communities studied in this volume—especially New York and

Chicago. Vélez-Ibáñez's analysis of poverty in Tucson points to the overwhelming importance of "funds of knowledge" shared in interdependent household clusters. Although a priori it makes sociological sense that concentrated poverty should destroy communities, these studies offer evidence that a different pattern emerges under certain circumstances. To use Grenier and Stepick's term, "social capital" also becomes concentrated.

In short, the concentration of poverty need not plunge a neighborhood into disarray, and these authors identify structural resources that ward off despair. This line of reasoning raises other issues. If it isn't just demographic shifts that weaken neighborhoods, then what is it? These questions strike at the heart of the underclass debate. The old, rancorous controversy about the usefulness of the "culture of poverty" concept questioned whether the poor adhered to a special set of self-defeating values, and if so, whether those values were powerful enough to make poverty self-perpetuating. That argument faded as research focused more effectively on the situational and structural sources of poverty. We do not intend to revive this controversy. It is all too easy to attribute the differences between Latino and black poverty to "the culture". This line can be invidious, pitting one poor population against another in its insinuation that Latino poverty is somehow "better" than black poverty. (Ironically, this would reverse another outdated contention—i.e., that Latinos are poor *because* of their culture.) These essays do not make that case; they emphasize structural factors. But their implication is clear: too little is known about poor communities of *any* ethnicity.

Other Aspects of Urban Space

The essays in this volume go beyond the question of concentration effects, and touch a wide range of other issues and conflicts over the uses of urban space. *Where* a poor neighborhood is located makes a difference.

First, some are targets for "gentrification". This is traditionally viewed as a market process by which old neighborhoods are revitalized and unfortunate poor people displaced. But there is a different perspective. Sassen (1989) argues that gentrification is best understood in the context of restructuring, globalization, and politics. It doesn't happen everywhere. In the sample of communities represented in this volume, gentrification, along with downtown revitalization and expansion, affects Latino neighborhoods in Chicago, Albuquerque, New York, and west side Los Angeles. In Houston, a variant of "gentrification" is documented. Apartment owners who were eager to rent to Latino immigrants when a recession raised their vacancy rates were equally eager to "upgrade" their tenants when the economy recovered and the demand for housing rose once again. Latinos were "gentrified" out of the buildings.

Second, Latinos are an expanding population in many cities, and they rub up against other populations. Most of the allusions to living space in this volume center on ethnic frictions accompanying the expansion of Latino areas of residence. Ethnic succession is explicit in Albuquerque and in Chicago, where Padilla discusses an area of Puerto Rican second settlement. It is implicit in East Los Angeles, with the Mexicanization of Chicano communities, and in Houston, with the immigration of Central Americans to Mexican American neighborhoods and the manipulated succession of Anglos and Latinos. In Albuquerque and East Los Angeles, Latinos are "filling-in" areas of the city, in a late phase of ethnic succession. Ethnic succession is *not* an issue in Laredo because the city's population is primarily of Mexican origin. It is crucial in Miami, where new groups of immigrants are establishing themselves within the Latino community: newer immigrants tend to move into areas vacated by earlier Cuban arrivals, who leave for the suburbs. In Brooklyn a different kind of urban ecological function is filled by the Puerto Rican barrio—that of an ethnic buffer between African American and Anglo communities. Los Angeles' Westlake area is most strongly affected by its location near downtown: it is intensely involved in both gentrification and problems of ethnic succession. Here the Central Americans displaced a prior population, and, in turn, their nascent communities are pressured by an expanding Koreatown to the west and by gentrification from the north and from downtown.

These details are important in themselves, but they also have implications for existing theories of how cities grow and how ethnic groups become segregated (and segregation is closely allied to poverty). Most such theories take the late nineteenth-century industrial city as a point of departure—a city with a strong central business district and clearly demarcated suburbs. In these models, immigrants initially settle in deteriorating neighborhoods near downtown. Meanwhile, earlier generations of immigrants, their predecessors in those neighborhoods, leapfrog out to "areas of second settlement", often on the edge of the city.

In this volume, only New York and Chicago fit this pattern; all the other cities have evolved differently. In the Mexican American Southwest, Chicano barrios were historically scattered throughout metropolitan areas, and this pattern still remains. Many Mexican enclaves evolved out of early labor camps, like one of the Los Angeles communities profiled in this book. Whole families emigrated or were imported into these camps to work at ranching, railway maintenance, citrus harvesting and packing, and brickmaking. As the population of southwestern cities boomed, many such settlements were wiped out, though some persisted, surrounded by new middle-class housing.

Thus it is no surprise that the "traditional" Rustbelt pattern of ethnic location and ethnic succession fails to appear in most cities discussed in this volume. New Latino immigrants are as likely to settle initially in communities on the edge of town (near the new jobs) as they are to move near downtown; or their initial settlement may be steered by housing entrepreneurs, as in Houston. The new ecology of jobs, housing, and shopping malls has made even the old Rustbelt cities like Chicago less clearly focused on a central downtown business district.

Housing for the Latino poor is equally distinctive. Poor communities in which one-third to one-half of the homes are owner-occupied would seem on the face of it to provide a different ambience from public housing—like the infamous phalanx of projects on Chicago's South Side that form part of Wilson's focus. (Unfortunately, none of the profiles in this volume includes housing projects.) In fact, in many southwestern cities home ownership among the Latino poor is relatively high. There is not as much ownership in East Los Angeles as in Albuquerque, Laredo, and Tucson, but it is a realistic aspiration. By contrast, New York, Chicago, Houston, and Los Angeles' Westlake are the communities in our sample in which Latinos are primarily dependent on rental housing. In Houston the excessive manipulation of rental housing added to the vulnerability of nascent Latino communities.

Finally, space is especially important when we consider Mexican American communities on the border. Mexican Americans in most border communities have important relationships with kin living across the border in Mexico, and this is certainly the case in Tucson and Laredo. But space is also important in economic matters. Shopping, working, and recreation are conditioned by the proximity of alternative opportunities on both sides of the border. And in Laredo the opportunities for illicit economic transactions also depend on location. The Laredo barrios in which illicit activities are most concentrated are located right on the Rio Grande River, where cross-border transactions are easier.

In sum, when we consider poor minority neighborhoods, we are drawn into a variety of issues that go well beyond the question of how poverty gets concentrated because middle-class families move out. We must look at the role of urban policy in addition to the role of the market. We must look at the factors that promote and sustain segregation. We must look at how housing is allocated, and where neighborhoods are located within cities. And, finally, we must look at how the location of a neighborhood facilitates its residents' activity in licit and illicit market activities.

The Role of the State

Most discussions of changes in poverty assume either a constant governmental role or a shrinking national welfare state. The profiles in this book contradict such a simple view. First, in many poor communities money derived from welfare makes a significant contribution to the local economy, and it is easy to forget that the underdeveloped American welfare state is more underdeveloped in some places—and for some people. California and New York supported welfare recipients at $850 and $806 a month for a family of three, respectively, in 1992—though of course living costs are also high. Illinois provides less, but is more generous than Arizona and Florida, whereas Texas is near the bottom, with a mere $476 a month (*New York Times*, July 5, 1992). The substantial differences in the amount of money available through AFDC means that poor families in Houston, Laredo, and Tucson may be driven to other expedients, and the patterns discerned in those cities should be viewed against this background. In addition, immigrants—whether documented or not—are not eligible for most welfare benefits, though their U.S.-born children are. Immigrant life and the search for work and housing are colored by this fact, and poverty at the neighborhood level is thus conditioned by policy made at the state and national levels.

Second, government has disinvested in these neighborhoods. During the War on Poverty, in the 1960s, community-based organizations appeared in most cities to serve a variety of needs unmet by welfare bureaucracies. These ranged from health care to services for families of prisoners. Most of those organizations disappeared during the 1980s. This aspect of welfare-state contraction—or government disinvestment—is easily overlooked. Once it was fashionable to criticize such organizations for their many inadequacies, but their departure meant that community resources were seriously depleted, as described by authors profiling communities in Brooklyn and Los Angeles. The authors of the Chicago and Brooklyn chapters also document the contemporary struggles of Puerto Ricans to establish organizational resource bases for their communities, and the same pattern is repeated among the Central Americans in Los Angeles. The chapter on Tucson shows how difficult this is even when a community has political autonomy. With the exception of the Cubans, ethnic politics has not yet provided a strong resource base for Latinos.

By contrast, the Cubans of Miami offer a prime example of government investment. Grenier and Stepick document the importance of the Cubans' "political capital". Government spending during the early stages of settlement was essential in permitting Cubans to translate their substantial human and financial capital into a thriving enclave economy, with Cuban professionals and Cuban-owned businesses. Unlike other Latino groups, Cubans had the political clout to make this happen.

Third, government involvement in urban space and urban housing are critical to the well-being of many Latino communities. We have noted New York City's enhancement of permanent poverty neighborhoods in the South Bronx through its ten-year plan for the city. Some of the communities discussed in this volume are also affected by downtown revitalization in which the role of government is all-important. The level of involvement varies substantially from city to city and from one period to another, and these variations affect the poor of all ethnic groups. They are more obvious for Latinos because so many live in states with a very short tradition of serious government help.

Conclusion

No matter what their particular focus, these authors respond directly to Wilson's work—to his conceptualization of an "underclass"; to his theory that urban poverty has become concentrated; that it has become concentrated as a result of the decline of the manufacturing sector and the out-migration of the middle class; and to his characterization of the underclass in relation to specific behaviors. But it is clear that to apply Wilson's analysis to the Latino situation requires considerable adaptation of the original formulation. For example, there is little debate that the nation as a whole has been profoundly affected by economic restructuring. But matters become more complicated when one looks at any given city—no matter what subpopulation is of concern—and even more complicated when one looks at Latinos. Again, though immigration is a relatively minor concern in understanding Wilson's subjects, it is a major phenomenon in most Latino communities, and is closely tied in with economic restructuring. It has a major bearing on Latino poverty. Finally, for Wilson urban space is largely a matter of "concentration effects", but for the communities profiled in this book, matters become much more complex.

In sum, the authors conclude that economic restructuring has been critical in increasing poverty in Latino communities. But the emphasis is on the complexity of economic restructuring rather than on the constriction of the manufacturing sector alone. These authors show how new Latino immigrants help to revitalize and stabilize impoverished Latino communities. They show how Latino communities may serve different ecological functions in the city—some as buffer zones between poor black and more affluent white communities, some as targets for gentrification. Although these studies document poverty and many problems, they do not portray the severe urban decay that Wilson describes in Chicago's ghettos. Some of the studies portray thriving ethnic enclaves with businesses owned by Latino residents, and strong interhousehold networks that cross class boundaries and mediate the effects of poverty. Finally, most authors describe poor Latino residents who are strongly attached to the labor market. Many of those who are unemployed are actively searching for work. Others are employed in the informal sector, where they work for wages so low it keeps them living below the poverty line. Still others are employed in the underground economy.

The "new poverty" described so effectively by Wilson for the black population of deindustrialized Chicago is directly applicable only to the New York and Chicago Puerto Rican communities in this volume: the deindustrialization framework simply does not work in cities that were never industrialized to begin with. Nevertheless, these studies indicate that national economic restructuring has affected all cities, even those most peripheral to mainstream trends. Again, immigration is of major importance even where there has not been deindustrialization, because most of the new jobs are in low-wage manufacturing and service occupations, and these jobs are easily filled by exploitable immigrants.

Each author viewed the community from a different perspective. Each has his or her own critique of the applicability of the underclass perspective, and each rejects and accepts portions of it more or less emphatically. To apply to Latino populations, it is clear that, at the very least, the underclass/deindustrialization framework must be expanded to take into account both the traditional and modern mixes of industry and of the informal economy in any given locale, along with immigration, the niches in urban space into which Latinos fall, and the extent of government investment. Even with such modifications, the perspective does not account for important cultural and historical differences in social organization between Latinos and others at the community and family levels. This is the substance of this book, the first major comparative application of the Wilson thesis to Latino poverty areas.

NOTES

1. The underclass concept was first used in this country by Gunnar Myrdal to refer to the long-term poor, those experiencing little or no advancement in spite of the postwar economic growth that provided rapid mobility for so many others. Myrdal believed that the formation of an American underclass had little to do with behavioral orientations but much to do with material deprivation and a lack of reasonably accessible avenues to mobility for those at the very bottom (Aponte 1991).

2. Tabulations from the 1990 census provided by the Population Division of the U.S. Bureau of the Census in June 1992.

3. A perfect case in point is the Panel Study on Income Dynamics (PSID), probably the most important social science data set for analyzing poverty and social mobility over time. Since its inception, the PSID over-sampled blacks, but it was not until 1990 that an effort was made to sample Hispanics.

4. Two books dealt with urban problems in a quasi-fictional manner in an attempt to humanize dry facts (Griffith 1948; Tuck 1956). Another, quantitative analysis was roundly criticized for equating East Los Angeles juvenile delinquency with "overconform[ity] to this [Mexican American] cultural pattern" (Heller 1966).

5. A shift to service economy often entails a shift to underemployment (i.e., full-time employment that pays below-poverty wages, part-time employment, and part-year employment). In 1980, this kind of underemployment was "most highly concentrated in the rapidly growing metropolitan areas of the South and West", with Albuquerque and Miami among the ten highest (Sheets, Nord, and Phelps 1987, p. 63).

6. The headquarters of 24 percent of the world's largest multinational corporations were located in Chicago, New York, and Los Angeles (Smith and Feagin 1987).

7. A census study shows that in poor Los Angeles neighborhoods both population and median household income increased between 1970 and 1980, whereas in Chicago and New York they declined precipitously (Weicher 1990). "Poor neighborhoods" refers to "groups of continuous low-income census tracts with 20,000 or more residents in the aggregate" in which 20 percent or more of the population were beneath the poverty line in both 1970 and 1980 (pp. 69–70). In Los Angeles, population in such neighborhoods increased by 13.5 percent, and median household income by 4.2 percent. But in Chicago population decreased by 25.9 percent and by 31.7 percent in New York. Median household income decreased by 26.8 percent in Chicago and by 22.8 percent in New York.

8. In Albuquerque, Kirtland Air Force Base has been a major employer, along with the Los Alamos and Sandia research complexes. In Tucson, Davis-Monthan Air Force Base is also very large, and

Hughes Aircraft dominates a thriving defense industry (Lucking-ham 1982).

9. The 1986 Immigration and Control Act apparently reduced undoc-umented immigration primarily through its legalization provi-sions, which permitted some 2.7 million undocumented workers to regularize their status (Fix 1991). Though this may have been responsible for a decline in the number of undocumented immi-grants apprehended in the late 1980s, a resurgence of apprehen-sions in 1990 indicates that the pressure for immigration remains high.

10. In New York, some of the high labor-force dropout rates among Puerto Ricans may be accounted for by competition with Domini-can workers.

11. Residents of black and Latino inner-city Milwaukee neighbor-hoods, for example, cited family networks as a significant resource (Moore and Edari 1989).

1

PUERTO RICANS IN SUNSET PARK, BROOKLYN: POVERTY AMIDST ETHNIC AND ECONOMIC DIVERSITY

Mercer L. Sullivan

R ECENT DISCUSSIONS of poverty among cultural minorities in the United States have focused primarily on African Americans. The perennial issue of the causal relationships between poverty and the behavioral deviance so often associated with poverty has again become controversial. Yet, Puerto Ricans in New York City are among the poorest groups of people in the United States—poorer than other Latino groups and also poorer than African Americans in the city or nationally. This chapter looks at the social and behavioral correlates of poverty among Puerto Ricans living in Sunset Park, Brooklyn.

It has now been fully a generation since Oscar Lewis' sensationalistic account of social deviance among Puerto Ricans in *La Vida* (1966) became the basis for the theory of a "culture of poverty". Lewis portrayed Puerto Ricans as mired in family strife and social deviance, unable to socialize their children to better themselves. His vivid and lengthy portrayals of a few highly deviant families created powerful public images of Puerto Ricans as deviants and of poverty as the product of culture and community.

Following Lewis' work, a number of more rounded community studies of poor African American neighborhoods argued against simplistic notions of culture as the cause of poverty by showing the wide range of life-styles in poor neighborhoods and by demonstrating the relationship of poverty and deviance to structural factors

1

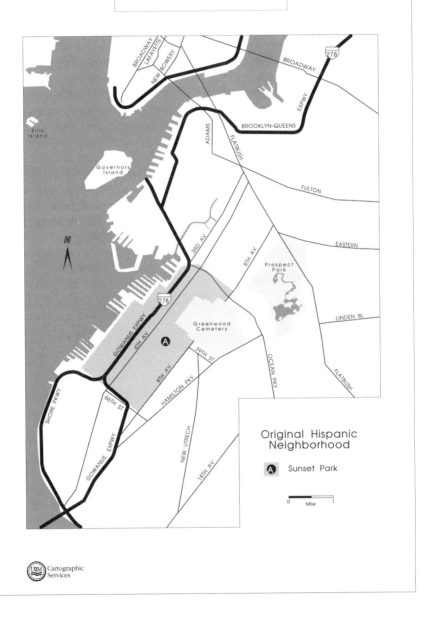

Brooklyn, New York Area

Ellis
Island

Governors
Island

N

BROADWAY LAFAYETTE

NEW BOWERY

BROADWAY

278

BROOKLYN-QUEENS

EXPWY

ADAMS

FLATBUSH

FULTON

3RD AV

8TH AV

EASTERN

Prospect
Park

278

GOWANUS EXPWY

4TH AV

Greenwood
Cemetery

LINDEN BL

A

39TH ST

OCEAN PKY

FLATBUSH

SHORE PKWY

66TH ST

8TH AV

HAMILTON PKY

NEW UTRECH

GOWANUS EXPWY

18TH AV

Original Hispanic
Neighborhood

A   Sunset Park

0   Mile   1

Cartographic
Services

such as labor market conditions and societal discrimination (Aschenbrenner 1975; Hannerz 1969; Ladner 1971; Liebow 1967; Rainwater 1970; C. Stack 1974).

After a period in which ethnographic studies of poor communities, along with the study of poverty generally, went into decline, the study of poverty at the community level has returned. This time the controversial theory has been that of the emergence of an "underclass" (Wilson 1987; Ricketts and Sawhill 1988). The package of concepts tied to that term includes both strong echoes of the "culture of poverty" and an explicit focus on the effects of economic restructuring.

Most of the empirical focus this time has been on African American neighborhoods. Yet, Puerto Ricans remain even poorer than African Americans, especially in areas of concentrated poverty within New York City. The reexamination of poverty at the community level demands close attention to Puerto Rican neighborhoods of New York City. This chapter examines the relationships of culture, community, poverty, deviance, and economic restructuring within one such neighborhood in order to advance understanding of how economic conditions and community social organization affect one another.

Despite the fact that economic restructuring has occurred nationally, its effects have not been uniform. Both African Americans and Latino-Americans have suffered disproportionately from economic restructuring, but there are significant differences among minority communities in how they have been affected and how they have responded.

The Puerto Ricans of Sunset Park include both upwardly mobile, working-class homeowners and families that have been dependent on welfare for more than one generation. Though Puerto Ricans constitute an ethnic plurality in the neighborhood, they are not a majority. They share the area with other poor and working-class Latinos, Asians, and non-Latino whites.[1] The range of life-styles in the neighborhood is also quite wide. By looking at how working-class and poor, mainstream and deviant live together in this neighborhood, this study of community social organization describes both some distinctive features of poverty among Puerto Ricans and the etiology of deviance in a community bearing the brunt of dislocations caused by economic restructuring.

Sunset Park's relationship to national and regional economic restructuring; its changing ethnic, class, and institutional structure; and the ways in which deviance is both generated and controlled are discussed below. The discussion is based on ethnographic data collected under the direction of the author and on published sources, including census data and a recent book by Louis Winnick (1990). The descriptions of Sunset Park are frequently contextualized by means of comparisons to other poor groups and neighborhoods in New York City and elsewhere.

Regional Economic Restructuring

Much of the recent discussion of poverty has focused on the effects of economic restructuring that accompanied the nation's deindustrialization during the 1970s. Regional and local processes of economic restructuring, however, have not been uniform. Economic restructuring in New York City has taken a distinctive path, leading to its current configuration of residual marginal manufacturing and highly developed regional and international service sectors. New York City has been experiencing deindustrialization for several decades. The shift toward a service economy has been more extreme than elsewhere. The timing and manner of Puerto Ricans' entry into this changing labor market have led to their current economic niche, characterized by low-wage jobs, high rates of welfare dependency, and widespread poverty (Tobier 1984).

Although manufacturing has been leaving New York City for at least fifty years, the continuation of a low-wage manufacturing sector was a primary reason for the in-migration of large numbers of Puerto Ricans in the period following World War II. Unlike the large Midwestern cities, New York City's economy was never based on a few large-scale industries such as steel and auto manufacturing. Although New York was a major manufacturing center and also a strong union town, manufacturing there was always scattered among many small firms, garment factories being prototypical. Wages were lower than in auto and steel plants, despite unionization. When the bulk of New York City's Puerto Rican population arrived during the 1950s, the garment industry was their main employer. Yet, both political power in the garment industry unions and high wages were denied them (H. Hill 1974).

As much of the garment industry and other manufacturing continued to leave the city, Puerto Ricans who had come to the mainland in search of employment were thrown out of work. By the late 1960s, they were already on the welfare rolls in large numbers. Since the 1960s, both these trends—the concentration of Puerto Rican employment in low-wage manufacturing jobs and the displacement of Puerto Ricans out of those jobs and out of the labor force entirely—have continued. Despite the massive deindustrialization of New York City, a significant manufacturing sector remains, and it depends on immigrant labor. Puerto Ricans remain concentrated there, but, as we shall see in looking more closely at Sunset Park, they are being displaced by more recent immigrants, who are more easily subjected to labor discipline because they lack the U.S. citizenship and mainland socialization of the established Puerto Rican population.

New York City also differs from other urban areas in the intensity of its shift toward a service economy. That shift has accompanied deindustrialization nationwide, but in few places to the same extent as in New York City. During the 1980s, the growth of the corporate service sector, serving both domestic and international clients, gave the New York economy a vitality that made it an exception to the conventional Sunbelt/Rustbelt opposition of growth and decline during that period (Drennan 1991). Service sector jobs, both high-wage and low-wage, however, require more education than blue-collar work, and thus have eluded many Puerto Ricans because of their low levels of education. Still, low-wage service employment has become the second-largest category of jobs for Puerto Ricans after manufacturing (Falcon and Gurak 1991).

The deindustrialization of the 1970s, therefore, was merely the continuation of a long-established trend among New York City's Puerto Ricans. During the 1970s, the concentration of Latinos in manufacturing actually increased, despite the continuing decline of manufacturing employment (Bailey and Waldinger 1991).[2] Together, the concentration of employed Puerto Ricans in low-wage manufacturing and service jobs and the displacement of many others from labor force participation have been the primary generating forces of widespread poverty in their neighborhoods.

Sunset Park and Puerto Ricans

Sunset Park in the early 1990s is an area of approximately two square miles and 100,000 residents,[3] of whom about half are Latino and about 40 percent are Puerto Rican. The western border of the neighborhood is the waterfront of New York Harbor, along which lies a large concentration of industrial, warehousing, and transportation facilities. This industrial spine continues with the water around the northern edge of Brooklyn and up the East River separating Brooklyn from Manhattan. Though much deteriorated from its prime during and after World War II, this area remains the largest concentration of blue-collar employment in New York City. The residential neighborhoods just behind this waterfront area were originally constructed to house the workers employed in these businesses. Originally populated by white ethnics, this area is now largely black and

Latino, primarily Latino, with Puerto Ricans comprising the dominant Latino category.

This arc is part of what has been referred to as the "Puerto Rican doughnut", actually more a croissant, that curves around three sides of predominantly black Central Brooklyn, New York City's largest area of African American and Afro-Caribbean settlement. The heavily Hispanic neighborhoods of Sunset Park, Red Hook, Williamsburg, and Bushwick enclose Central Brooklyn's Fort Greene, Bedford-Stuyvesant, Flatbush, and Brownsville. Sunset Park itself is a mixed area of Latinos and whites that is bordered by the more affluent and predominantly white neighborhoods of Bay Ridge, Borough Park, and Park Slope. This type of settlement pattern, with Latinos living more intermixed with whites than are blacks and with Latino neighborhoods separating predominantly white and predominantly black neighborhoods, is not unique to New York but is in fact common across the country (Massey 1979).

The development of a large Puerto Rican community in Sunset Park has taken place over a sixty-year period. Throughout this period, economic restructuring and associated political decisions have continuously affected the ecological, political, and demographic profile of the neighborhood, eventually producing today's mixture of both very poor and upwardly mobile Puerto Rican families living alongside other poor and working-class non-Puerto Rican Latinos, Asians, and whites.

Although there is considerable intermixture of both ethnic and income categories throughout the neighborhood, there is a social gradient that conforms in a general way to the ecological gradient defined by the declining elevation from Eighth Avenue on the neighborhood's inland border to Second Avenue near the waterfront.

This settlement pattern is illustrated in Table 1.1. The sub-areas

TABLE 1.1

Household Poverty, All Latinos and Puerto Ricans,
by Neighborhood Subarea

	Household Poverty	All Latinos	% Puerto Rican among Latinos
Sub-Area 1	43.9%	78.7%	88.0%
Sub-Area 2	32.4%	68.6%	74.9%
Sub-Area 3	24.4%	52.6%	77.2%
Sub-Area 4	20.1%	29.4%	74.3%
Sub-Area 5	22.4%	21.3%	62.6%

indicated in the table are five bands of census tracts. Sub-Area 1 comprises the tracts nearest the waterfront, Sub-Area 2 the tracts just behind them going up the hill, and so on through Sub-Area 5, along the Eighth Avenue edge of the neighborhood. The population figures of the tracts in each sub-area have been averaged. The figures show that as one approaches the waterfront, the population generally becomes progressively poorer, more Latino, and more Puerto Rican.

The blighted area around Third Avenue, above which rises the elevated Gowanus Expressway, is the locus of the most concentrated poverty. The creation of this blighted area dates back fifty years to the construction of the expressway, opened in 1941, long before the arrival of large numbers of Puerto Ricans in the area. Robert Caro, in his biography of Robert Moses, describes how Moses ignored pleas from community leaders to route the expressway along Second Avenue, next to the factories and warehouses of the vast Bush Terminal, rather than along Third Avenue, then the heart of a neighborhood of predominantly Scandinavian immigrants that was "poor, but clean poor". After the expressway was constructed, Third Avenue degenerated into an unsavory neighborhood of derelicts, prostitutes, and roving "fighting gangs, Irish and Puerto Rican teenagers, seeping down from the notorious Red Hook section" (Caro 1974, pp. 520–525). By 1950, Latinos still accounted for only 2 percent of the neighborhood's residents (Winnick 1990, p. 92).

A small number of Puerto Ricans have lived in Sunset Park since the 1920s. Local lore traces their arrival to their disembarkation from ships of the Marine Tiger Company that docked along the waterfront. They came primarily from two towns in Puerto Rico, Hatillo and Aguadilla, whose names are still incorporated into the names of several social clubs in the neighborhood. These early immigrants provided a template for the large Puerto Rican in-migrations of the 1950s and 1960s. To this day, many of the neighborhood's residents can still trace their roots to these areas. This settlement pattern is less cosmopolitan than in other of the city's Puerto Rican neighborhoods such as El Barrio (East Harlem) or the South Bronx. As a result, Sunset Park has more of a small-town atmosphere than these other neighborhoods.

One community activist refers to the neighborhood as "este pueblito" when he discusses the extent to which local people live most of their lives within the boundaries of the neighborhood. The fact that there are still a lot of jobs in the neighborhood—albeit low-wage, insecure, and not plentiful enough—means that local residents are less compelled than residents of many other neighborhoods to travel to Manhattan for work. Cheap housing and a once plentiful supply of unskilled jobs along the waterfront were the attractions leading to large-scale Puerto Rican in-migration after 1950.

During the following two decades, there was a major population turnover throughout Brooklyn, as jobs disappeared and many white residents fled the northern and central parts of Brooklyn for southern Brooklyn and the suburbs, to be replaced by blacks and Hispanics. The population of the borough shrank by half a million between 1950 and 1980. By the late 1960s, seven of the eight piers of the Bush Terminal had closed (Winnick 1990, p. 89). The resulting exodus of the white ethnics once employed there created many housing vacancies. As the housing stock had always been quite modest and now was aging, many units became available at very low prices.

Responding to these vacancies were poor and upwardly mobile Puerto Rican families, both from the island and from more crowded areas of the city from which they were uprooted by urban renewal. Many young, working families bought their first homes here. Others, non-working and welfare-dependent, settled in the very cheap and poorly maintained buildings closer to the waterfront.

In 1961, the city dealt a further blow to the already blighted area around Third Avenue by passing a zoning resolution prohibiting residential improvements between Third and Second Avenues in a vain attempt to stimulate industrial revitalization along the Bush Terminal. This resolution sealed the doom of most of these blocks, although the final results were not felt for another twenty years. In the early 1980s, a wave of arson swept through this area displacing thousands of very poor, mostly Puerto Rican families in the course of a year.

During the 1960s, the local housing market was a gamble for many Puerto Rican families. Some won. As their homes increased in value, they sold them for a profit and joined the leading edge of more successful Puerto Ricans leaving the city for the suburbs. Others lost, victimized by unscrupulous real estate agents who induced them to buy at inflated prices with mortgages they could not afford.

During the 1970s, Sunset Park became progressively more Latino. During this same time, it also lost in overall population, a decline of about 9 percent. Median income declined as poorer Latinos replaced more affluent non-Latino whites. The Latino population became more diverse. Puerto Ricans accounted for nearly 90 percent of the area's Latinos in 1970 but only 80 percent in 1980 (Winnick 1990, p. 116).

During the 1980s, many of the new arrivals in the neighborhood were Asian and non-Puerto Rican Latinos. Among these non-Puerto Rican Latinos, Dominicans were the most numerous, followed by

Central and South Americans (Winnick 1990, p. 146). Both the Dominicans and the Asians tended to be more prosperous than the poor Puerto Ricans concentrated near the waterfront. Dominicans, for example, operated almost as many small businesses in the neighborhood as Puerto Ricans, despite their much smaller numbers (Waldinger 1990), while Asians owned their own homes at rates similar to non-Latino whites and much higher than for Puerto Ricans.

An additional small stream of middle-class in-migrants during this period were non-Latino whites who came in search of housing bargains, although gentrification as such has not been extensive in this neighborhood. Reliable information on Central and South Americans is scarce, but ethnographic data suggest that many of them are employed at higher rates than Puerto Ricans in the neighborhood poverty areas but work for illegally low wages, living in very crowded conditions and sending much of their earnings back to their countries of origin (Sullivan 1989a).

Ethnographic data present a picture of a marginalized work force, in which many people do work but often sporadically and under illegal conditions. Many of the more stable families are supported by men working steadily at manual jobs. The neighborhood's largest employer, the Lutheran Medical Center, employs over 2000 people under honest and humane conditions, though many of the jobs are low-wage. Other employment patterns, however, are far less stable. Women work seasonally in some of the small manufacturing firms or for very low wages in service jobs. Young men find occasional work on the loading docks, either for minimum wage or for daily, off-the-books pay on an as-needed basis. Young men also complain that many of the operative jobs in the factories are closed to Puerto Ricans because employers intentionally hire undocumented aliens and then illegally hold back part of the wages their books say they are paying them, knowing that their immigration status will keep them from complaining to the authorities. Many men also work either in unskilled service jobs or in off-the-books construction. These patterns of irregular work often alternate or combine with welfare enrollment.

The social and economic position of Puerto Ricans in Sunset Park thus presents a very mixed picture. One portion of them are upwardly mobile, often homeowners. Another and probably larger portion of them are very poor—welfare-dependent and living in officially female-headed households. Many of these very poor families are residentially concentrated between Fifth Avenue and the waterfront. In 1987, 25.1 percent of the neighborhoods' households had incomes below the poverty line, and 14.5 percent received public assistance (Stegman 1988, p. 158).

One useful indicator of this mixed socioeconomic picture is provided by comparing home ownership rates for different ethnic
groups within the neighborhood, as in Table 1.2 below. The home
ownership rate of 14.1 percent for Latinos is well below those for
whites and Asians. Nonetheless, it is also substantially higher than
in the South Bronx, New York City's largest area of concentrated
Latino poverty, where ownership rates are between 2 and 5 percent
(Stegman 1988, p. 166). Thus, Sunset Park has many poor Puerto
Ricans and some areas of concentrated Puerto Rican poverty but also
other Puerto Rican families who are young, upwardly mobile, and
homeowners.

The pattern of population succession just described differs markedly from that described by Wilson (1987) for black, inner-city Chicago, in which a black middle class allegedly fled neighborhoods
formerly characterized by class integration. In Sunset Park, there
was a replacement of working-class by poor residents during the
1960s and 1970s, leading to a smaller, poorer population in the
neighborhood as a whole. However, the working-class people who
fled were primarily non-Latino whites, and those who replaced
them were both working-class and poor Puerto Ricans along with
working-class Asians and working-class and poor non-Puerto Rican
Latinos. The 1980s then saw a further exodus of poor Puerto Ricans,
who fled to Williamsburg and other poorer neighborhoods as they
were displaced by the burning of the housing stock to the west of
the Gowanus Expressway.

The following sections of this chapter describe the social organization of the neighborhood's ethnic and economic diversity within
various institutional domains. A central concern of the underclass
debate has been the effects of economic restructuring on neighbor-

TABLE 1.2

Housing Tenure by Race and Hispanic Origin, 1980

	Renters		Owners		Total		Owners as Percent of Ethnic Group
	Number	Percent	Number	Percent	Number	Percent	
Whites	13,490	54.7	5,805	73.9	19,295	59.3	30.1
Blacks	503	2.0	112	1.4	615	1.9	18.2
Asians	668	2.7	289	3.7	957	2.9	30.2
Hispanics	10,009	40.6	1,648	21.0	11,657	35.8	14.1
Total	24,670	100.0	7,854	100.0	32,524	100.0	24.2

Source: Winnick, 1990.
Note: Details may not add to total because of rounding.

hood institutions. Wilson's theories have portrayed the erosion of local institutions and family breakdown as key mediating links between economic displacement and the crystallization of patterned deviant behavior. The evidence for the existence of these community processes in Sunset Park is quite mixed. Despite the emergence of considerable poverty among Puerto Ricans in Sunset Park, including local areas of concentrated poverty, the neighborhood has shown considerable institutional resilience in several sectors along with evident stress in others. In addition, despite the presence of high rates of officially female-headed households, patterns of family formation and household structure differ markedly from these patterns among either blacks or whites.

Political Organization

In the political arena, Sunset Park's Puerto Ricans have not been able to use their local plurality to gain control of the major local elective offices, those for city council, state legislature, and Congress. (As this is being written, federally mandated redistricting for the New York City Council has just gone into effect, one possible but far from certain result being the first Latino representative from Sunset Park.) Those offices, as well as that of head of the powerful local planning board, have been held entirely by whites, mostly of Irish or Italian descent. Since the late 1960s, however, a coalition of white, church-based liberals and grass-roots Puerto Rican community organizations has sometimes managed to give effective voice to the concerns of Puerto Ricans and other Latino and poor people in the neighborhood. This coalition has had some success in developing a network of antipoverty initiatives more extensive and effective than those in many other poor neighborhoods of the city.

This coalition was initially sponsored by a major neighborhood institution, the Lutheran Medical Center (LMC), part of the neighborhood's institutional heritage from its Scandinavian past and an important local employer and provider of medical services. The catalyzing situation was a decision by the city to transfer the Fort Greene Meat Market to Sunset Park's industrial area. Local activists opposed this decision because of the noxious nature of the business. In 1969, LMC worked together with a local confederation of grass-roots Latino organizations called UPROSE (for United Puerto Rican and Spanish Organizations of Sunset Park-Bay Ridge) to organize a protest against this decision.

Though they failed in that attempt, the organizing activity had several significant results. First, they drew concessions from the city to help with future efforts to redevelop the neighborhood. Second, they founded a local redevelopment organization, the Sunset Park Redevelopment Committee (SPRC), which, working out of the LMC, operated successfully for several years building and rehabilitating low-income housing. SPRC also served as an effective advocacy organization, bringing a wide variety of antipoverty funds into the neighborhood. The organization was headed by a young, college-educated Puerto Rican male.

One of SPRC's major victories was in helping to obtain special designation in 1979 of Sunset Park as a Neighborhood Strategy Area, a city classification entitling the neighborhood to preferential access to a number of benefits including Section 8 subsidies for low-income housing. This designation came only after an internal political battle between SPRC and middle-class white community leaders who resented the poverty designation and the subsidizing of poor, Latino residents (Winnick 1990, pp. 101–113). SPRC and UPROSE found important allies in the surrounding middle-class neighborhoods, particularly Bay Ridge, because residents of those neighborhoods thought it in their interests to stabilize Sunset Park as a buffer between them and even poorer, and blacker, neighborhoods (Lugo 1979, personal communication).

LMC also made a crucial decision to relocate within the neighborhood, rather than moving to the more affluent Bay Ridge. In 1977, they opened a new facility in the heart of the blighted area west of the Gowanus Expressway. This decision had several positive consequences for poor people. Over 2000 jobs remained in the neighborhood, many of them low-skill jobs employing poorly educated Latinos. The major supplier of medical services to the poor also remained in place. In addition, LMC's relocation served as a catalyst for the development of a small area of new, low-income housing adjacent to the hospital. This area was the only part of the corridor between Second Avenue and the expressway to escape the massive arson-related depopulation in the early 1980s.

SPRC's leading role in community redevelopment continued until 1986, when a series of financial scandals crippled its ability to continue its work. Although it is now dormant, the legacy of its housing development remains. UPROSE also remains a significant voice commanding attention from the local planning board and other centers of power.

Any discussion of antipoverty programs and social services in Sunset Park must include mention of two notable church-sponsored youth programs. One of these, the Center for Family Life, is administered by Roman Catholic nuns and enjoys a national reputation for its youth and family services. The other, the Discipleship, is run by a Lutheran minister who provides housing for homeless youths and provides a round-the-clock crisis and referral center for troubled youth. Though not run by Puerto Ricans, these organizations provide extensive and valuable services to many poor and troubled families within the neighborhood.

The significance of these antipoverty programs and services should not be overemphasized, however. Though more extensive than in other poor neighborhoods of the city and, in one case, nationally known, they still fall far short of the need. For example, the Center for Family Life was the subject of a *Time* magazine Christmas cover story during the 1980s, yet youths living only a few blocks away and very much in need of their services were unaware of their existence.

The political clout of Puerto Ricans in Sunset Park is also weak compared to their numbers. Voter registration and electoral participation are low, and major political offices are controlled by non-Latino political clubs outside the neighborhood. Puerto Ricans generally lack political power proportionate to their numbers throughout the city (Falcon 1988).

Religious Organizations

The antipoverty efforts of the LMC and church-based service agencies exemplify the important role played by local churches in attempting to deal with the problems of poor Latinos. These organizations have provided direct services and brokered a substantial flow of antipoverty funds into the area. However, many Puerto Ricans and other Latinos have relatively low levels of involvement with the mainstream churches. Some Latinos do participate in both Spanish-language and regular English-language services in these churches. In general, however, the religious affiliation of most Puerto Ricans in the neighborhood, and elsewhere for that matter, could be described as either inactive Roman Catholic or intensive Pentecostal.

The small Pentecostal congregations constitute very tight sub-communities within the neighborhood. They meet several times a week with whole families coming together for several hours. Either as congregations or as cooperating individuals, these groups own small bundles of real estate and provide dense networks of mutual support for their members. Many of their members are the young, hardworking, upwardly mobile families of the neighborhood. The Pentecostal churches are not connected to mainstream politics in the same way as the more traditional churches but rather form small, independent self-help communities.

Commerce

The commercial areas along the neighborhoods' avenues are busy and crowded, with many small stores operated by local residents. Fifth Avenue is the main artery for Latino shopkeepers and customers. A study of ethnic business in the neighborhood compared small businesses in terms of the financial and social capital of proprietors and whether or not their customers were co-ethnics. Asian and non-Latino white proprietors tended to be older, more educated, and more highly capitalized than Latino proprietors. Asian and Latino businesses also differed in that Asian owners sold primarily to non-Asians while Latino businesses sold to Latinos. On the whole, the Latino businesses were smaller and more marginal than non-Latino businesses. A disproportionate share of Latino businesses were operated by Dominicans compared to their share of neighborhood population, again a reflection of poverty concentration among Puerto Ricans (Waldinger 1990).

Despite the small, often marginal nature of their businesses, Puerto Rican commerce does constitute a substantial ethnic enclave economy within the neighborhood. This situation contrasts with that in predominantly black neighborhoods in the city and elsewhere, where the lack of local businesses operated by local residents has often been noted (Glazer and Moynihan 1963).

Apart from the businesses along the bustling retail strips, small bodegas are scattered throughout the Latino blocks of the neighborhood. Ethnographic work with local families has documented the complex role of the bodega in poor areas. Poor families buy most of their groceries there, despite the fact that prices are much higher than in the more distant supermarkets, because they receive credit. This credit is essential to those whose money runs out between welfare checks or sporadic paychecks, but it comes at a high price. Bodega proprietors keep the tabs and are often thought to add charges quite arbitrarily, especially for customers already behind in payments. Families down on their luck may be forced to move or walk a great distance to find a new source of credit if they fall too far behind. The bodega owner thus serves as both merchant and banker and becomes a key figure in the micro-neighborhood. The bodega itself becomes a major nexus of interaction and gossip. Yet, the hours are long and economic viability is uncertain.

The community features and processes just described—home ownership, the emergence of political advocacy, physical redevelopment, the presence of youth and family services, commercial vitality—all differentiate Sunset Park both from stereotypical black, "underclass" areas as well as from neighborhoods of more concentrated

Puerto Rican poverty within New York City, notably the South Bronx and Brooklyn's Williamsburg. In addition to the bustling Latino marketplace along Fifth Avenue, many predominantly Puerto Rican streets in Sunset Park are lined with very modest but neatly maintained homes housing two or three families that attest to this neighborhood's status as a step up from poverty.

Despite this, there are also many very poor people in the neighborhood, both concentrated toward the waterfront and scattered elsewhere throughout. The behavioral deviance stressed in writings about the culture of poverty and underclass formation is readily evident. Specifically, there are high rates of school-leaving and female-headed households, and crime and drugs are serious problems in the neigborhood. The rest of this chapter examines these aspects of life in Sunset Park.

The emphasis in the following discussion is not just on the existence of behavioral deviance but on the ways in which these problems are specific to this neighborhood: how local conditions both generate and control deviance and how these local patterns of deviance do or do not resemble patterns in other neighborhoods, particularly the poor, African American neighborhoods in Chicago, New York City, and elsewhere that have provided existing stereotypes of underclass formation. In education, for example, Puerto Ricans have lower rates of school attainment than blacks. Their rates of early, out-of-wedlock childbearing, however, appear to be lower. Beyond these quantitative differences, moreover, there are significant differences in the ways in which behavior is patterned by community norms, resources, and social organization.

Education

Since Sunset Park's Latinos are younger and have larger families than non-Latinos, the neighborhood's public schools are 85 percent Latino, far out of proportion to the Latino share of overall population, which is under 50 percent (Winnick 1990, p. 94). Educational levels of adults are low. In the neighborhood as a whole, only about 40 percent of adults have a high school education. In the predominantly Latino census tracts, less than a third of the adults have completed high school. Nor is this low level of educational participation restricted to adults. Over 40 percent of young people aged 16 to 19 in the neighborhood as a whole and 60 percent in predominantly Latino census tracts are not enrolled in school (U.S. Bureau of the Census 1983). The local public schools are overcrowded and in very poor physical condition, to such an extent that they are seen by local real estate agents as serious barriers to attracting more middle-class residents. Parochial schools, a major resource for working-class families throughout the city who seek better than public education at less than private fees, have experienced sharply declining enrollments for years.

Although Latinos lag behind both blacks and whites in educational achievement across the country, in part because of language barriers, the social ecology of Sunset Park suggests additional factors that restrict educational attainment. The high level of concentration of employed residents in factory jobs and other types of manual work means that credentials and skills acquired through formal education have less relevance to career paths than for workers in other sectors of the economy. For example, in some black neighborhoods, as many of 40 percent of residents are employed in government jobs for which civil service requirements make formal education a necessary prerequisite.

Comparative ethnographic work among young people in Sunset Park and two other neighborhoods—one poor and African American, one working-class and white—showed the important influence of both culture and local labor markets on the school-to-work transition. Puerto Rican youths left school even earlier than their black or white peers in the other neighborhoods, even though school completion rates in those neighborhoods were also low. Yet, the Puerto Rican youths were in the labor market to a greater extent than their black peers during the teen-age years. Even though they were not able to find as much work as they desired and received lower wages than their white peers when they did work, local factories, small private landlords, and auto repair shops did provide them with a certain amount of sporadic employment (Sullivan 1989a).

Responses to teen pregnancy in these three neighborhoods also showed this tendency of local Puerto Rican youths to leave school and assume adult roles at earlier ages than their peers elsewhere. The young Puerto Rican couples in Sunset Park were generally expected by their families to leave school and try to provide for the child immediately. In the black and white neighborhoods, in contrast, abortion rates were much higher. Young black mothers and fathers were more likely to continue their education (Sullivan 1989b).

The school-to-work transition pattern for Puerto Ricans in Sunset Park is one of early school-leaving and labor force entry. Yet, this early labor force entry is into a very low-wage and insecure sector of the economy. Even though they start work early, their subsequent labor market careers include many spells of joblessness and severe restrictions on the kinds of jobs for which they are able to compete.

Thus, although Sunset Park's proximity to the deteriorated but still substantial industrial spine of the city seems to be associated with somewhat earlier labor market entry and higher levels of labor force participation and employment than is found in predominantly black neighborhoods, low levels of education confine many Puerto Rican workers to low-wage jobs. This is a particularly serious disadvantage in an extremely service-oriented economy such as that of New York City. As noted earlier, the Latino share of manufacturing jobs actually increased during the 1970s (Bailey and Waldinger 1991). Overcrowded and undermaintained schools exacerbate these educational problems rooted in local labor market patterns.

Crime

Sunset Park has had substantial crime problems over the last twenty years. The blighted area around Third Avenue has been a high-crime area since the construction of the Gowanus Expressway fifty years ago, long before the major influx of Puerto Ricans and other Latinos into the area. As the neighborhood became poorer and more Latino, however, the crime worsened and spread. Three specific crime patterns during the 1980s were fighting youth gangs, auto theft, and drug traffic.

Youth gangs came to prominence in the neighborhood in the late 1970s and early 1980s. Youth gang activity in New York City had previously peaked during the 1950s "West Side Story" era and then had faded away with the heroin epidemic in the 1960s. When youth gangs returned in the mid-1970s, they appeared primarily in Latino neighborhoods and Chinatown, almost as if the city's newest immigrants were claiming their chance at this urban tradition. Puerto Rican gangs appeared in the South Bronx in the mid-1970s, although neither the South Bronx nor Chinatown gangs were youth gangs because they included older members and were involved in organized crime.

By the early 1980s, Sunset Park had developed classic fighting youth gangs that drew a great deal of press attention for the large number of murders they committed on one another. These gangs—the Assassinators, the Turban Saints, the Maseteros, and the Dirty Ones being the most prominent—had well-defined colors and turfs and pursued violence as a kind of recreation rather than as a means toward an end such as financial gain. They were so prominent that all local youth had to be aware of territorial boundaries. One of the youth programs mentioned earlier, the Discipleship, came into being when a young Lutheran minister's church service was invaded by a gang and he decided to devote his life to the young people of the community.

By the mid-1980s, however, the youth gangs had run their course. Their members had either grown up and straightened out or they had moved into more profit-oriented forms of crime, particularly drug sales and auto theft.

Sunset Park has a very high volume of activities related to auto theft. Residents of Manhattan who find their cars stolen are sometimes told by the police to go look for them underneath the Gowanus Expressway. The local auto theft tradition has a long history: some of its current Puerto Rican practitioners can trace lines of recruitment going back to the Italians and Irish who preceded them in the neighborhood. The many abandoned buildings and whole deserted blocks west of Third Avenue provide ideal spaces for stripping cars. Many small shops for mechanical repair and body work are scattered throughout this part of the neighborhood, and the Atlantic Avenue corridor, which is a major locus of auto shops, is not far away.

The tradition of auto work is strong among local residents. Many of the shops are legitimate, but many others are "chop shops" and still others combine both legitimate and illegitimate activities. The proximity to the waterfront allows many stolen cars to be chopped up and their parts shipped to South American countries. Both teenagers and adults do the actual stealing, ranging throughout Brooklyn and over into Manhattan, Queens, and beyond, while adults take supervisory positions in a substantial underground industry.

Many of New York's neighborhoods, including some that are not among the poorest, have very serious problems with drug traffic, Sunset Park among them. Again, the most visible traffic during the 1980s was around Third Avenue. During the early 1980s, heroin traffic was especially prominent here. Adult male addicts lived in groups in abandoned buildings and supported their habits by prizing copper from the abandoned piers, stealing automobiles, and other forms of theft, with some occasionally shipping out to sea for a few months to clean their systems out while they worked cleaning the insides of tankers.

In the mid-1980s, the police department began a major campaign to curb flagrant heroin dealing on Manhattan's Lower East Side, another Latino neighborhood that served as a major metropolitan heroin marketplace. The police campaign known as "Operation Pressure Point" displaced some of that traffic to the area west of Third Avenue. During that period, the scenes on some of the side streets were truly terrifying: dozens of addicts in the middle of the street being herded about by dealers carrying baseball bats and guns.

The crack cocaine trade was actually somewhat slower to emerge in the Third Avenue area than in some other parts of the city, perhaps because of the tight control of the heroin trade, but crack traffic was established with a vengeance by the late 1980s.

During the early 1980s, the efforts of community residents to obtain police protection were frustrated. The neighborhood is served by two precincts, the 68th and the 72nd. Cooperation with the 72nd was problematic but was eased somewhat by the presence of a Puerto Rican community affairs officer. In contrast, community leaders described the attitudes of officers in the 68th as "protecting Bay Ridge from Sunset Park".

By the mid-1980s, however, the juxtaposition of major drug traffic on one side of the neighborhood with the viable commercial districts and relatively peaceful blocks of homeowners just a few blocks to the east created a perfect opportunity for special police interventions. To date, several such interventions have taken place. First, the police department decided to inaugurate its Community Patrol Officer Program (CPOP) in the 72nd Precinct. This program was New York City's bid to join the national trend toward moving officers out of cars and reactive policing to foot patrols and systematic cultivation of good working relationships with community residents. The program was highly popular with merchants and many residents and has since been replicated throughout the city.

Subsequently, the 72nd was also the first precinct in this part of Brooklyn to be the site of the saturation drug-busting task forces known as the Tactical Narcotics Teams. In the early 1990s, the 72nd has again been chosen as the demonstration site, this time for the Model Precinct program, which attempts to integrate community policing methods into all aspects of the precinct's operations. These programs have markedly improved the relationship between the police and many local residents, especially merchants and homeowners, but there remains a large segment of the population that is alienated from the police and officials of all sorts.

Despite these substantial problems with crime and drugs, however, it should also be noted that Sunset Park does not have a reputation as one of the highest crime areas in the city, nor does it appear as such in police statistics. For example, its rates of reported crimes are much lower than those either in the predominantly African American precincts of Central Brooklyn or in the predominantly Latino and Puerto Rican precincts of the South Bronx. Much of the interpersonal violence in Sunset Park has been associated with conflicts between parties who know one another, such as warring youth gangs or rivals in the drug trade. The sense of danger from an unknown predator, while higher than in middle-class neighborhoods, is not as palpable in Sunset Park as it is in many other poor neighborhoods of the city.

Families and Households

Household composition and family formation patterns have been at the center of much of the discussion of the effects of economic restructuring on poor neighborhoods. Declining rates of marriage and rising rates of family formation through out-of-wedlock births to teen-age mothers have been cited as evidence of family breakdown and increasing intergenerational transmission of poverty, especially among blacks (Wilson 1987; Ricketts and Sawhill 1988).

Nationally, Puerto Rican households are far more likely to be female-headed than those of whites or of other Latino groups (Tienda and Glass 1984; Ventura 1984). In Brooklyn in 1986, the out-of-wedlock birth rate for Puerto Ricans was 61.9 percent, slightly lower than the 65.4 percent for blacks but much higher than either the 12.6 percent for whites or the 41.2 percent for other Latinos (City of New York 1986). Puerto Ricans thus seem at first glance to resemble blacks very closely in their family patterns, with both groups deviating very strongly from other major groups in the United States.

This superficial resemblance, however, obscures some very pronounced differences between Puerto Ricans and blacks. Despite high rates of officially female-headed households, family formation patterns among Puerto Ricans in Sunset Park diverge significantly from those in poor black neighborhoods in New York City and elsewhere. New York City health statistics reveal sharp differences between the fertility and family formation patterns of Latinos and those of blacks and whites. Tables 1.3 and 1.4 are based on birth and abortion statistics from selected Health Areas in Brooklyn. The figures for Latinos below are from Sunset Park and Williamsburg, those for whites are from Sunset Park, Borough Park, and Greenpoint, and those for blacks are from Central Brooklyn. Although Puerto Ricans are not separated from other Latinos in these figures, Puerto Ricans constitute a very substantial majority of Latinos in these areas.

Table 1.3 shows the different outcomes of teen-age pregnancies by ethnic group, controlling for Medicaid status as a poverty indicator. It shows that poor pregnant teen-agers are far more likely than non-poor to carry their pregnancies to term. Within each income group, however, Latinos are far more likely than either blacks or whites, whose abortion rates are basically similar, to carry to term. This is clearly a cultural difference.

TABLE 1.3

Pregnancy Outcome by Race/Ethnicity
Controlling for Medicaid Status

Medicaid

	White (N = 162)	Black (N = 665)	Latino (N = 756)
Abortions	27.8%	34.3%	17.6%
Births	72.2%	65.7%	82.4%
Total	100%	100%	100%

Chi-Square p = 0.0000.

Not Medicaid

	White (N = 430)	Black (N = 663)	Latino (N = 488)
Abortions	77.9%	83.9%	66.8%
Births	22.1%	16.1%	33.2%
Total	100%	100%	100%

Chi-Square p = 0.0000.

Source: Mercer L. Sullivan, "Patterns of AFDC Use in a Comparative Ethnographic Study of Young Fathers and Their Children in Three Low-Income Neighborhoods." U.S. Dept. of HHS, ASPE, 1990.

A similar analysis of legitimacy rates for births again shows clear class and ethnic differences. Non-poor teen mothers of all cultural groups are much more likely than poor teen mothers to be married by the time their babies are born. Latinos fall in between whites and blacks in marriage rates within both income groups.

What these analyses show is that, although rates of female-headed households are high for both Latinos and blacks, the processes of family formation leading to these household composition outcomes are quite different. Pregnant blacks who avoid becoming unwed teen mothers are more likely to do so by means of abortion, while Latinos are more likely to do so by getting married.

Ethnographic work in these same areas reveals further distinctive processes of family formation among Puerto Ricans in Sunset Park that are not discernible in census or health statistics. Although eth-

TABLE 1.4

Legitimacy by Race/Ethnicity,
Controlling for Medicaid Status

Medicaid

	White (N = 117)	Black (N = 437)	Latino (N = 623)
Not Legitimate	43.6%	97.3%	79.8%
Legitimate	56.4%	2.7%	20.2%
Total	100%	100%	100%

Chi-Square p = 0.0000.

Not Medicaid

	White (N = 95)	Black (N = 107)	Latino (N = 162)
Not Legitimate	37.9%	88.8%	48.1%
Legitimate	62.1%	11.2%	51.9%
Total	100%	100%	100%

Chi-Square p = 0.0000.

Source: Mercer L. Sullivan, "Patterns of AFDC Use in a Comparative Ethnographic Study of Young Fathers and Their Children in Three Low-Income Neighborhoods." U.S. Dept. of HHS, ASPE, 1990.

nographic data do confirm high rates of female-headedness, they also suggest that male participation in households is greater than that reflected in statistics. In a study for the Census Bureau, we compared the results of an ethnographic block census with the household count of the block performed by census employees around the same time. We found that the census had undercounted adult males living in households by 20 percent (Sullivan 1990), which is very close to the Census Bureau's own estimates of its undercount of black and Latino men (Hainer et al. 1988).

Ethnographic work also suggests that marriage and co-residence are more common among Puerto Ricans than among blacks (Sullivan 1989b) and that the practice of common-law marriage (documented for Puerto Ricans by Falcon and Gurak, this volume) is far more common among Puerto Ricans than among blacks or non-Latino whites. Many Puerto Rican couples in Sunset Park live together and refer to themselves as "husband" and "wife" even though they are not legally married. Falcon and Gurak report common-law marriage rates of nearly 30 percent for mainland Puerto Ricans, and ethnographic work in Sunset Park suggests the same pattern. Another distinctive cultural practice among young Puerto Rican parents is that the young mother often moves in with the young father's family, a pattern rarely seen in ethnographic work with lower-income blacks or non-Latino whites (Sullivan 1989b).

The functional importance of non-legal unions among poor people can be quite significant. As Jencks and Edin (1990) have recently shown, welfare recipients are almost universally unable to survive on welfare benefits. In this situation, concealing marriage can allow two people to combine meager incomes without the woman's welfare check being cut back. This situation offers a tempting explanation for the prevalence of common-law marriage, except that it does not explain differences between poor Latinos and poor blacks in the prevalence of this practice. In addition, it does not explain the fact that common-law marriage has been relatively common in Puerto Rico for decades, since before widespread welfare enrollment. Indeed, some family histories gathered in Sunset Park show a pattern of common-law marriage reaching back generations. On the other hand, ethnographic data also confirm that many couples in Sunset Pack do combine incomes illegally and in full knowledge that they are avoiding welfare regulations.

What may have happened is that a cultural pattern rooted in an island past has become functionally adapted to a new set of structural constraints defined by the welfare system. Together the official statistics and the comparative ethnographic work suggest two patterns. First, enduring conjugal relationships and cohabitation with or without legal marriage are more common among Puerto Ricans than among blacks. Second, it is also true that these unions are fragile and that structural unemployment does separate males from households among Puerto Ricans more often than among whites.

If these patterns are being correctly measured and interpreted, it would appear that the effects of economic restructuring on family life do bear some similarity between Puerto Ricans and poor blacks but also diverge in significant ways along cultural lines. Although blacks and Puerto Ricans in these neighborhoods have similarly high rates of officially female-headed households, Puerto Ricans probably have higher cohabitation rates than indicated by official statistics. Further, the family formation processes that lead to these household patterns appear to be quite different.

Conclusion

This chapter has surveyed the ecology, demographic profile, and social organization of Puerto Ricans in an ethnically and economically diverse neighborhood on Brooklyn's waterfront. The neighborhood and its inhabitants have been compared at various points to other poor neighborhoods and poor groups in New York City and elsewhere in an effort to ascertain the effects of economic restructuring and how they vary by neighborhood and cultural group.

If there is a Latino "underclass" in the United States (Moore 1989), it is most likely to be found in areas such as the blocks of Sunset Park near the waterfront. Yet, the complexity of the life in Sunset Park belies many aspects of the stereotypes of poverty associated with the notion of an "underclass", or, for that matter, of a "culture of poverty". Such sweeping and stereotypical labels inevitably cloud the diversity of life-styles in any neighborhood and obscure positive forms of organization and adaptation.

A number of differences have been noted between the Puerto Ricans of Sunset Park and the residents of stereotypical "underclass" neighborhoods in which concentrated poverty is associated with deteriorated neighborhood institutions, family disintegration, crime, and social isolation generally. Yet, the deleterious effects of economic restructuring are still amply visible in Sunset Park. Despite the presence of working-class homeowners, some vital institutional sectors, and family and household patterns that differ significantly from those of other cultural groups, Sunset Park is home to many very poor Puerto Ricans who have been displaced over time from the manufacturing sector that originally drew them to the mainland and to this neighborhood. Crime, family stress, and low rates of participation in schooling, electoral politics, and other mainstream institutional sectors are widespread. Sunset Park offers simultaneous evidence that some Puerto Ricans are upwardly mobile community builders and that many others are now suffering enormously, as individuals and as members of a community, from economic restructuring.

Community studies such as this chapter and the others in this book are vital for improved understanding of poverty. If the "underclass" debate has had one beneficial effect, it has been to refocus attention on the fact that poverty affects people not just as individuals but also as members of communities. Yet, very little of the considerable scholarly activity generated by the debate has been based on studies of community process. Local-level statistics alone will never be able to answer questions about social process at the neighborhood level. Qualitative data and analysis are needed in order to understand such things as how deviant and mainstream values and behaviors coexist and how people adapt collectively to material deprivation. Both the strengths of local groups and the specificity of their problems tend to get lost in bare statistical tabulations of rates of non-mainstream behavior.

NOTES

Many people have contributed over the years to my knowledge of Sunset Park. I owe special thanks to Antonia Caban, Sister Geraldine, the Reverend Doug Heilman, Wilfredo Lugo, Adalberto Mauras, and Antonio Valderama.

1. Subsequently, the term "whites" will be understood to mean "non-Latino" whites, unless otherwise stated.
2. Bailey and Waldinger's figures do not separate Puerto Ricans from other Latinos.
3. Some demographic tabulations to follow are based, for technical reasons, on a population of 85,000.

2

BARRIOS IN TRANSITION

Joan Moore and James Diego Vigil

L os Angeles has long been the Chicano "capital" of the
United States, housing more people of Mexican descent than
most cities in Mexico. Many of Los Angeles' Chicanos are
poor, and virtually all of Los Angeles' increase in poverty
between 1969 and 1985 was because poor Latinos increased by more
than half a million (Ong 1988). Los Angeles, then, is a good place
to see how well arguments that are derived from experiences with
other minorities and economic structures in other parts of the country actually help explain Chicano poverty.

This chapter will focus on change in four separate Chicano barrios
in Los Angeles County.[1] Reflecting their origins in labor camps as
well as immigrant enclaves, they range along a continuum from
central city to rural (see map). Only by looking at this range of
settlements can we understand the complexity of Chicano poverty
in the Los Angeles area. These are not the most poverty-stricken
barrios: in 1980 only 5 percent of Los Angeles' Chicanos lived in
communities with more than 40 percent poor (Ong 1988). But these
four neighborhoods are poor: poverty levels in 1980 ranged from 20
to 35 percent of each barrio's population. Briefly, this is what they
look like:

The barrio that is nearest to downtown, White Fence, is one of
the westernmost neighborhoods inside the long-standing Chicano

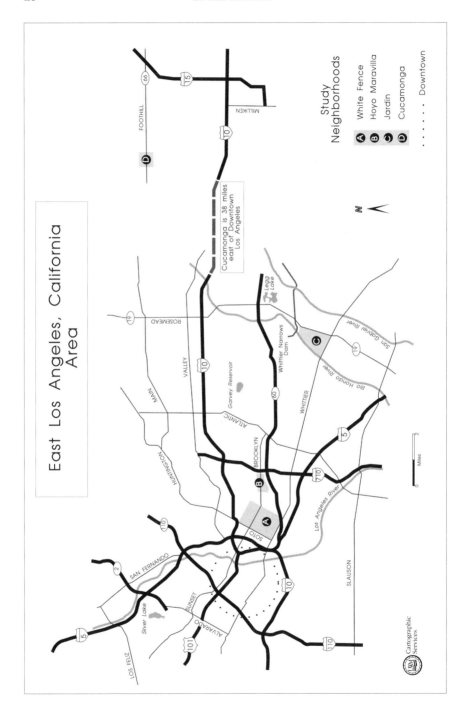

East Los Angeles, California Area

Cucamonga is 38 miles east of Downtown Los Angeles

Study Neighborhoods

Ⓐ White Fence
Ⓑ Hoyo Maravilla
Ⓒ Jardin
Ⓓ Cucamonga
· · · · · · Downtown

Cartographic Services

concentration that is called East Los Angeles (see Romo 1983). In the 1920s and 1930s, the barrio's first Mexican residents came to work in brickyards, packinghouses, and railroads, building small houses in the ravines of what was then an affluent Anglo neighborhood. The barrio had a strong local identity centered on its church. By the 1970s Mexican Americans dominated the community, and it was among the poorest in the county. Today the barrio is still full of the empty lots and the dirt footpaths that mark the neglected areas of the city.

The second, Hoyo Maravilla, is also in East Los Angeles, east of White Fence, just outside the Los Angeles city limits. Settled by Mexicans in the 1920s and 1930s, it is ecologically isolated, in a "hole," or arroyo. Its early Mexican residents built shacklike homes that were periodically inundated when the "dry" riverbed flooded. By contrast with White Fence, El Hoyo Maravilla was semirural. Many of its residents worked in nearby Japanese-owned market or truck gardens. By the 1970s the residents of El Hoyo Maravilla were fully integrated into the urban labor market, though still among the poorest communities in the County.

The third, Jardin, is now surrounded by suburban housing in the city of Pico Rivera. For many Chicanos in East Los Angeles in the early days, Pico Rivera was "suburbia", the American Dream. Jardin started out as a low-income, Anglo housing tract in periodically flooded terrain near the Rio Hondo river, about 6 miles from downtown Los Angeles. Mexicans began to move in during the 1940s, working in the local citrus and avocado orchards, and by the 1960s it was a mixed Mexican and white working-class area. The socially mobile Chicanos living there worked hard at various agricultural and industrial jobs.

The fourth, Cucamonga, started out in the 1920s as an all-Mexican farm laborers' settlement in the middle of a vineyard, close to citrus groves just east of the Los Angeles County line on the western edge of San Bernardino County. As recently as the 1970s it was a desperately poor barrio of 2600, with dirt streets and no sewers, but surrounded by bright new middle-class housing tracts.

All four of these communities have been profoundly affected by ecological and economic changes that have altered the entire Los Angeles metropolitan area, and it is to those changes that we will now turn. First, we will flesh out our description of the barrios by discussing the population shifts in this portion of the Los Angeles metropolitan area that spreads east from downtown. Second, we will discuss the broad economic changes. There has, indeed, been economic restructuring recently, but it is not quite the same as in Rustbelt cities of the Middle West. Third, we will turn to what we see as some of the major institutional changes over the past twenty years. Finally, we will look at street problems and how they have changed.

Population Changes

Los Angeles grew enormously and almost continuously between 1930 and 1990, adding more than 6 million people for a total of nearly 9 million residents. From a rather small minority in 1930, Latinos[2] expanded to form almost 40 percent of the county's population by 1990.[3] Between 1980 and 1990 their numbers grew by an astonishing 70 percent, led by immigration from Mexico as well as from Central America, but also fueled by a high birth rate.

East Los Angeles, the most massive concentration of Mexican Americans, starts just east of downtown and continues for dozens of miles. The history of the White Fence, El Hoyo Maravilla, and Jardin barrios is part and parcel of the filling-in by Mexican Americans of the area east of the Los Angeles River. For example, in 1960 the general area that contains El Hoyo Maravilla was two-thirds Hispanic. By 1980 it was 94 percent Hispanic. And, further east, in 1960 the general area that includes Jardin was only 26 percent Hispanic, while by 1980 it was 76 percent Hispanic (P. Garcia 1985).

During the 1970s and 1980s, immigrants from Mexico settled heavily in and around Los Angeles' central city (P. Garcia 1985). The barrios that are immediately adjacent to downtown Los Angeles thus tend to be very poor, and home to large numbers of Mexican immigrants.[4] The neighborhoods are shabby, with people spilling out of overcrowded dwellings onto the streets. The stores and street vendors on nearby busy streets obviously cater almost exclusively to immigrants. The farther east one goes, in general, the less immigrant-dominated and the less poverty stricken the neighborhoods become, though there are still pockets of severe poverty.

White Fence and El Hoyo Maravilla, a little farther east of downtown, house larger proportions of U.S.-born Chicanos. Although recent immigrants were an increasingly significant fraction of these neighborhoods in the late 1980s, they did not dominate the scene, nor was there much overt extreme poverty. Housing in both neighborhoods was old,[5] small, and crowded, and in 1980 close to 20 percent of the homes had no heat whatsoever—a problem even in balmy Los Angeles. However, many of the homes had been upgraded by their owner-occupants. Many houses in both barrios had been recently restuccoed, and in White Fence new houses were built on the few remaining empty lots. (Close to 40 percent of the residents in these communities owned their homes in 1980.) Real estate prices increased as they did in the rest of the county. Most new immigrants had jobs, and were managing reasonably well. Nearby arterial streets in White Fence, closer to downtown, catered somewhat more to recent immigrants than in El Hoyo Maravilla, farther east, but both neighborhoods were taking on a more mainstream appearance, surrounded by minimalls, chain grocery stores, and fast-food outlets. Some of the smaller mom-and-pop stores had vanished.

Nonetheless, in White Fence and El Hoyo Maravilla, there were signs that not all was well. As far back as 1980, both communities were still very poor, with more than a third of the population in poverty, compared with less than a fifth of the county as a whole.[6] Homeless men began to appear on the streets in the mid-1980s. They could be found sleeping in the park that nestles in El Hoyo Maravilla or even begging on the sidewalks of the busier streets. Many of them were older members of the barrio street gangs—former heroin users and former prisoners whose family members had died or had finally rejected them. Some were recent immigrants who had not found a niche for themselves. Jardin, still somewhat "suburban", was spared the more obvious manifestations of these problems, as was Cucamonga. Neither Jardin nor Cucamonga seemed to be deeply affected by the rapid changes that influenced the barrios closer to downtown.

If White Fence, El Hoyo Maravilla, and Jardin evolved as part of the Chicano filling-in of Los Angeles' East Side, Cucamonga, on the rural fringe of the metropolis, had quite a different history. In its early years, the Cucamonga barrio was a colony of agricultural laborers, working in the vineyards and orchards. The general area was the farming and truck-crop basket of Los Angeles. But by the mid-1970s it had become the new exurbia for Los Angeles and even for Orange County commuters. The changes in the Cucamonga barrio were thus dominated by the mobility patterns of middle-class whites. Land near the barrio was still available for new middle-income bedroom housing tracts, and the small agricultural workers' settlements were engulfed by the growth.

Immigration has always been a factor in the lives of all in these barrios, particularly those near downtown. But the massive surge in immigration during the 1980s was a major factor of change in all four barrios, and we will allude to it throughout this chapter. In Los Angeles in general, Latino immigrants are more likely to live next door to native-born members of their own group than are immigrants of any other ethnic group (White 1988). Mexican immigrants, in particular, tend to seek out Mexican American areas; many, of course, come to live with relatives.

The composition of the schools is yet another indication of the importance of continuing immigration. "Latinization" processes are at work throughout the Los Angeles area: by 1991 the city schools were 70 percent Latino. For example, Jefferson High School, in South Central Los Angeles, was once 90 percent black, and clearly recognized as African American; by 1991 it was 90 percent Latino. In 1974 most of the students in Garfield High School, the school that serves El Hoyo Maravilla youngsters, were third- and fourth-generation Chicanos, but by 1988 the student body was predominantly first and second generation. This generational transformation was also reflected in greater use of and fluency in Spanish, and preference for "Mexican" as an ethnic identity label.

Economic Changes in Los Angeles County

Los Angeles has been the outstanding national example of a Sunbelt boom town, most recently symbolized by a spectacular rise in the cost of housing. For example, the median sales price of an existing single-family home leaped from $87,400 in 1980 to $201,034 in 1989—more than double the national average (*New York Times*, July 3, 1990; United Way 1988). Actually, Los Angeles has seen a series of economic booms. Each involved significant economic restructuring, and each involved a somewhat different mix of industries. Each had different implications for poor Chicano communities.

Before World War II, only a minority (18 percent in 1940) of Los Angeles' workers were employed in manufacturing. There was no strong, unionized, blue-collar tradition. Citrus, motion pictures, petroleum, and tourism dominated the economy. At the end of the war, Los Angeles experienced a major boom and industrial shift. Not only was there an increased demand for consumer goods, but the cold war and the Korean conflict extended the demand for the machines and weapons of war. The military industry—aerospace in particular—began to dominate manufacturing, supplying 36 percent of its employment in 1957 (California 1989). Much of the boom was based on a change from the simple production of airplanes to sophisticated aerospace, missile, and electronic technology. This involved a rapid shift from skilled to professional labor.[7] Thus by the late 1950s Los Angeles was already beginning a pattern that became familiar in the "post-industrial" 1980s—increasing proportions of professional and clerical workers and declining proportions of blue-collar workers (Meeker 1964, pp. 43–46).

At the same time, other sectors of manufacturing were also expanding. Though Chicanos and other minorities were largely excluded from the excellent high-tech jobs, they *were* being hired in more traditional manufacturing plants. Notably, in White Fence, El Hoyo Maravilla, and Jardin, these included the large-scale auto assembly, tire, auto parts, and steel factories that skirted East Los Angeles. All were unionized, "core sector" plants, with nationally recognizable names. In addition, secondary-sector enterprises, like the garment, shoe, and furniture factories, were important local employers. There were also vegetable packing and other food-processing plants, and—especially for White Fence—the slaughter-houses and cattle pens near downtown. East of the area, especially in Jardin, Mexicanos also continued to work in the citrus groves and market gardens, and some gained skills in construction industries—carpentry, masonry, and cement—that catered to 1950s and 1960s suburban housing needs.

The 1970s brought another wave of substantial economic restructuring. Combined with large-scale immigration, it had major consequences for East Los Angeles. There was a short recession following the Vietnam War. But then in the 1970s and 1980s Los Angeles experienced another boom in high-tech manufacturing and also—a new factor—a boom in the financial and managerial sectors associated with the city's emerging "Pacific Rim" orientation. This time, however, traditional core-sector manufacturing did not expand: it declined rapidly. The city saw "an almost Detroit-like decline of traditional, highly unionized heavy industry." Not surprisingly, very low-wage manufacturing and service jobs expanded (see Soja, Morales, and Wolff 1983, pp. 211ff).[8]

Effects of economic change on the four barrios.   The changes in the mix of manufacturing jobs during the 1970s and 1980s had a major impact, especially on the communities we study. The heavily unionized industries that were located nearby all but vanished.[9] White Fence, El Hoyo, and Jardin are not far from the City of Commerce, which had been the home of several "good", traditional industries. Even in 1970 such firms were beginning to leave. By 1978 there were only 761 manufacturing firms in Commerce—a 25 percent drop from 1970 (TELACU 1978). Between 1978 and 1982 another 200 firms in and near East Los Angeles closed their doors, and with them went another 70,000 jobs (Kort 1990). Further, poor-paying, non-unionized jobs in manufacturing enterprises (like the garment shops) and in service industries (like restaurants and hotels) expanded dramatically. Ong calls this "low wage reindustrialization".

And in concert, the 1970s and 1980s saw a dramatic increase in immigration from Mexico and Central America to Los Angeles County (McCarthy and Valdez 1986; Muller and Espenshade 1986; Ong 1988). As always, the East Los Angeles communities like White Fence and El Hoyo Maravilla were home to many immigrants. In 1980, almost half of the residents of these communities were Mexican-born, and the proportion certainly increased during the 1980s.

The most important economic effect of the large-scale new immigration was that it coincided with—and probably stoked—local economic restructuring to drastically constrict the job opportunities available to Chicanos in the area. New immigrants from Mexico and Central America could usually get work. Hispanics[10] filled virtually all of the new low-wage jobs created in manufacturing during the decade. The net effect was that by the end of the decade, the earnings of Hispanics in Los Angeles County had, on the average, declined rather substantially by comparison with Hispanics elsewhere in the nation (McCarthy and Valdez 1986, p. 44). If immigrants fail to find work, they have difficulty surviving; they are not eligible for public assistance. Many are undocumented, adding to what some authors call "perhaps the largest pool of cheap, manipulable, and easily dischargeable labor of any advanced capitalist city" (Soja, Morales, and Wolff 1983, p. 219). To put it crudely, Mexican immigrants were more likely to get jobs than were Chicanos in the same community.

Zeroing in on our particular neighborhoods, almost half of the White Fence and Hoyo Maravilla residents were still, in 1980, working in manufacturing, but these were less likely to be good jobs. White Fence is within easy commuting distance of the expanding downtown garment industry in Central Los Angeles, for example. Many of the garment factories are run as sweatshops. Conditions are not good, and workers—many of whom were immigrant women—continue to be badly exploited. Downtown also houses low-wage job opportunities in big new hotels and restaurants. In general, Los Angeles' Latinos "do not face the same spatial mismatch experienced in Black ghettos" (Ong 1989, p. 206), partly because so many Latino barrios are near downtown, and partly because, as Ong argues, the availability of cheap labor has attracted some new developments in their own barrios. In White Fence, El Hoyo Maravilla, and Jardin, the informal economy proliferated, as we discuss later.

The broader economic changes had a somewhat different effect in Cucamonga. The first generation had labored for low wages as regular/seasonal workers. Generally, low-skilled, low-paid occupations dominated these first years—grape and citrus picking, packing, and processing, work as railroad section hands or in road gangs. With the passage of time, education, relaxation of racist barriers, and familiarization with American opportunities permitted some of the second generation to secure employment in small industries, like the Frito-Lay (corn and potato chips) factory and a foundry producing auto tailpipes. Others moved up to find permanent semiskilled jobs (e.g., as janitors and cooks in schools and local businesses). However, when the housing tracts began to appear in the area, thriving grape, citrus, and railroad operations were curtailed or closed down; the foundry moved to Mexico. The largely untrained and ill-prepared population were left with few employment outlets. In addition, by the 1970s a large influx of undocumented immigrants, mostly male, appeared in the barrio and took what few vineyard and citrus jobs were available. With new housing and new people, new industries and plants also appeared. But the new industries (like so many contemporary enterprises) were concerned with service and electronics, requiring even more education and training. Thus macro-changes acted with job competition to hasten the marginalization of local Chicanos.

Institutional Changes

Thus far we have argued that the interaction of demographic and economic changes in Los Angeles had profound effects on the well-being of the poverty-level Chicanos living in these four barrios. In this section we will discuss other changes at the local level, beginning with shifts in commercial institutions and going on to shifts in other major institutions.

Commercial institutions. In some communities throughout the nation, Latinos have been able to establish a strong economic base *within* the community itself: in Miami, for example, Cubans own and operate most of the enterprises that serve the Cuban community. This type of "enclave economy" has not developed in East Los Angeles. Instead, there is a kind of hybrid economic development. At the neighborhood level, many of the Chicano-owned mom-and-pop stores foundered, and were replaced by small businesses in new minimalls. Although local people tend to own most of the independent restaurants, bars, and drugstores, they work only as managers or lower-level employees in the small chain outlets that dominate the minimalls. At the same time, chain stores maintain an important hold on the grocery business in East Los Angeles, and one of the largest food chains in Southern California has found profit in a Mexican-style marketplace—the Tianguis supermarket located at the edge of East Los Angeles.

In White Fence and El Hoyo Maravilla, the informal economy burgeoned—particularly among immigrants following time-honored strategies for making a little money. Along the main streets bordering White Fence and El Hoyo Maravilla one could buy fresh fruit, hot corn on the cob, tamales, cigarettes, and cheap merchandise from unlicensed immigrant street vendors—estimated by one source at between 2000 and 3000 (*Los Angeles Times*, June 27, 1990). They worked under constant threat of fines and police confiscation. At most freeway ramps and many intersections vendors sold bags of fruit, and men tramped endless miles peddling ice cream along the streets of the barrios. At an estimated forty sites (Cornelius 1990), young men, mostly immigrants, clustered early every morning to sell their labor to anyone who passed by—gardeners, restaurant owners, construction contractors, homeowners. Less than a half mile from Jardin stands a construction materials yard that every morning had close to eighty immigrant workers for hire. In East Los Angeles many U.S.-born Chicanos were also working in the informal economy, usually for cash, but also for food, for services, or for furniture. Yard sales of used clothing and household goods were common. On the other side of town, in the more affluent sections of Los Angeles, Spanish phrase books to facilitate communication with one's maid or gardener were being sold in local drugstores, and immigrant labor was so plentiful that some jobs—like car washes—were being de-mechanized. It was cheaper, as well as more elegant, to have your car washed by hand.

Family. The intense concern about the rise in female-headed households as a result of family impoverishment seems somewhat irrelevant in the two inner-city barrios. Thus in White Fence and El Hoyo Maravilla, in 1980 close to 80 percent of the families with children under the age of 18 were headed by a married couple. That certainly is not grounds for complacency about the structure of the family, but neither is it grounds for the kind of deep concern that has been expressed about, for example, Puerto Rican families.

However, such aggregate figures conceal a good bit of internal variation. We would expect, for example, that the more American-ized Mexicans of second and third generations would show a different family structure from immigrants'. Heavy immigration means that there are still many traditional family networks, particularly of the extended family type. However, more and more Mexican American families are beginning to work out an egalitarian, dual leadership arrangement or are simply single-parent households. Finally, we would expect that some fraction of the poorest or most street-oriented families would in fact be disorganized (cf. Moore and Vigil 1987). In this regard, it may be somewhat surprising that in El Hoyo Maravilla and White Fence, even among those families that might be considered "problems" (in that their children were in gangs), almost two-thirds were headed by a married couple.[11] A more complete breakdown was possible for one segment of the Jardin barrio. Among sixty-nine families, the Mexican-born were the largest, with an average of 5.5 individuals, and the Mexican Americans were the smallest, with an average of 3.6 members. Somewhat surprisingly,

the "cholos", street-oriented families, were mostly female-centered
and were also the largest, averaging 6.2 members. What this suggests is that immigration strongly colors, adding nuances and subtle-
ties here and there, any analysis of Mexican family life and structure.
With the addition of new immigrants to enliven and regenerate Mexican culture, the contrast in family styles and patterns is made even
wider.

*The disappearance of community-based organizations and the
growth of political representation.* There were other changes,
equally important, and easily overlooked by researchers who have
not been familiar with these communities over time. All four of these
neighborhoods were profoundly affected in the late 1960s and early
1970s by the flurry of institutional development in which the Chicano movement and the expanded "Great Society" interacted to produce a wide range of community-based organizations. One of the
biggest institutional changes may have been that those programs
were destroyed.

This statement requires some background. From a national perspective, the worst race riot in decades occurred in Watts, the black
section of Los Angeles, in the summer of 1965. Existing institutions,
along with the fledgling local offices of the War on Poverty, were
slowly propelled into a series of confrontations with newly activated
civil rights groups—Chicano as well as black. For example, with
Chicano high school dropout rates about 40 percent in East Los
Angeles schools and close to 80 percent in Cucamonga, education
was long a concern among Mexican Americans, and was a prime
target of change. Thus one of the first overt manifestations of the
Chicano movement in Los Angeles was the dramatic staging in 1968
of a week and a half of protest-oriented "blowouts" from several
schools (see Acuña 1981). The focus was on the high schools that
serve White Fence and Hoyo Maravilla and surrounding barrios.
Cucamonga had a similar blowout two years later, centering on elec-
tions to the Board of Education. The climax of the Chicano movement was the August 29, 1970, Chicano Moratorium march in East
Los Angeles, which drew demonstrators from barrios throughout
the region. The event ended in death and destruction: a crowd dispersed by police and tear gas reacted by looting and destroying
stores in the commercial section of East Los Angeles.

Between 1965 and 1972 federal antipoverty measures generated a
"massive increase" in federal expenditures for social welfare (Katz
1986, p. 257). In East Los Angeles the effects were visible and important in every neighborhood. There were new community-based organizations bringing pressure not only on schools but on health and
mental health-care institutions, on law enforcement, and even on

the Immigration and Naturalization Service. Cucamonga, still a rural enclave, had only a multipurpose "contact" station to serve these main needs. In East Los Angeles, job training and job development programs proliferated. One (the Mexican-American Opportunity Foundation) was located right in the White Fence barrio. Teen Posts and Neighborhood Youth Corps programs began to spring up throughout the area, including an innovative out-of-school program for gang youngsters. Easily reached, culturally accessible agencies appeared in every barrio, meeting needs that had been so badly served by existing institutions that they led to the stereotype that Mexican Americans were a "hard-to-reach" population. They were *not* hard to reach: it was just that few had tried to reach them in ways that were culturally cued to community networks and habits.

Funding for even the most "radical" of the Model Cities agencies lasted through the early 1970s. Thus undocumented immigrants could get legal advice; heroin addicts, gang youth, and ex-offenders could turn to grass-roots agencies to help them reintegrate into conventional society. These agencies were generated by and supported by significant groups of "respectable" leaders within the community, as well as by the newly mobilized ex-offenders (see Moore 1985 for an analysis of the fluctuation in attitudes toward street problems in East Los Angeles).

Gradually, however, the welfare state contracted again. By the late 1970s, new budget constraints combined with a series of intra-agency scandals to destroy most of the agencies dealing with street problems, leaving them to an enhanced police force. A few agencies became institutionalized—mainstreamed—offering greatly expanded mental health services, for example. Others became absorbed into existing institutions so that the visible, accessible grass-roots-staffed community-based agencies all but disappeared.

Meanwhile, beginning in the late 1970s, a growing political power had by 1991 put local Chicanos from East Los Angeles into both houses of the state legislature, into the City Council, into additional congressional seats, and, after a lengthy legal battle, into the County Board of Supervisors. But growing political representation did not compensate for the loss of community-based organizations. The welfare state had shriveled, and there was simply no money available for social programs, no matter how effective the new local politicians might be.[12]

Schools. The mainstream institutions have, in general, become somewhat more responsive over time. For example, we refer to the schools at several points during this chapter. Though leaders of the Chicano movement "blowouts" interviewed in 1988 saw little change in the schools since their protests in the 1960s (Woo 1988), it is clear that many school programs now exist that were unheard of in the earlier generation. Bilingual education has become entrenched, for example, despite problems in implementation because of a shortage of funding and of well-trained teachers, and reports of continuing resistance from older staff. Nonetheless, there are obvious problems for Chicanos in the system. White flight, combined with the increase in the Latino population, meant that the Los Angeles school system became predominantly Latino. The proportion increased from 19 percent in 1966 to 59 percent by 1988, particularly notable in the lower grades. Between 1969 and 1986 Latinos in elementary school increased by 134 percent, whereas students of other ethnicity declined by 57 percent. Performance on standardized test scores in reading and math were close to the statewide bottom for both 3rd and 12th graders in the system, and 56 percent of the Chicano students who entered the 10th grade in the fall of 1986 failed to register for 12th grade in the fall of 1988. The system had failed to attract Hispanic teachers: in 1988 only 11 percent of the teachers were Latino. Year-round schools were instituted in some overcrowded Latino areas of the system, with generally inferior results, especially for students with limited English proficiency (Castellanos et al. 1989). In an even more disturbing vein, in the early 1990s budget cutbacks in California eliminated English-language classes for immigrants who are under the amnesty program of the Immigration Reform and Control Act. From a high of $133 million in 1988 to a proposed level of $40 million for 1992, this shortfall virtually ensures that educational and employment mobility will be severely affected (*Los Angeles Times*, June 19, 1991, p. 1B).

Health and mental health. Similarly, by the late 1980s the nearby County Hospital was much better equipped than in the 1960s to deal with Spanish-speaking clientele, and East Los Angeles also had both a large new health clinic and a greatly expanded mental health facility. All of these new efforts were working: for example, one sensitive indicator of the health status of a population is the neonatal death rate, and in the health districts that include White Fence and El Hoyo Maravilla both the neonatal and the fetal death rates declined between 1981 and 1986.[13]

Health and mental health problems remained, of course. Many were associated with other changes in the communities. Thus immigrants were reportedly showing up with "Third World" diseases like tuberculosis and various dysentery-producing infections whose sources were unfamiliar to local physicians.[14] Local schools were overcrowded and had many transient pupils, and schools were losing control of immunization. As a consequence, there was a measles epidemic in 1990. Sexually transmitted diseases were a problem, with gonorrhea being especially troublesome. The incidence of AIDS had been quite low (in 1986 there were only 11 cases reported in the East Los Angeles Health District), but by 1991 an AIDS advocate reported that the County Hospital had close to 800 Latino patients, of whom nearly a third were immigrants. (AIDS had been detected as undocumented immigrants went through the amnesty processes.) As of 1991 the stigma surrounding AIDS was seriously inhibiting educational efforts, and local priests were opposing efforts aimed at AIDS prevention. Substance-abuse treatment programs were virtually unavailable.

Health-care advocates had been active since the 1960s and 1970s, and new ones appeared. But fiscal problems at every level of government reduced health and mental health services. Eleven County mental health clinics were closed, and El Centro Human Services Corporation, a mental health facility serving a large portion of East Los Angeles, had to curtail services for monolingual Spanish-speaking patients and to concentrate on crisis intervention, abandoning long-term approaches to therapy because of a $1 million county deficit. Despite significant accomplishments, then, both new problems and reduced funding were inhibiting health-care efforts.

Churches. One further institutional shift may be important. The Catholic churches in the area continued to attract members, and began to engage in significant social action efforts. UNO, the United Neighborhood Organization, was a social action effort organizing parishioners to press for changes in local conditions of life. The organization put pressure on a supermarket chain to improve the quality of its products and services, put pressure on insurance companies to combat high rates, put pressure on politicians for improved transportation and for elimination of a toxic waste dump, and put pressure on a corporate office park to provide new jobs.

The number of small, storefront, evangelical Protestant churches also increased dramatically, especially in El Hoyo Maravilla. Some, like the one discussed below, expanded so rapidly that they could embark on ambitious building programs. There is an extensive literature on how extended kinship networks function in poor Mexican and Chicano barrios, but the activities of these churches have been neglected. They serve important social service functions—for many very poor people, and particularly for immigrants.

In a typical instance, a Tijuana family moved to Los Angeles as members of an energetic small sect, which established its church in East Los Angeles in the early 1980s. Its members pooled their resources to build an impressive structure that looms over the freeway. The father was helped by the church to immigrate to Los Angeles. When he became seriously ill, he was joined by his family, and jobs were found for his wife and two oldest children. In time, his sisters and their families also immigrated to Los Angeles and jobs were found for their families. Of the eight family members over the age of 18, six were working. There were six children under the age of 16—all in school, and all doing well. The church is their American lifeline. They found their current two-bedroom apartment through their church. (The landlord is a fellow member.) The church helps them with food and furniture, and they supplement this help by energetic scavenging. The church helped them take advantage of the amnesty program, and by the end of the decade family members were all getting their permanent resident visas, borrowing money for the filing fee from church members. And the church helped the father of the family to get on Medi-Cal (the California version of Medicaid) when he got sick. The church is also their social lifeline. They go to church early every morning; when they have parties, it is church members rather than fellow workers or neighbors who attend; and they give quite a bit of money to the church.

Similar churches also serve significant functions for many street people in these communities. Victory Outreach, for example, is an affiliate of the Assemblies of God, which established missionary churches in various barrios of Los Angeles. Their purpose was to revitalize gang members and drug users through an evangelical process of being "born again" (see Vigil 1982).

What these pentecostal churches do *not* do is protect the immigrants from the kind of exploitation that the 18-year-old daughter in this family experiences in her job in an Asian-owned sweatshop. These churches may have provided some compensation for the vanished grass-roots community organizations of the 1970s, but the emphasis on social justice and direct action that characterized the Chicano movement is absent. In addition, community-based organizations provided a way for their workers to make their way up the organizational ladder—often into stable city jobs—and the pentecostal churches provide no such ladder.

Street Problems in the Four Communities

As discussed in the Introduction to this volume, the "underclass" argument was based on changes in Chicago's black ghettos. It implied that economic restructuring and the exodus of respectable residents out of poor neighborhoods ("concentration effects") both undermine institutions of socialization and social control. As a consequence, street problems mushroom, and norms that help contain illicit economic activities are weakened. We have demonstrated that there has been economic restructuring in Los Angeles, but our four barrios have not seen Chicago's "concentration effects". Local helping institutions were undermined because of political shifts rather than because of population shifts. What, then, has happened with street problems and the illicit economy? Have they mushroomed, as they did in Chicago?

We will focus our discussion of this issue on the barrio gangs, long a hub of a complex mesh of street problems. They are not a numerically important factor in the barrios, but their prevalence is a decisive measure of community health. On the one hand, they are a direct cause of concern: even relatively peaceful gangs make residents worry about violence. On the other hand, their presence indicates the weakness of both the institutions of socialization (schools and family) and of transition from adolescence to young adulthood (the labor market).

Chicano gangs in Los Angeles go back a long time—to the 1920s, in some cases. By the middle of 1989, Los Angeles law enforcement counted a total of 770 gangs in the metropolitan area. Although the Crips and Bloods (both black) received most of the media attention, Latino gangs were actually more numerous, accounting for 56 percent of the total number of gangs in the Los Angeles metropolitan area (Los Angeles Sheriffs Department 1990). Each of the four barrios we studied housed an active street gang.

The oldest is in El Hoyo Maravilla, whose youth gang goes back to the 1930s. Maravilla had its zoot-suiters, and during the "Zoot Suit Riots" of 1943 Maravilla gang boys and invading sailors confronted one another right inside the barrio. El Hoyo Maravilla was one of the earliest of the Chicano gangs to become involved in serious drugs. During the late 1940s heroin was first used by gang members, and the barrio soon became a center for heroin marketing. By the 1950s, imprisonment on drug related charges became almost routine for a significant fraction of older gang members.

The White Fence gang appeared in the mid-1940s. The gang soon gained a name as one of the more violent groups in the area. By the 1980s the gang was claiming an enormous territory, but the "heart of the neighborhood"—the principal hangout for the gang—was much as it had been for decades.

In Jardin, the gang got started in the 1950s/60s. In junior high school, they met other young Mexicans like themselves who were bused from gang barrios. Barrio rivalries at school, coupled with school problems, worked in concert with broader economic and social marginalization (Vigil 1988) to create a street gang. By the mid-1960s there was a very well established gang tradition with all the drug, conflict, and youth camp/prison problems associated with the classic barrio. Most of the members were cholos (i.e., "multiple marginality"), whose parents were immigrants who had somehow lost out in improving their lives. These families live in the oldest, worst-looking houses in the barrio, with the largest number of household members, suffering the most family stress and facing the most serious schooling difficulties. The rest of the Jardin youth still consider it worthwhile to struggle against barriers and obstacles, and there are enough success stories to point that way. Only the choloized families (Moore and Vigil 1987) had either given up the effort or somehow lost their coping skills and were considered the marginal, the "raspa" (flakes) of an already marginalized community.

The Cucamonga gang came even later. The barrio, known as "Northtown", was ecologically separated and socially stigmatized. But the high school was situated some distance in the foothills in the midst of an area of upscale, middle-class white residents. Barrio students bused to the school were rejected, isolated, and alienated. Antagonism and hostility dominated relationships between Mexicans and whites (both school personnel and majority students), including the predictable early school year fights and riots. By the 10th grade most of the students, especially the males, dropped out. By the third generation (approximately, the 1950s/60s), Cucamonga began to see cholo youth grouping together as a kind of gang. Despite efforts to nip the process in the bud, by the late 1960s the Cucamonga Kings was an entrenched street gang.

Both the White Fence and El Hoyo Maravilla gangs were sporadic targets of programs from the 1940s on (see Moore 1991). During the War on Poverty, gang programs developed in Jardin as well. In all three neighborhoods, the programs temporarily ameliorated the worst effects of choloization. For a largely unemployed, choloized youth population, these programs occupied much of their idle time, redirected them in constructive ways, and most importantly, put some money in their pockets to keep them out of trouble. Without question, gang violence was lessened if not curtailed in this period. Teen Post personnel operated more diffusely, bringing rival gangs to the negotiating table. For a while the Great Society was working.[15]

But the programs, for both street youth and street adults, *were* sporadic and inconsistent, and began to disappear in the 1970s as money grew scarce and local programs were hit by scandals. The dismantling of the federal government's efforts to address the poor and dispossessed had a major effect in all three communities. This retreat tended to exacerbate choloization. Street problems seemed to mount. New and destructive drugs were introduced. During the 1970s, intergang violence escalated to the point that it had become the leading cause of death for Hispanic teen-aged males in Los Angeles County (Loya et al. 1986). The gangs were left to one another—and to the police (see Moore 1985). Thus youth gangs persisted in all four barrios through the late 1980s and 1990s, with some modification. In more recent years, the youth gangs had clearly become entrenched, quasi-institutionalized agencies of socialization, and more influential in the lives of their members (see Moore 1991 for a full analysis of changes, focusing on El Hoyo Maravilla and White Fence). By 1975, when we conducted small-scale household surveys in White Fence and El Hoyo Maravilla, more than half of the respondents complained about street problems. Visible violence (both gang-related and not gang-related) and thefts from homes were particularly troublesome. More than 40 percent of residents in both neighborhoods felt unsafe on the streets. Few at that time, however, said they would turn to police or jails for help with street problems (see Moore et al. 1978 for details of the survey). In contrast, in Cucamonga, with eleven homicides between 1977 and 1978, extensive police sweeps (with law enforcement personnel scouring houses looking for drug dealers) were generally supported by a desperate community.

Did economic restructuring affect the gangs? Apparently it did, but in a rather subtle way. Gang members had more trouble "maturing out" of gang involvement because they had more trouble finding jobs. The gang structure in both inner-city neighborhoods, but especially in White Fence, began to change as young adults continued to hang around on the streets with their homeboys and homegirls, rather than finding jobs. By the 1980s the industries had changed and there was new competition for unskilled work from undocumented Mexicans living in the barrios. This former gang member was 31 when interviewed in 1988:

> (What didn't you like about that job?) Well, I didn't like the way they were running it. After a while they started firing la raza, well, you know, the Chicanos, and hiring the border people. (They started hiring wetbacks?) Yeah, they started hiring them. Throwing us out. They give them a lower income. Not that I don't blame them for coming over and wanting some money, but . . .

Was there more drug dealing among the gangs? Did the illicit economy prosper under these circumstances? The extensive publicity given to drug dealing among South Central Los Angeles gangs (Crips and Bloods) might lead one to expect that these East Los Angeles gangs developed in the same way. In fact, in the late 1970s there was talk that the Mexican Mafia, a prison-based supergang, was trying to move into big-time drug dealing. However, when White Fence and El Hoyo Maravilla gang members were interviewed in 1990, the drug-marketing pattern appeared to be very much as it had been for decades—a few members were dealing drugs, but the activity was not organized and did not include the entire gang or even a substantial portion of it.

Cucamonga continued to be anomalous, its street problems never under control. In the early 1980s, sheriff/law enforcement sweeps were common, and near riots regular events. Problems with social control and other public institutions had always been a part of the barrio's history, and street problems of this marginalized population were no exception.[16]

Conclusions

All of these communities have undergone three major changes within the past decade or so. First, economic restructuring combined with immigration to change the economic opportunities for poor Mexican Americans throughout the Los Angeles metropolitan area. Second, all of these communities have become increasingly "Mexicanized", with a number of consequences.[17] And the third major dimension of change was the disappearance of accessible community-based organizations as the welfare state contracted in the 1980s.

What are the consequences of these changes? First, there are probably more underpaid people in these communities than in the past, with fewer local government-funded institutional resources to meet their needs. However, in most households somebody is working, and there are compensations. Our case history, for example, shows the extensive coping mechanisms provided, for some community members, both by a large household with many kin and by the fail-safe back-up of an evangelical church. And, even though the 1990s are an era of welfare state contraction, these poor communities now have a stronger political voice than ever before, and thus more effective channels to air their grievances. Good manufacturing jobs have vanished, but the informal economy flourishes, with the Mexican-born the most visibly involved. Chicanos, for lack of anything better, are also increasingly involved. This means that there are more people whose wages are not enough to support a family, and who have neither health insurance nor other fringe benefits of core-sector jobs.

Street problems persist. The gangs in White Fence and El Hoyo Maravilla continue to recruit, but there are very few Mexican-born youngsters among them. The White Fence gang in particular prides itself on recruiting only Chicanos, despite its members' preference for the term "border brothers" instead of pejorative terms like "wetback" or "TJs". It is very probable that the renewed presence of

Mexican families in the neighborhood has slowed the process of choloization. They may be poor, and poverty may have become more concentrated, but they are conventional families with high family solidarity, and they tend to reenergize the social controls in the neighborhood. Conversely, however, a new crop of Latino gangs are sprouting up as immigrants in some formerly gang-free neighborhoods begin to adopt the gang traditions of older Chicano barrios.

Finally, perhaps the most surprising finding is that the kind of violent drug-marketing illicit economy that characterizes many black communities in Los Angeles did *not* develop—at least not in the early 1990s. Interviews in 1988 and 1990 show basically very little change in the gang members' involvement with drug marketing. There *are* more elaborate drug operations, with beepers and runners, but they were not based in either one of these barrios. Instead, the street people hang around, perennially caught up in adolescent cholo concerns.

Are there differences along the urban-rural continuum? Our answer to this question must be guarded, because we do not have data that are precise enough to pinpoint differences. Our impressions are that there are substantial differences between Cucamonga and the other three communities, but that White Fence, El Hoyo Maravilla, and Jardin differ only in degree. The three latter barrios have all felt the impact of the same kind of economic restructuring—to a greater or lesser degree—while Cucamonga's experiences are somewhat different. Similarly, the Mexicanization of the barrios has affected the city communities quite differently. Institutionally, the city barrios have always been more complex and better off than either the suburban or the exurban barrio, and this differential continued throughout the War on Poverty era and through to the present day.

In conclusion, these communities are clearly not the demoralized, devastated inner-city neighborhoods that Wilson depicted in Chicago. There is no reason to expect to find the same patterns, or even similar patterns. One difference that is of overriding importance is the fact that there has been continuous immigration into these barrios. The upwardly mobile men and women who leave the barrios generally have been replaced by a stream of newcomers either from Mexico or from other Chicano areas in the Southwest. These newcomers have usually been exploitable both because of their economic marginality and because of their strong commitment to work. But their constant presence has other implications as well. The use of Spanish is a necessity in those barrios, for example, and other aspects of Mexican culture are regenerated as well.

Thus, unlike the situation that Wilson (1987) depicted for black

Chicago, there has been no sudden, abrupt "exodus" of middle-income residents from the barrios, with an attendant loss of institutional support. Instead, Chicano men and women have steadily moved out of poor neighborhoods when they could afford to move to middle-class settings (cf. Grebler et al. 1970). But they never leave a social vacuum behind. Typically their parents and some of their siblings remain; immigrants move in; the institutional structures change, but are not undermined.

A final sharp difference is that Los Angeles' Mexican-origin poor have never been exclusively concentrated in inner-city "ghettos". Small, poor Chicano barrios have always been scattered throughout the metropolitan area, just as the original work sites were scattered. As early as the 1940s and 1950s, such colonies were being surrounded by new housing tracts built for middle-class Anglos. Old *colonias* became pockets of Chicano poverty encapsulated in suburban and exurban locations, and the process continued through the 1980s.

The theoretical framework that Wilson developed has been enormously fruitful. It called the attention of the social science community to real and important changes in the nature of poverty in America's inner cities. Economic restructuring has been of major significance in virtually all large cities, but the ways in which it works itself out depend on many other variables.

NOTES

1. We have been studying these communities for many years. The work in Jardin and Cucamonga was of long duration. Vigil worked in both barrios as a youth counselor, with intensive interaction with the youth of Jardin in 1966–1967. Later, in 1986, he returned to Jardin to compile household data for the U.S. Bureau of the Census. He began to study Cucamonga in the middle and late 1970s and utilized youth and adults from the community as field workers. Since 1974 Moore has been working in White Fence and El Hoyo Maravilla, focusing on several funded research projects in which she used a collaborative approach: former members of the quasi-institutionalized gangs in the two barrios were involved in all phases of the research (Moore 1977; Moore et al. 1978; Moore, 1991). Most of that research has concentrated on the barrio gangs, with a general interest in the community as well. Both Moore and Vigil have taken an eclectic approach, drawing on life histories, key informants, participant observation, surveys of community residents and of gang members (Moore et al. 1978; Moore 1991).
2. Wherever possible, we have reported data for Mexican-origin populations. However, in many cases it has not been possible to obtain

national-origin data, and in such instances we have used "Latino" and "Hispanic" interchangeably to refer to the broader population group.

3. In the nineteenth century, of course, Mexican-origin people were the majority population of Los Angeles throughout most of the century.

4. In 1980, the majority (53 percent) of residents of the poorest predominantly Hispanic census tracts (poverty rates of 40 percent or more) were foreign-born (Ong 1989).

5. In 1980, in Los Angeles County as a whole only one-third of the housing was older than thirty years, but the majority of buildings—66 percent—in Boyle Heights (the community in which White Fence is located) and unincorporated East Los Angeles (the community in which El Hoyo Maravilla is located) were that old. Forty-five percent of the County's dwelling units were owner-occupied in 1980: in the census tracts that formed the White Fence and Hoyo Maravilla barrios the proportions—37 percent and 40 percent, respectively—were comparable.

6. "Poverty" refers to the proportions living at or below 125 percent of the official poverty line. 1980 data were for Boyle Heights (in which the White Fence barrio is located) and unincorporated East Los Angeles (in which the Hoyo Maravilla barrio is located), and are obtained from special tabulations made by Los Angeles' United Way. We are grateful to the organization's research director, Marge Nichols, for her generosity with these data. Somewhat different figures were used by Ong (1988) to show that while the total poverty rate in Los Angeles increased from 11.0 percent in 1969 to 14.8 percent in 1985–1986, the Latino poverty rate increased from 16.6 percent to 25.3 percent.

7. Thus in 1955 three-quarters of the aerospace employees were production workers, but by 1961 only 54 per cent were (Lane 1975, p. 21).

8. Thus between 1970 and 1980 low-wage manufacturing jobs accounted for 53 percent of the city's growth in employment. Moderate-wage jobs accounted for only 7 percent, and high-wage manufacturing for 11 percent (McCarthy and Valdez 1986, p. 40).

9. As Sassen notes (1988, p. 161), 75 percent of the workers in the most unionized industries lost their jobs between 1978 and 1988. These industries included auto production, rubber tires, auto glass, steel, and steel products. By contrast, some 80,000 jobs were created in the garment industry.

10. In the period discussed here, these jobs in Los Angeles were often filled by undocumented workers from Central America as well as Mexico.

11. This statement refers to a retrospective study of men and women who had been in youth gangs in El Hoyo Maravilla and White Fence during the 1970s. Sixty-four percent of this probability sam-

ple of gang members were living with both parents when they were in their early teens (Moore 1991).

12. California was particularly hard-hit because of the passage of Proposition 13, which severely limited the amount of revenues that could be raised through the property tax.

13. In the East Los Angeles Health District, which includes El Hoyo Maravilla, the neonatal death rate in 1981 was 8.3/1000 live births: by 1985 it was 7.9/1000 live births, and by 1986 it was 5.26/1000 live births. In the Northeast Health District, which includes White Fence, the neonatal death rate in 1981 was 7.7/1000 live births: by 1985 it was 5.25/1000 live births, and by 1986 it was 4.20/1000 live births (County of Los Angeles 1982, 1986).

14. In 1985, the shigellosis rates for the East Los Angeles and Northeast Health Districts were 60.6 and 39.8/100,000: in 1986 they were 32.4 and 35.0, respectively. In 1986, the salmonella rates for the districts were 18.3 and 26.5/100,000: in 1986 they were 28.8 and 34.1. In 1985, the tuberculosis rate for the two districts were 23.5 and 35.0/100,000, and in 1986 they were 16.2 and 32.5, respectively (County of Los Angeles 1986). Local informants reported in 1991 that there had been a recent alarming rise in tuberculosis, largely attributed to Asian immigration.

15. In addition, the Chicano movement had inspired Chicanos in prison, and when they came back to the streets they persuaded the Model Cities programs to provide help for both drug users and ex-offenders (Moore et al. 1978).

16. For instance, in the early part of the century "Americanization" programs in the local school district were aimed at improving the lot of Mexican children in separate "Mexican" schools and programs. The latter experiences are recounted bitterly and resentfully by elderly adults who attended these schools.

17. "Mexicanization" is parallel to Wilson's "concentration effects". Wilson is concerned with the exodus of a distinctive population; we are concerned with the ingress of a distinctive population.

3

CENTRAL AMERICANS IN LOS ANGELES: AN IMMIGRANT COMMUNITY IN TRANSITION

Norma Chinchilla, Nora Hamilton, and James Loucky

Central Americans and the Los Angeles Economy

DURING THE 1980s Southern California, and specifically Los Angeles, became known as a major growth center in the United States and U.S. capital of the Pacific Rim. Among the factors allegedly contributing to Los Angeles' growth were its diversification and flexibility in shifting from declining industries in traditional manufacturing to expanding industries in both nondurable consumer products and high-tech industries, and particularly to services related to international trade—wholesaling, shipping, banking, and insurance (*The Economist*, 1988–1989; Anderson 1989).[1] At the same time, the region concentrates, in a limited geographic space, most of the contradictions of late twentieth-century capitalism, with its extremes of wealth and poverty; high-tech Sunbelt industries and decaying traditional or Rustbelt manufacturing; overdeveloped and overpriced downtown and suburban real estate with deteriorating inner-city ghettos beset by gangs, drugs, and crime; high-salaried, skilled professional and technicians and unskilled, low-wage service and sweatshop workers (Soja et al. 1983; Davis 1987; Sassen 1988).

Underlying these contradictions, which have been intensified in the recession of the 1990s, is the global restructuring of capitalism, which in the Los Angeles area takes the form of a juxtaposition of

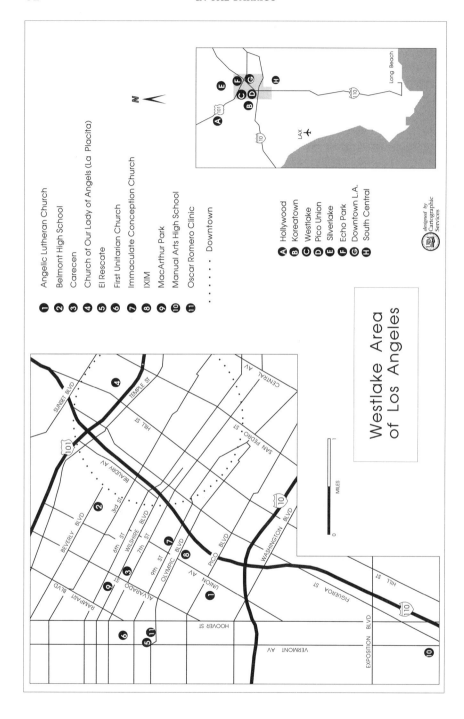

1 Angelic Lutheran Church
2 Belmont High School
3 Carecen
4 Church of Our Lady of Angels (La Placita)
5 El Rescate
6 First Unitarian Church
7 Immaculate Conception Church
8 IXIM
9 MacArthur Park
10 Manual Arts High School
11 Oscar Romero Clinic
· · · · · · Downtown

A Hollywood
B Koreatown
C Westlake
D Pico Union
E Silverlake
F Echo Park
G Downtown L.A.
H South Central

designed by
Cartographic
Services

Westlake Area
of Los Angeles

international capital and international labor—specifically first world capital, European and particularly Japanese as well as U.S., with increasing input from other Asian countries—and Third World labor, composed largely of Latino and Asian immigrants. Approximately 130 foreign banks operate in Los Angeles, and by the end of 1988 Japanese banks controlled 11 percent of the assets in Los Angeles banks, while Japanese investors controlled 30 percent of the downtown buildings.

Immigrant labor has been a second major factor in shifting the economy as well as the demographic makeup of Los Angeles, which has been characterized as the "capital of the Third World" (Rieff 1991). Latinos and Asian Americans, combined with African Americans, now constitute a new majority in Los Angeles. Because these groups are employed in low-wage manufacturing and service jobs, many of which other Americans will not take (Cornelius 1989, pp. 38–39), the growing gap between the wealthy and the poor is often reinforced by racial, ethnic, and national differences.

This chapter focuses on one of the fastest-growing immigrant groups in Los Angeles—the Central Americans. Although Central Americans have been coming to Los Angeles for decades, it was in the late 1970s and 1980s that their numbers began to escalate. Salvadorans, who constitute the largest number, have been variously estimated at 300,000 to 500,000 in Los Angeles County, and Guatemalans at 120,000 to 200,000; the total number of Central Americans in Los Angeles is estimated at 500,000 to over 1 million. While Central Americans have historically come to Los Angeles for a series of reasons, most who came to Los Angeles in the 1980s were fleeing from war and deteriorating economic conditions in their own countries. The majority were undocumented, and because many came after 1981 an estimated three-fourths did not qualify for the amnesty program of the Immigration Reform and Control Act (IRCA).

Most of this population is relatively new, and was less directly affected than other ethnic groups by the decline of traditional manufacturing industries. With some exceptions, the Central American immigrant population, along with other Latino immigrants, has been drawn into the low-wage occupations servicing both the growth sectors of Los Angeles and those benefiting from this growth—the high-skilled technicians, professionals, real estate brokers, and others: workers in the growing number of restaurants and hotels; janitorial workers in the high-rise buildings of downtown Los Angeles, Century City, and other parts of the city; domestic workers, gardeners, construction workers, and so on. Others were employed in small-scale industries such as furniture manufacturing and especially the apparel industry, which in turn experienced a regeneration in the area during the mid-1980s due in large part to the presence of Third World immigrant labor. A certain proportion are self-employed, and many of these immigrants service the new Central American population itself through markets, import houses, stores and restaurants, and street vending, providing products and services the new Central American population cannot obtain elsewhere, or can obtain only with difficulty or at higher cost.

But although they were not directly affected by the loss of traditional industry jobs, Central Americans have been indirectly affected. The jobs they obtain in low-wage manufacturing or service industries are for the most part dead-end jobs that lack the possibilities for good wages and promotion of traditional manufacturing jobs. The effect of the loss of better work opportunities on traditional communities—increased poverty and dependence on welfare and the growth in drug trafficking and crime—have also affected the communities in which Central Americans live. The recession of the 1990s has in fact forced increasing numbers of Central Americans into the "informal" economy, in some cases selling products and services out of their homes, and some have gone into the sale of drugs and other illicit activities.

Focus of the Chapter

Although our concern is with the Central American population in Los Angeles in general, this chapter will be focused on the Westlake area west of downtown Los Angeles[2] and bounded by Figueroa Street (near the Harbor Freeway) on the east, Washington Avenue (roughly adjacent to the Santa Monica Freeway) to the south, Vermont Avenue to the West, and Temple Street (near the Hollywood Freeway) to the north. The southern part of this area, which extends north from the Santa Monica Freeway to Olympic, has been designated Pico Union (after the two streets that dissect the area). This term is often informally applied to the Westlake area as a whole. There is also a narrow corridor along the Harbor Freeway north of Olympic and directly west of downtown Los Angeles that has been designated Central City West. Both of these areas have been targeted for redevelopment at various times, and there is relatively extensive information on the two that can, with reservations, be applied to the area as a whole.

The Westlake area appears to epitomize the concept of deteriorating inner cities described in the literature on economic restructuring and the "underclass": low-skill but well-paid jobs disappear; unemployment grows; levels of crime and delinquency increase; middle-class and stable working-class families move out; and the institutions they support, such as churches, schools, and stores, move, decline, or close down, leaving a concentration of the very poor and unemployable, dependent on insecure, low-wage jobs, welfare, and/or crime. The solution of many developers and planners is urban redevelopment and gentrification, a solution that often entails the removal of poor families to make room for middle-class residents and/ or consumers, or commercial and/or financial interests. In the specific case of Pico Union and the surrounding area, proximity to downtown Los Angeles has led to plans to turn it into a bedroom community for downtown office workers or to expand offices and commercial buildings into the area (Davis 1987).[3]

The development of this area over recent decades, however, suggests another possibility—and an alternative source of dynamism to the urban redevelopment strategy. On the one hand, the area does indeed display many of the characteristics of a declining neighborhood: the departure of many of the better-off residents; a high incidence of high school dropouts; an increase in crime, drugs, and gang activity, aggravated by the psychological and mental problems experienced by some Central Americans as a result of political persecution and war; and a decline in physical infrastructure and traditional institutions. On the other hand, there are elements of a self-rejuvenation: while many leave the neighborhood for outlying suburbs as soon as they are economically able, the numbers are more than offset by the constant influx of new population; existing institutions, such as churches, have expanded their activities, and dozens of new institutions and hundreds of small businesses have emerged to service this growing population; stores, markets, restaurants, and street vendors providing a variety of foods and other products from El Salvador and Guatemala contribute to the bustling street life and ethnic identity of the neighborhood. These changes have in fact resulted in other types of urban problems, ranging from congestion to deterioration in housing stock owing to overcrowding to pressures on schools and other institutions that must service a larger population with limited resources. But these are the problems of a dynamic community, not those of a deteriorating neighborhood in which the only solution is urban renewal. The past activism of the Pico Union residents, as well as the nature of the problems they confront, also indicates that the community itself should be directly involved in the planning and implementation of solutions.

Westlake: The Geographic Context.   During the 1860s the area west of Figueroa began to be developed as a fashionable residential area for downtown employees and professionals, a process that was accelerated with the real estate boom of the 1880s. The discovery of oil in the fashionable Temple Beaudry Hill area (in the northern section of Westlake) in the 1890s changed the character of that neighborhood, which became the center of the Los Angeles oil industry, with some 500 oil derricks—some of which still operate—sharing the landscape with Victorian mansions (Levin and Associates 1988, pp. 2–3). In the 1920s, and especially in the 1930s and 1940s, residents began to move to the new suburbs created with the decentralization brought about by the automobile, and the commercial districts of downtown Los Angeles began to extend westward along the major east-west arteries. The former residents were replaced by rural Mexican Americans, forced off their land by the new suburban development, and by Mexican immigrants (Pico Union Neighborhood Council 1971). Subsequently it became a point of entry for other immigrant groups, including Puerto Ricans, Cubans, South Americans, and Filipinos and other Asian groups at different times, and for Central Americans in the 1970s and 1980s. As described by an area resident, in the 1960s parts of Pico Union were still predominantly Anglo or European, and it was regarded as a "suitcase" area for people who worked downtown; after six or seven years they would get better jobs, move out, and other groups would come in (Cruz 1990). By 1980, however, Pico Union was 75 percent Latino, and various Asian and Latino groups were predominant to the north and west.

As of 1970, an estimated 71 percent of the construction in the Pico Union area dated from before 1933, another 11 percent from 1933–1934, and the remaining 18 percent occurred within the next 26 years. Since that time there has been limited new construction, notably by the Community Redevelopment Agency (CRA). A major part of the Pico Union infrastructure, especially the housing, is at least sixty years old. In Central City West, as of 1980, 51 percent of the housing stock was pre-1940 and an additional 28 percent was built in the 1940s. According to an analysis of alternative housing production programs for Central City West, only 8–10 percent of the housing units were considered to be in sound condition; over 90 percent are deteriorated or in need of moderate to heavy rehabilitation (Robert Charles Lesser and Co. 1988, pp. 6–7). As noted above, housing in this area has been depleted through demolition of an average of 268 units per year between 1980 and 1988, largely to make space for new commercial and residential development (Hamilton, Rabinovitz and Alschuler 1989, p. 46, App. 1).

Reflecting the pattern of urban development of older cities, much of the area is mixed residential and commercial, with commercial activity continuing to expand along the main east-west arteries that cross the neighborhood—Beverly, Third, Sixth, Wilshire, Seventh,

Olympic, and Pico, as well as major north-south streets such as Hoover and Alvarado. For most part this is strip commercial and retail activity, with an extension of downtown office and commercial buildings along the Wilshire corridor and to a lesser extent Beverly and Olympic.

The area under study is bounded on the north by Silverlake and Echo Park—mixed communities but predominantly middle class; on the east by the civic center and downtown Los Angeles; on the west by Koreatown, which has been expanding into the Westlake area; and on the south by South Central, formerly a predominantly African American area into which Central Americans and other Latinos have been moving over the past decade. The growing presence of Asians and especially Koreans in Westlake is evident in several Korean churches and the fact that various buildings and stores in the area are now Korean-owned.

Since at least the 1920s and 1930s, Pico Union has been a point of entry for immigrants, especially Latinos. According to the 1980 census, the population of the northern Pico Union area (between Hoover, Ninth, Figueroa, and Pico) was between 70 and 90 percent of Spanish origin, predominantly Mexican but with a substantial (25–35 percent) "other Spanish origin." Because this designation excludes Mexicans, Puerto Ricans, and Cubans, a substantial proportion of this "other" population was presumably Central American, although an unspecified proportion of South Americans are also included. The area north of Ninth was also substantially Hispanic, with an important minority of Asians. According to one estimate, the population of Pico Union increased by 75 percent between 1969 and 1989, with most of the increase attributed to the immigration of "non-Mexican" Latin Americans, who now represent about 50 percent of the total, with approximately half of this group constituted of Salvadorans and most of the rest Guatemalans and Nicaraguans. Projections of the Central City West population, however, suggest that after increasing 20 percent in the 1970s it may have stabilized or declined in the 1980s, at least partly due to the demolition of as many as one-third of the housing units in the area, with the resultant relocation of population. The composition of the Central City West population has apparently also shifted, with an increase in the proportion of Asians (especially Chinese and Vietnamese in addition to Filipinos) and particularly Central Americans, and a corresponding decline in the number of older Mexican families (Hamilton, Rabinovitz and Alschuler 1988, pp. 7, 23, 33–34, 39–40). The dramatic growth in Central American immigration to the Westlake area in the 1980s has increased the density of the area and intensified pressures on housing, schools, and other institutions. Described by one observer as a "pulsating area," Westlake is characterized by a growing population in which people moving out of the area are more than compensated for by new immigrants coming in.

The influx of immigrants into the area as well as the demolition of the housing stock in the Central City West (northeast) portion of Westlake has aggravated pressures on housing. North of Olympic there is a particularly dense core of multifamily residential neighborhoods running east and west between Third and Sixth, where a large number of Central Americans are located, including several thousand indigenous Mayans from Guatemala. The area north of Third to Beverly Boulevard is characterized as medium density with mixed single/multiple family residential areas. From Sixth Street south to Olympic there are mixed medium- to high-density residential and commercial buildings, while the Pico Union area, south of Olympic, as well as the area north of Beverly Boulevard tend to be predominantly single-family neighborhoods with a few multifamily dwellings (Meyer and Allen Associates 1988).

Even in areas such as Pico Union, however, pressures on housing have increased: according to one informant, a house that previously had two inhabitants might now have six. In more densely crowded areas, family rental units may be occupied by three or four families. Over 97 percent of the Central American workers covered in our survey lived in housing with more than one adult per room, a common definition of overcrowding, and nearly 60 percent were in housing with three or more per room. In the crowded corridor between Third and Sixth, it is common for four to eight residents to share a single room unit that rents for $450 to $500 per month. These are often young single men, but there are also cases in which two or more families incorporating fifteen or sixteen persons may share two rooms.

A 1971 survey of a targeted redevelopment area within Pico Union revealed a relatively high level of transiency; 40 percent of the Mexican/Mexican American population and 45 percent of the other Latin (especially Cuban and Puerto Rican) population (which together constituted about 60 percent of the total) had been there less than three years; only 16 percent of the Mexicans and 7 percent of the other Latinos had lived there for five years or more. Over one-third of the area's population stated that they would be moving in the next two years. Most (90 percent) rented their units. While many expressed satisfaction with the area, most indicated that few or none of their best friends lived there, and a majority (55 percent) thought of it as "just a place" they happened to be living rather than a place where they belong (Pico Union Neighborhood Council 1971).

Nevertheless, the Pico Union area has elements of stability. A survey of businesses in Pico Union in 1971 found that the majority planned to stay and expand, and that one-third of the employees were from the area, although a subsequent (1979) survey indicated that this proportion had dropped by 20 percent. Of the businesses surveyed in 1979, two-thirds had been in business for ten years, and two-thirds (not necessarily the same, but obviously overlapping) anticipated remaining at their present location for more than three years (Economic Resources Associates 1979, p. 32).

Pico Union residents have joined forces on several occasions to combat the deterioration of the area as well as projected plans of developers and real estate interests to target the area for redevelopment. A group that began meeting at the Temple Methodist Church in the 1960s formed the Pico Union Neighborhood Council (PUNC), which successfully promoted improvements in street lighting, safety, and child care. Subsequently, with the assistance of technical advice from UCLA and other sources, PUNC succeeded in channeling a CRA development project toward needed construction of low-income housing and rehabilitation of substandard housing. Later, when developers tried to clear out forty families to build a Pep Boys headquarters, the community formed a new organization, People United to Save Our Community (PUSOC), to fight the project; although the families were eventually forced to move, they received relatively good resettlement benefits, given the CRA's past record (Diaz 1991; Haas and Heskin, n.d., pp. 7–13).

As indicated above, the interest of developers and real estate brokers has shifted to Central City West, where the process of demolition of old housing and construction of new residential and commercial buildings has already begun. Pressures from a strong grass-roots tenants'-rights organization have led developers to include low-cost housing and amenities such as parks and child-care centers as well as more expensive residential and office buildings in the plan (Clifford 1990; Lowe 1991).

The Central American Community in Westlake

Central Americans coming to Los Angeles, and specifically to Westlake, confronted the immediate necessity to find work and a place to live; like other immigrant groups, many were responsible for earning enough to send home to support families remaining behind. Those who came in the 1980s in some cases confronted additional difficulties and psychological problems resulting from the experience of war and violence in their home countries. Many Central American immigrants left members of the family behind; parents would leave children with grandparents with the hope of earning enough to send money back home for support; parents sent children to live with little-known relatives in the United States; sometimes individuals came alone, leaving both spouse and children in the home country.[4] In some cases reunification occurs; often, however, the separation becomes permanent, or reunification after numerous years of separation and diverse experiences is painful and difficult. In other cases, separated spouses may take up with a new partner. The experience of broken families and of war and violence in Central America have been factors in mental and psychological problems experienced by some Central American immigrants.

At the same time, networks of relatives and friends are important for Central Americans coming to the United States. Our study of the owners of Central American enterprises in Los Angeles found that 55 percent had received some help—chiefly housing—from relatives already in the United States when they arrived. A subsequent study of Central American workers found that 66 percent had received help from relatives in housing, 47 percent had received financial help, and 37 percent had received help in finding jobs. Over 40 percent of the workers stated that additional family members had come since their arrival, and over 48 percent anticipated that family members would come in the future. Among the owners of Central American firms (who for the most part had been here for a longer period of time), over 75 percent stated that relatives had moved here after their own arrival. This suggests that for at least some of the Central American population, family networks are an important source of support and stability.

Many Central Americans, despite their low wages, succeeded in sending money to families in their home countries at least occasionally—and often monthly—which again indicates the importance of family, social networks, and/or household structures in strategies of survival. As noted above, the influx of Central Americans into the Westlake area has put extensive pressures on housing, often with additional relatives and in some cases several families sharing a given rental unit. But for the families involved, it means that the incomes of various household members can be pooled to pay for rent, housing, and other necessities. Managers of overcrowded rental units are willing to look the other way in return for a monthly "silence" fee averaging $10 per person per month; renters look upon this as part of the informal housing cost. Families sharing housing also help each other out with child care and share other responsibilities such as house cleaning and recreational activities such as Sunday trips to the park. New arrivals who have not found work, or household members who are temporarily unemployed, can be accommodated for limited amounts of time. Thus households, even of unrelated adults, are not only economic units but also social units.

Pressures on housing have resulted in many Central Americans leaving the area. Those who can afford to may move to predominantly Anglo or established Mexican and Mexican American suburbs within Los Angeles or in Orange county (e.g., Torrance, Santa Ana, Van Nuys, Long Beach); within Los Angeles county some move north to Echo Park or Hollywood (although housing possibilities are limited here as well); some go east into predominantly Mexican areas such as Highland Park and El Sereno; and some move south into what have previously been predominantly African American areas— the northern area of South Central (around U.S.C.) or further south into Watts and Compton. Although the latter are also high-crime areas, families can often rent a house with a yard for the same amount they pay for a crowded apartment in Westlake. By the end of the 1980s, an increasing number of new immigrants were going directly to areas outside of Westlake where their families or neighbors had established themselves, but substantial numbers of newcomers continued to swell the population of Westlake.

The undocumented status of the more recent immigrants and the fact that many did not speak English meant that the majority were relegated to low-wage service or manufacturing jobs—building maintenance, restaurants and hotels, construction, the apparel industry, and domestic service. Because of their undocumented status, and in some cases the experience of persecution of union activists in their own countries, some Central Americans are afraid to join unions and/or to demand better wages or working conditions. Labor relations are also complicated in several industries in which companies do not hire directly but subcontract with other companies or contractors, as is the case with the garment industry and building maintenance (janitorial) work.

Nevertheless, several unions in industries where undocumented workers now constitute a significant portion of the work force have launched aggressive unionization campaigns. One of the most successful has been the Justice for Janitors campaign of the SEIU (Service Employees International Union), which has reversed the 1980s trend toward de-unionization of janitorial workers in Los Angeles and has organized workers of several cleaning companies responsible for building maintenance downtown and in other parts of the city.[5]

In contrast, only about 3 percent of workers in the garment industry—chiefly immigrant women, the majority (75 percent) Latina, followed by Asian—are organized. Many earn less than the minimum wage, and a majority work for piece rates. There are also many reports of home work and child labor. Garment workers are at the bottom of a stratified hierarchy in the highly volatile and competitive apparel industry and are hired by contractors who are operating at a very narrow profit that can be easily wiped out; up to one-third of contractors go out of business in any given year (Bonacich 1990).[6] Contractors are themselves often recent immigrants; in Los Angeles they are chiefly Korean. Unionization is also discouraged by the ease with which manufacturers can shift production to Mexico or other countries in which wages are less than $1 per hour.

New immigrants to the area may join day laborers at pickup points at various locations in the city and county, where they hope to obtain a day's work—or, if fortunate, work for several days—in construction, gardening, home repair, and similar jobs. Immigrants lacking the networks of family, friends, and neighbors that constitute an important source of information about jobs are forced into this segment of the labor market. Although some skilled workers can make a substantial income as day laborers (a few day laborers are documented and/or skilled workers who have been in Los Angeles for several years), for most work is at best uncertain, and contracting for work in this manner involves a high level of risk. Aside from the fact that only about 20 percent of the day laborers may obtain work on any given day, pickup points have been subject to raids by the Immigration and Naturalization Service (INS). In numerous cases unscrupulous employers, taking advantage of new immigrants' lack of documentation and English-language ability, have refused to pay for a day's work or have paid less than promised.

A significant and growing proportion of the population is self-employed, many of them as street vendors.[7] Some skilled workers find it more profitable to work for themselves than for others; a skilled mechanic can make more money fixing cars on the street than he might in a garage earning $5 per hour.

Among the self-employed, the role of street vendors has been particularly controversial.[8] As indicated above, street vending is prohibited by law in Los Angeles (in contrast to most other major U.S. cities) except in very specific circumstances. However, street vending has existed for decades and has grown especially rapidly since the mid-1980s due to the growth in the number of immigrants from countries where street sale of food and merchandise is widely accepted, and to the limits of other employment possibilities. But street vending may also be preferred to other jobs available to immigrants, especially for women with small children. Some vendors may earn up to $100 a day—as much or more than they would earn in low-wage factory or service jobs, although this is exceptional.

The growth of street vending has been particularly important in the area under study, along certain major streets and avenues intersecting the area, as well as in the area of Our Lady Queen of Angels Church. And street vendors can be found in other areas of the city, including Hollywood and East Los Angeles, and several other cities of Los Angeles county. Products sold include clothing, jewelry, tape cassettes, and household goods; and mangos and other fresh fruit, as well as cooked foods such as tamales and chicharones. Although the sources of their products vary, much of the fresh fruit is bought at central markets, cooked food is prepared at home, and other merchandise is purchased from downtown wholesalers.

Some critics of street vending, including the police, associate it with drugs, and vendors have sometimes been included with drug dealers in police sweeps of areas such as MacArthur Park (Tobar 1990; Bayette 1990). Other critics complain of such factors as congestion, littering, and health hazards from the preparation of food in unsanitary conditions. Among the most vociferous critics are area merchants, who complain of unfair competition, since street vendors do not pay rent, taxes, or insurance and may choose to sell only at peak hours rather than throughout the day.

Street vendors and their advocates argue that vending increases the street life and vitality of the affected areas—for the most part Latino neighborhoods—aside from making goods available to residents who would otherwise not be able to afford them. They claim that street vending actually prevents drug dealing; they cite examples in Pico Union, Hollywood, and Venice in which the role of vendors in keeping drug dealers out of the area has been recognized by community residents and merchants. Problems of littering, congestion, and competition, as well as issues related to health, can be handled through regulation rather than by prohibiting street vending.

Street vending is the tip of the iceberg as far as informal activities are concerned: many residents work directly out of their homes in such activities as shoe repair, making their services known through word of mouth or other informal contacts. The current recession has increased reliance on the "informal economy" as opportunities for formal employment are reduced.

Within the Westlake area, unemployment is high by regional standards, especially among recent immigrants. According to one long-term resident of Pico Union, among those who have been there a year or less 50 percent may be unemployed at any one time; for the rest of the population it is about 10 percent. In Central City West, the 1980 census indicated that approximately 30 percent of the population experienced some period of unemployment in the previous year (Hamilton, Rabinovitz and Alschuler 1988, p. 46).

However, there is little evidence of a correlation between unemployment and dependence on welfare. An estimated one-third of the population in Pico Union receives some form of welfare payment, but this includes members of the working population whose wages are insufficient, or who lack health benefits or experience unforeseen emergencies. In Central City West, over 50 percent of the households earned less than $15,000 in 1979, yet only 15 percent reported receiving public assistance. New arrivals, especially those who are undocumented, are much less likely to apply even for benefits for which they or their children are eligible, such as AFDC, due to fear of the INS or to lack of knowledge. Our survey of Central American workers in the Los Angeles area indicates that fewer than 10 percent have received any kind of welfare payment.

Interethnic Relations

The search for jobs and affordable housing, as well as conditions in Los Angeles in general and in Westlake in particular, have placed Central Americans in close contact with other ethnic groups. A 1989 description of MacArthur Park suggests the ethnic diversity of Westlake: by day, at various times and at various locations, the park is a haven for Korean Seventh Day Adventists, Armenian pinochle players, and Central American families and vendors. Around its perimeter are markets and restaurants offering Guatemalan and Salvadoran food and products.

But in fact, interethnic relations are more complex than this scenario suggests. As noted above, there is a substantial Asian population in Westlake, chiefly Chinese, Filipino, and Vietnamese in the northern section, and Koreans in the areas closest to Koreatown. Koreans have bought into the area; many own the buildings in which Central Americans and other Latinos live and work, and increasing numbers own businesses in the area. Many Central Americans work in situations with several different ethnic groups or in which their boss or supervisor is of a different nationality or group.

Evidence based on interviews with business owners/self-employed and workers is mixed. Among business owners, reactions were roughly equally divided between those who said there were no serious tensions and those who said there were. Among the latter were several who mentioned discrimination by Anglos, particularly by the police and government agencies. Central American workers also mentioned discrimination by Anglo and Asian supervisors and contractors.

Asians were also predominant among other ethnic groups mentioned by Central American business owners; complaints generally focused on their competitiveness in business. Several of the business owners rented from Koreans; one complained that when a Korean bought the building the rent was doubled, and another indicated concern that the Korean owner was trying to drive him out. Interestingly, the latter responded to the question about interethnic tensions that there were none, suggesting that respondents may have understated the existence of tensions. A few swap-meet vendors also complained that the swap-meet houses were Korean-owned, and that Korean vendors were given the best posts. There were some in both groups who complained of African Americans, associating them with gangs or drugs. According to some informants, there is considerable prejudice against African Americans; some Latinos consider them lazy, and cases were mentioned in which Latino apartment owners refuse to rent to African Americans. Many African Americans in turn believe that immigrants, especially undocumented workers, take jobs at lower wages, thereby lowering wages for everyone.[9] Clearly distinct perspectives are involved: immigrants, whose point of reference may be severe economic exploitation and even political repression at home, see low-wage U.S. jobs and long hours of work as an improvement over their former life or at least a means for a better life in the future; African Americans, whose point of reference is the U.S. consumer society and who have struggled for generations for equal opportunity, see such jobs as a regression to an earlier period of exploitation, a perspective that may be shared by some older Latino residents. It is likely that the children of today's immigrant population will see U.S. society rather than the experiences of their parents as a point of reference.

Another area in which ethnic antagonisms have emerged is in ethnically divided neighborhoods, in which older residents perceived that new groups are coming in and taking over their neighborhood.[10] Although most of the self-employed/businesspersons lived in predominantly Anglo or mixed neighborhoods, the majority of the Central American workers in our study live in predominantly Latino or African American neighborhoods. Here the picture is mixed. One observer reported ethnic and even national segregation among buildings, with Hondurans in one building, Salvadorans in the next, and tensions between the two. There are undoubtedly situations in which a building manager from a specific country will show preference to his/her own compatriots, as may also occur with foremen in a given workplace. But there are also multiple-unit buildings with different Latino groups and in some cases African Americans and Asians.

About 30 percent of the immigrant workers we interviewed work in environments that are predominantly non-Latino or mixed. A number mentioned ethnic conflict in their work place (33 percent) or serious ethnic tensions in general (40 percent). A Guatemalan man, for example, felt there were conflicts at his office where African Americans, Mexicans, Central Americans, other Latinos, and Vietnamese worked, due to nationality and language differences. Another Guatemalan attributed the serious tensions he had noticed to a lack of cultural education—a lack of understanding of the culture of each group. Anglos in particular, he noted, are not biculturally educated. Others suggested that workers in mixed workplaces get along well but tend to associate with their own ethnic group.

One of the most striking findings was the presence of tension or conflict *within* the Latino community. Several of the small-business people spoke of the lack of cooperation among Latinos, in contrast to the Asian groups. As expressed by one: "El latino no cree en el latino." More specifically, several business owners and workers reported antagonisms between Mexicans and Central Americans, or more specifically Guatemalans or Salvadorans. Central American as well as Mexican workers pointed out tensions among Latinos. According to a Guatemalan worker: ". . . los mexicanos creen que ellos son los dueños de Los Angeles, e insultan a los centroamericanos." Some complain that Mexicans don't want to accept other cultures, and that in schools, for example, Mexican holidays and events are celebrated but not those of other Latin cultures—although this may be changing. A Mexican noted: "Los Latinos somos muy agresivos entre nosotros mismos." Again, competition for jobs is sometimes a factor: one Salvadoran woman stated that Mexicans feel that Central Americans have taken their jobs.

This is not to imply that interethnic relations are necessarily antagonistic. Several Central American business owners expressed admiration for the solidarity among the Asian community. Some workers who cited specific ethnic groups as problematic claimed to have friends among the same groups. Spokespersons at Manual Arts High School, which was nearly 100 percent African American ten years ago, noted that Latinos and African Americans appeared to get along well; one informant suggested that this may be due to the fact that the shift to a predominantly Latino population had been gradual, in contrast to the Compton area, where the change had been more abrupt and tensions are high.

Many of these antagonisms or tensions can be traced to power relations: landlord vs. renter, supervisor or contractor vs. worker, and so on. In other cases, tensions reflect the fact that the different groups are victims of a process of economic restructuring and the resulting inegalitarian socioeconomic system in which the opportunities of all are severely constricted. Whether the "new majority"—within which the Central Americans are now an important element—will be able to unite to assert their right to equal opportunity or will be divided by interethnic antagonisms will be an important determinant of the future of the city.

Elements of Deterioration

Having examined the Central American community in Westlake and its relationship to other ethnic groups, we return to the questions raised earlier about elements of deterioration versus those of regeneration in the area and among the Central American community. Like many of the poorer areas of Los Angeles, Westlake has been afflicted by crime, drug trafficking, and gangs. Police records for the Rampart Division (which encompasses Westlake) show that crime is high relative to most other areas of the city and is growing; according to one police officer, crime increased by 25 percent in 1989–1990: "Rampart is a combat zone, comparable to Lebanon." Homicides in the Rampart Division increased from 68 in 1988 to 121 in 1990 and 116 in the first nine months of 1991.

Streets and intersections in the area are pickup points for drug dealers and buyers, who can take advantage of easy access to freeways and east-west commuter routes, and a large proportion of the consumers are from outside the neighborhood. As described by an informant who accompanied the police in watching a major pickup point (in the area between 11th and 12th Streets, Lake and Alvarado), the occupants of the first four cars that stopped to buy drugs were, respectively, a white man, a young woman (blonde "U.S.C. type"), an Asian family, and an African American man. Control of drug import and distribution clearly seems to lie outside the community, although area residents, particularly gang members, are involved in selling on the street, where they can earn more than at entry-level cleaning and restaurant work.

The high level of crime and drug dealing in Pico Union led to the establishment of police barricades at key intersections and the dispatch of 160 police officers to the area. Many residents approved of the measure, hoping that it would lead to an overall decrease in crime in the area. By most accounts the operation succeeded in removing the drug trafficking from MacArthur Park, which had been a major drug center, and did reduce crime, at least temporarily. However, crime increased in the area adjacent to Rampart during this period, and drug dealing and consumption have subsequently increased on streets near the park and in alleys behind offices and businesses. Criminal activity, whether drug-related or not, has become bolder; as stated by one resident who was robbed three times, "It doesn't matter whether it's day or night."

Some residents as well as community activists have also complained of police brutality in dealing with alleged drug suspects and gang members (Davis 1990). The police have also openly collaborated with the INS, turning over individuals who are picked up for whatever reason—and in at least one case a group that had called the police to protest a crime—to immigration officials, with the result that they are often confined and may be deported. Police-INS collaboration—and in some cases experience with the brutality of police and military in their own countries—discourages the undocumented from reporting crime. Despite the visible deployment of law enforcement units, including some moderately successful efforts to improve police-community relations, crime has continued to plague the area, most of it directly linked to the drug market and gang activity.

Although drugs are relatively new to the area, gangs have been there for a long time. One of the oldest is the 18th Street gang, which was relatively small in the 1960s but is now the largest in the area. Unlike many of the others, which are primarily or exclusively of a given racial, ethnic, or national group, the 18th Street gang is multiethnic, including Latinos, African Americans, and Anglos. Over the past decade Salvadoran gangs such as Mara Salvatrucha have proliferated and are reputedly among the toughest in the area; there are also several predominantly Guatemalan and Honduran gangs, although membership in some cases (e.g., the Crazy Aces) includes several nationalities. Even when gang divisions may be primarily ethnic or national, membership in a gang apparently supersedes nationality in importance for identification.

Assessments as to the number of gang members vary. According to one source, only about 2 percent of the young people in the Pico Union area belong to gangs. But teachers at Manual Arts High School, located southwest of the Pico Union area at Vermont and Martin Luther King Boulevard, estimate that approximately 10 percent of the students are in gangs, with an additional proportion who are on the periphery of gangs—seeing them as destructive but attractive at the same time. Belmont High, located in the Westlake area, also has a large number of gang members, although both schools have generally been successful in keeping gang conflicts off campus.

Police records for the Rampart Division show that juveniles accounted for 15 to 30 percent of arrests for homicides,[11] presumably reflecting deaths caused by gangs. Shoot-outs among rival gangs are common. Observers contend that most gang crime is among gang members, but innocent people, including children, are killed in drive-by shootings. During the month of October 1991 four children in the area were seriously injured by gangs; in one case a 15-month-old toddler was scalded when gang members broke into the apartment of his mother, who had complained to the police about drug dealers outside her building, and threw a cup of steaming soup at her (Hudson 1991). Police officials who have worked in the area believe that a majority of gangs are involved in narcotics, at least as users, and that many are involved in the drug trade.

The younger generation and children of Central American immigrants, growing up impoverished in a society of relative abundance and a culture that prizes material possessions, are more likely than their parents to be dissatisfied with a survival standard of living. The fact that half of the students in such schools as Manual Arts drop out before finishing, often forced to work, like their parents, in dead-end jobs, suggests that the problems of gangs, drugs, and other illicit activities are not likely to go away.

By the early 1990s, the deterioration of conditions in the area and lack of security had become acute. Numerous residents have been robbed at knifepoint or gunpoint. Drug addicts can be seen using needles in the alleys. In some parts of the area parents are afraid to let their children out on the streets, even during the day. At Belmont High School, teachers and administrators stand outside on the sidewalk at the beginning and end of the school day, providing a kind of buffer zone to protect students entering or leaving school. Residents as well as people working in the area speak of a growing, pervasive sense of fear.

Elements of Regeneration

Within the context of deteriorating conditions and limited resources, there are also elements of regeneration: some existing institutions have expanded their role, and new institutions have been created in efforts to meet the needs of the Central American population, often with the active participation of the Central Americans themselves.

Institutional support. Like other poor neighborhoods, Westlake has been negatively affected by the California tax revolt and resulting shortages of fiscal resources that have affected the institutions of the area, including schools, health centers, and recreation facilities. Aside from added pressures on institutions owing to the population growth the neighborhood has suffered from the disappearance of the MacArthur Park YMCA, as well as the general scarcity of recreational facilities. Other institutions, however, have not only maintained their presence in the area but have expanded their functions in an effort to meet the challenges resulting from the growth and changing needs of the population.

Among the latter, churches have been particularly important in building a sense of community and in expanding their activities to respond to the growing number of new immigrants and the changing composition of their parishioners. The vast majority of Latinos are Catholic by birth, and although many are not practicing, for others the church constitutes an important community as well as spiritual center. Catholic churches have doubled or tripled their Sunday masses in Spanish; the Church of the Immaculate Conception had only one Spanish mass out of seven in 1968; today seven of nine Sunday masses are in Spanish, with Central Americans representing approximately 90 percent of the Spanish-language population. Immaculate Conception and other churches have opened their facilities to Central American and Mexican groups, providing ESL (English as a Second Language) and literacy training, immigration counseling, transportation to shelters, and other services.

Protestant and nondenominational churches have also sought to promote a sense of community, and recently Evangelical churches have moved into the area. The first Unitarian Church and Angelica Lutheran Church have provided facilities and support for numerous immigrant and refugee groups, and the latter has opened its facilities to other congregations, including indigenous Mayan evangelicals. Several other churches have also expanded their athletic and recreational programs in an effort to compensate for cutbacks in recreation in the area.

One of the most activist churches in working with Central Americans, the Church of Our Lady Queen of Angels at La Placita, is located outside the Westlake area north of the civic center. Aside from making its facilities available for numerous functions of the Central American community, the church was declared a sanctuary for refugee families from El Salvador and Guatemala, and by the middle of the 1980s it was widely known among Central American migration networks as a place where one could go for help. Subsequently the church offered its facilities for day laborers and street vendors, with the latter selling to parishioners attending mass on Sunday, and allowed homeless men to sleep there at night. As a result of a change in the leadership of the church at the end of the decade, however, the church at La Placita has taken a less visible role.

Schools in the area have also sought to serve their changing and growing population within the context of overcrowded facilities, high dropout rates, and limited resources. Belmont High School has an enrollment of approximately 4500, among the largest high school populations on a single campus in the United States. Forty percent of the student body are Mexican, 40 percent Central American, and the rest predominantly Asian. Many students enter with no English-language ability, and about half are, or have been, in English as a Second Language (ESL) programs. The dropout rate is high, but of those who graduate about 80 percent go on to college or vocational school. Many teachers have extended their work hours without pay in efforts to help students who might drop out, and graduates from Belmont High who have gone on to college recall with gratitude the encouragement and support of particular teachers and administrators at Belmont. Belmont also offers its facilities for adult education and recreational programs.

Several city or countywide programs explicitly oriented to problems of drugs and gangs operate in the area, among them DARE (Drug Awareness Resistance Education), which operates from the Sheriff's Department, and the police-sponsored Explorer Scout program, which targets young people who might become gang members. Immigrants' rights and human rights organizations have also incorporated Central American youth in their programs.

New institutions. The presence of a large and growing community of Central American immigrants has also led to the formation of a host of organizations in the Westlake area, often at the instigation of the immigrants themselves and explicitly oriented to their needs, among them the Central American Refugee Center (CARECEN) and El Rescate, which provide a range of services including food provision, English-language training, legal counseling, and in some cases representation for immigrants seeking asylum or threatened with deportation; the Guatemalan Information Center, a source of refugee assistance as well as information regarding Guatemala and the Guatemalan community in Los Angeles; the Oscar Romero Medical Clinic; and IXIM, an organization oriented to the indigenous Q'anhob'al community and other Mayan groups in Los Angeles, to mention a few. Although some have moved outside the area, they continue to serve the Central American population, and others have expanded their activities to respond to new needs and problems. An example of the latter is CARECEN, which established a program for day laborers and has worked with the city in setting up a pilot project to systematize the hiring process and to protect laborers from fraudulent practices by their employers; it has also provided counseling for the Association of Street Vendors (discussed below). With the passage of the Immigration Reform and Control Act (IRCA) in 1986, CARECEN, El Rescate, and other groups extended their activities to assist immigrants eligible for amnesty. Subsequently, the work of these organizations expanded to assist applicants for temporary asy-

lum under provisions of Temporary Protected Status, which grants
temporary stay to immigrants from countries experiencing extreme
hardship and was finally extended to Salvadorans at the end of 1990.
Currently, many of these organizations are assessing the implications of the Salvadoran peace accords for their continuing work with
the Central American community in Los Angeles.

With the assistance of these and other organizations, Central
Americans have had an important impact on city politics. In the
mid-1980s a controversy broke out over the issue of declaring Los
Angeles a sanctuary for Salvadoran and Guatemalan refugees. Although the issue was eventually decided negatively, it publicized
the situation of Central American refugees in Southern California,
as has extensive and generally sympathetic coverage of related issues
by the *Los Angeles Times* and other media. In 1986 Mayor Tom Bradley formed the Mayor's Advisory Committee on Central American
Refugees, which sponsored formal hearings on the situation of Central American refugees. In the fall of 1989 the City of Los Angeles
launched a project to provide protection, counseling, and information to day laborers, about half of them Central Americans.

In the meantime, street vendors—chiefly Central American—
formed the Association of Street Vendors, which has lobbied for
legalization of street vending in Los Angeles. In 1989 City Council-
man Michael Woo formed a Task Force on Street Vending in Los
Angeles, which met over the next year and a half to analyze street
vending in Los Angeles and other U.S. cities and to make recom-
mendations to legalize and regulate street vending in Los Angeles.
Aside from its input to the Task Force, the Street Vendors Association has also worked with city health officials and police officers
on issues related to the regulation of vending and the treatment of
vendors. In January 1992 the City Council agreed to draft legislation
permitting street vending in special districts, chiefly in neighborhoods where they now sell, including Pico Union—an important
victory for the association (Sahagun 1992).

Business firms and the self-employed. Another striking change
in the 1980s has been the growth of Central American businesses in
the area to serve the growing Central American population. Our
survey of Central American enterprises in Los Angeles suggested
that while the majority of business owners came to Los Angeles
prior to 1980 (in our sample, two-thirds of the total), most of the
businesses (77 percent) were opened after 1980 (i.e., at a time when
the Central American population in Los Angeles was expanding rapidly). Of the eighty-three businesses surveyed, 53 percent hired Central American workers (in many cases, members of their own families) and 59 percent had predominantly Central American customers.

Several of the businesses are explicitly oriented to the Central American population, among them restaurants, bakeries, markets, travel agencies, and import houses. One may eat at restaurants serving Guatemalan, Salvadoran, or Nicaraguan food; buy beer, toys, shoes, and even lingerie imported from Central America; and enjoy mangoes, cut fruit, or *aqua de coco* from street vendors. Many of these firms and vendors thus help to reinforce the ethnic identity of the neighborhoods—a process that is reinforced by the sponsorship of cultural events and soccer teams by business groups. Other firms have a networking role, linking Central Americans to the national or local economy or society—for example, providing notary services, insurance, or tax counseling for new arrivals lacking information about the intricacies and demands of U.S. society, and extending the markets of the larger economy by making nationally produced items available to a Central American clientele that might have difficulty obtaining them otherwise.

A special case of networking consists of the express courier services established at various locations in Westlake and other parts of the city since the early 1980s. These ensure that mail, money, and merchandise sent by Central Americans to families at home reach their destination, whether it is the capital city or a remote village. Because this assurance applies to merchandise as well as letters and remittances, Central Americans are able to buy and send TV sets, stereo systems, VCRs, and other products that they might be reluctant to purchase otherwise. More generally, business owners provide linkages to the overall economy in several ways: those who live in other areas use income to pay taxes, mortgages, rent, and so on to a different region and/or economy; they buy most of their merchandise from the economy; and they enable the community to buy merchandise that might not otherwise be available (Chinchilla and Hamilton 1989).

The institutional and organizational vitality of the Central American community in Westlake raises questions about any facile, one-sided interpretation of the area as depressed and deteriorating. Churches, schools, and other institutions have transformed and expanded their activities to incorporate the growing Central American populations, and new institutions have been formed, many at the instigation of the Central Americans themselves, to meet the changing needs of the community. Central American markets, restaurants, bakeries, and vendors help to reinforce the ethnic identity of the community, while other firms provide linkages to the national or local economy. The mobilization and organization of sectors of the community around specific issues demonstrates a continuation of the activist tradition of community involvement.

Conclusions

As an area of acute urban deterioration, which at the same time constitutes an entry point for a growing and dynamic immigrant population, the Westlake area epitomizes the conception of a deteriorating urban area in some respects but contradicts it in others. It reportedly leads the city as an area of violent crime, drugs, and gang activity; it is also an area of high transiency, with a substantial proportion of the population moving to other parts of the city or region when opportunity permits. At the same time, as noted above, it is an entry point for Central American immigrant groups who have brought skills, organization, and vitality to the area; churches, schools, immigrant and refugee organizations, restaurants, markets, and other firms and agencies provide a rich institutional life.

Westlake concentrates many of the diverse effects of the global economic restructuring that has penetrated Los Angeles. Thus the causes of the problems of Westlake, and to a large extent the solutions to these problems, lie outside the area itself. The current recession has deepened these problems, owing to cutbacks even in low-wage production and service jobs, and many of the youth, confronted with a bleak future, are tempted into the fraternity of gangs and the lucrative potential of drugs.

Programs that are strictly place-oriented (i.e., focused on the physical improvement of the area without regard to its current inhabitants) tend to displace the problems without resolving them, as appears to have occurred with the police barricades program. In the past, urban renewal programs often meant "urban removal"—forcing low-income residents to look for cheaper housing elsewhere. Indeed, as noted above, the high cost of housing, which has increased as Koreatown moves east and Koreans and other groups buy into the area, has led many Central Americans to move south into traditionally African American neighborhoods in search of cheaper housing.

Rather than high-cost programs that displace residents, limited resources would be better spent in expanding programs oriented to the population of the area and enabling old and new institutions to meet new challenges—whether it involves education about drugs, expanded recreation facilities, legal counseling for refugees, or keeping students in high school. The Central City West project, which incorporates the demands of low-income tenants in the area for affordable housing and other amenities such as parks and child-care facilities, might offer a new model for development in low-income neighborhoods in the future, but in the recessionary climate of the early 1990s the ability of communities to elicit such amenities will probably be severely curtailed. In any event, the resourcefulness and skills of the Central Americans who have made the difficult journey to Los Angeles and learned to cope with a new environment will continue to constitute an important asset in meeting the challenges of a complex urban community.

Postscript: Central Americans and the L.A. "Riots" of 1992

While media discussions of the April 29–May 1 disturbances in Los Angeles tend to focus primarily on relations between whites and African Amerians and between African Americans and Koreans, the impact of the riots on Los Angeles' Central American community is frequently ignored or misunderstood. South Central Los Angeles, the initial focal point of violence, burning, and looting, was the same geographical area of the city where the Watts riots occurred in the summer of 1965. In the intervening years, however, the ethnic make-up of the area had changed, just as it had in the city overall. Latinos made up less than 2 percent of Watts' population and 10 percent of the population of Los Angeles at the time of the Watts riots, but they accounted for and were estimated as half the population of South Los Angeles and 40 percent of Los Angeles, according to the 1990 census. By Thursday, April 30, 1992 (the second day of the disturbances), neighborhoods like Pico Union also resembled war zones as an estimated 1000 businesses, owned by Latinos as well as Koreans, burned, leaving some residents without housing and others without jobs. Despite residents' and business owners' complaints about the absence of police when the majority of the destruction took place, Latinos turned out to be the majority of those arrested, many for curfew violations and looting when security forces did finally mobilize. The Sheriff's Department analysis of riot-related arrests revealed that 45 percent were Latino, 41 percent were African American, and 12 percent were Anglo, with 60 percent of the arrestees lacking prior criminal records. Those arrested included Central American and Mexican immigrant women, caught leaving grocery stores with diapers and food and other basic necessities. Of the riot-related deaths, 25 were African American, 19 were Latinos, and 10 were Anglos (R. Martinez 1992).

Inflammatory comments at the time of the riots by conservative politicians, anti-immigration forces, and, most notably, Police Chief Darryl Gates (who publicly blamed "illegal aliens" for much of the pillage) did little to calm Central American and Mexican immigrants' fears that they might be blamed for the riots. Los Angeles police

violated the official policy of not turning over suspected undocumented immigrants to the INS, resulting in the deportation of a
large number, and brought in 400 Border Patrol agents (an armed
agency of the INS) to patrol Latino neighborhoods, including Pico
Union. The patrol cars, distinctive green-and-white vehicles, caused
widespread fear of mass deportations. A widely repeated early official estimate of one-third of those arrested being undocumented immigrants was eventually dropped to 10 percent, but little was done
to repair the damage that might have been created in the public
mind. "This was basically throwing gasoline onto a fire", said Madeline Janis, executive director of CARECEN. "There was almost a
feeling that someone was exacting vengeance against the community."

Adding to the trauma for many Salvadorans and Guatemalans
was the similarity between the disturbances and the conditions of
violence and civil war from which they had fled. Flashbacks to
scenes repressed or forgotten caused many adults and children to
seek treatment for symptoms of post-traumatic stress syndrome.

In an attempt to give Central American immigrants—documented
and undocumented—a stronger, more audible voice in the political
landscape of the city and neutralize the effects of scapegoating,
CARECEN, El Rescate, and other immigrant groups and service
centers have become actively involved in efforts to rebuild the city.
These efforts have given the Central American community a visi-
bility and access to decision-making groups not previously available
to it. Over the long term, however, the key to the Central American community's voice and political influence is the formation of
stronger Latino and multiracial coalitions that can play a consistent
role in city politics in alliance with other progressive organizations.

APPENDIX 3A: INTERVIEWS

Julie Aha and Jon Schafer, Justice for Janitors, July 12, 1990
Alice Callaghan, Para los Niños, July 27, 1989
Bill Cruz, Community Development Specialist, Pico Union,
    Community Redevelopment Agency, July 18, 1990
David Diaz, urban planner, May 1991
Leo Estrada, School of Architecture and Urban Planning, Oc-
    tober 18, 1990
Joe Favatella, Counselor, Belmont High School, November 7,
    1991
Eduardo Gonzalez, Central American Refugee Center
    (CARECEN), September 1990
Madeline Janis, Central American Refugee Center (CARE-
    CEN), October 1990

Anne Kamsvaag, Coalition for Humane Immigrant Rights of Los Angeles (CHIRLA), July 21, 1989

Philip Lance, Episcopal Minister, October 1991

Richard Mendelhall, Custodian, Immaculate Conception School, November 8, 1991

Anthony Mischel, Labor Defense Board, July 27, 1989

Michael Oppenheim, Josh Peshult, and Mary Jane Thompson, Manual Arts High School, May 22, 1990

Ana Perez, Belmont High School graduate, May 1991

Robert W. Riley, Captain, Los Angeles Police Department, September 6, 1991

Joan Ririe, Principal, Belmont Community Adult School, November 7, 1991

Jeff Stansbery, ILGWU, July 1989

Hector Tovar, *Los Angeles Times*, June 1991

NOTES

1. This concept of Southern California as a high-growth area has been challenged in the 1990s due to cutbacks in the defense industry, difficulties in the financial and real estate markets, and slowdowns in construction, retailing, and aerospace industries (Stevenson 1989; Peterson 1991).

2. Aside from secondary sources, census data, newspaper reports, and documents on Pico Union and Central City West, this chapter draws upon information from informants who have lived or worked in the area or who are knowledgeable about the Central American population in general. It also draws upon two surveys carried out by the authors: the first of Central American businesses in Los Angeles, the second of Central American and Mexican workers. The study of Central American enterprises was made possible by a grant from the Inter-University Program for Latino Research and the Social Science Research Council. The study of Central American and Mexican workers was funded in part by a grant from the Division of Immigrant Policy and Research, U.S. Department of Labor. It should be pointed out that these surveys are based on snowball sampling, and their findings cannot necessarily be generalized to the Central American population. However, they provide insight into the range of experiences of Central Americans in the Southern California area. In the chapter we will clarify to what extent information applies to Central Americans in the region as a whole or to the specific area under study.

3. Prior to the current recession, developers and planners were promoting a combined residential and office development of Central City West.

4. Our survey of Central American workers in Los Angeles found

that in more than 60 percent of the cases of those with children, some or all of the children were living outside the United States, and over one-third of those married were separated from their spouses. Since this was not a random sample, however, it may not be representative of the Central American population as a whole.

5. In the early 1980s, janitorial workers in Los Angeles were organized and earning approximately $12.00 per hour. By 1983, however, a number of non-union cleaning companies hiring undocumented workers as well as non-English-speaking legal immigrants had emerged, forcing unions to roll back wage demands. By early 1988, union membership had been reduced from 6000 to 2500 while wages and other benefits dropped to $4.00 per hour. The aggressive Justice for Janitors campaign has succeeded in reversing this trend in Los Angeles and other cities; by the end of 1989 some 55 percent of the workers cleaning buildings in downtown Los Angeles were organized, and in the summer of 1990 the union succeeded in organizing the workers of an international cleaning company who worked in many of the buildings in Century City. Although union wages, at $5.00 to $6.50 per hour, are not at their 1980 level, unionized workers also receive health insurance and other benefits, in contrast to non-union workers who generally receive only the minimum wage.

6. Typically, a contractor may receive $6.50 for blouses that cost $5.00 to produce—but may sell for $50–$100 each at the retail level.

7. There are also a large number of stores and shops in the Pico Union area run by Central Americans, but most of the owners live in other parts of the city.

8. Information on street vending is based on meetings of the Task Force on Street Vending in Los Angeles. See especially Fujimoto and Janis 1990.

9. Most studies of immigrant labor suggest that although this is a widespread perception, only in relatively few cases have immigrants taken jobs wanted by African Americans or other U.S. citizens. In some cases, such as the garment industry, much of the industry would go abroad in the absence of cheap immigrant labor. In others, such as hotels, African Americans often hold supervisory positions among the cleaning staff. Janitorial work would seem to be one example where the growing presence of a large immigrant population facilitated the decline in wages and working conditions, although other factors were also involved (Loucky, Hamilton, and Chinchilla 1989).

10. Two major examples in Los Angeles have been Monterey Park, which was predominantly Anglo and Latino until the growth of the Chinese population in the 1980s, and Compton, a black neighborhood with a growing Latino population.

11. This information is based on the Monthly Report of crimes and arrests in the city of Los Angeles for the month of May. It includes year-to-date (i.e., January–May) statistics for 1989 and 1990.

4

CUBANS IN MIAMI

Alex Stepick III and Guillermo Grenier

C UBANS ARE different. Just ask them. Miami Cubans commonly assert that they have "made Miami what it is today" through their hard work and "Cuban ingenuity". Indeed, Miami is the only U.S. city where Hispanic immigrants have managed to create a successful and self-sustained ethnic economy in which the primary problems are not unemployment and welfare but sources of capital and expanding markets. Cubans are undeniably the most successful Hispanics in the United States and apparently do not belong in a book addressing Hispanic poverty. Cubans are important to the issues of this volume, however, for two reasons: (1) not all Cubans are successful and those who are poor have played an important role within the community; and (2) Cubans have received probably more welfare than other Hispanic groups, but they have used it to establish an entrepreneurial enclave rather than becoming welfare-dependent. The critical question for this volume is, therefore, what allows this accomplishment. In this essay, we address these two concerns by first describing the social and economic structure of the Cuban community and then arguing that its relative success is based on three forms of capital—social, economic, and political—that have produced an extraordinary solidarity among Cubans in Miami that helps raise some from poverty, ameliorates it for others, and masks it for many. Before concluding, we discuss the economic basis for the perception that Miami Cuban success has

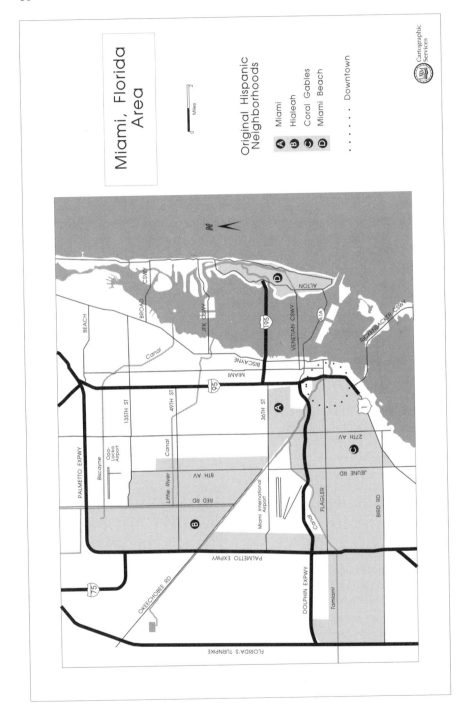

Miami, Florida
Area

0 — 2 Miles

Original Hispanic
Neighborhoods

Ⓐ Miami
Ⓑ Hialeah
Ⓒ Coral Gables
Ⓓ Miami Beach
· · · · · · Downtown

Cartographic
Services

come through displacing native African Americans in the local economy. Many non-Cubans in Miami, both black and white, commonly believe that Cubans have achieved success at the expense of blacks. We argue that the data do not support this hypothesis, but that Cuban success and Cuban community solidarity have created and exacerbated tensions and conflict between the Cuban and African American communities.

Cuban Economic Success

By every measure, Cubans are the most economically successful of U.S. Hispanic groups (see Table 4.1).[1] Both nationwide and in Miami they have higher individual and family incomes, more businesses, professionals, and executives, higher levels of education, and greater political power than other minorities. Cuban immigrants also advance economically more quickly than Mexican immigrants and receive a higher return on their education than Mexican immigrants (Portes and Bach 1985).

In Miami, Cubans played a pivotal role in transforming the local economy from domestic tourism and retirement into what has been described as the capital of the Caribbean and even Latin America.[2] Cuban immigrants frequently headed the import and export companies, the banks that financed the transactions, and the smaller trans-

TABLE 4.1

Income, Affluence, and Poverty
Dade County 1980

	Median Family Income	Percent Poverty	Percent Income Above $35,000	Inequality Measure
Whites	$25,700	7.9	33.8	.288
Hispanics	$20,200	16.9	17.5	.283
Blacks	$16,200	29.5	11.8	.309

Source: Profile of the Black Population, Metro-Dade Planning, 1984. Massey & Eggers 1990.
*The Inequality Measure represents the proportion of families that would have to shift income categories to achieve an even distribution. See Massey & Eggers, p. 1160.

portation and service companies that allowed Miami to displace New Orleans as the important U.S.–Latin American link. Although Miami has only 5 percent of the U.S. Hispanic population, with nearly 30,000 Hispanic businesses, it has by far the highest per capita rate of Hispanic businesses in the United States (O'Hare 1987, p. 33) and close to half of the forty largest Hispanic-owned industrial and commercial firms in the country. As Figure 4.1 demonstrates, between 1970 and 1980 the number of Hispanic executives nearly quadrupled, while the number of Hispanic professionals in Miami more than doubled. There is also no doubt that Cubans in Miami have achieved significant wealth and local power, exercised through the increasing number of elected officials (including a U.S. congressional representative and the mayor of Miami) and such organizations as the Cuban American National Foundation, the Latin Builders Association, the Hispanic Builders Association, and the Latin Chamber of Commerce.[3]

Nevertheless, not all Miami Cubans are rich and powerful businessmen. Even the fact of business ownership is somewhat misleading. Of the nearly 25,000 Hispanic-owned and -operated busi-

FIGURE 4.1

*Occupations of Employed Persons
Dade County, 1970 and 1980 (Tens of thousands)*

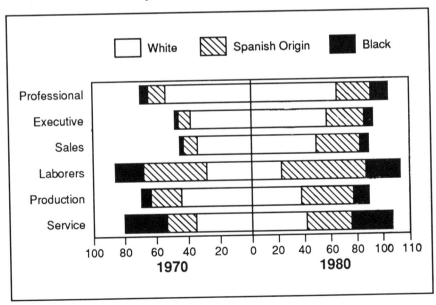

Source: U.S. Census 1970 and 1980.

nesses in 1982; only 12 percent had paid employees, and together they generated a total of only 18,199 paid jobs (Diaz-Briquets 1984), a number only slightly higher than the number of Hispanics in Dade County who belong to unions.[4] Indeed, Hispanics in Miami are over-represented in manual occupations, working primarily as laborers, craftsmen, and service workers (see Figure 4.1).

Most recently arrived Cuban immigrants first work in Miami for other Cubans (Portes, Clark and Manning, 1985). For the new immigrants, the jobs offer the advantages of requiring no language training and the opportunity to work with compatriots. For the employers, the new immigrants offer a cheap source of labor. Frequently working conditions are informal, that is, in violation of labor law and abysmally equal to those endured by the most exploited undocumented alien in other parts of the United States (Stepick 1989, 1990; Fernandez-Kelly and Garcia 1989). Miami's apparel industry, the third largest in the United States, was created in the 1960s by relocated northeastern entrepreneurs specifically because of the new supplies of female labor that Cuban immigration provided. The local firms expanded rapidly and continued to prosper throughout the 1970s and early 1980s because of their low labor costs and their ability to informalize production through subcontracting to women who worked in their homes. A similar pattern occurred in the local construction industry, in which Cuban labor and Cuban firms undermined union labor through lower wage rates and fewer benefits. In the restaurant industry, Cubans have employed their recently arrived compatriots at less than the minimum wage.

These low wages are reflected in surveys of new immigrants and the 1980 census income figures for employed Cuban females. Immigrants who arrived in the mid-1970s and the Mariel Cubans who arrived in 1980 both had poverty-level incomes for a few years after they arrived (Portes and Bach 1985; Portes and Stepick 1985). But within three years their incomes had improved notably, with 1970s immigrant Cubans advancing more quickly than a comparable group of Mexican immigrants, and 1980 Mariel Cubans outstripping a comparable group of Haitian immigrants in Miami.

In contrast to recently arrived Cuban male workers, Cuban females generally continue to have low incomes long after they arrive. Cuban female annual income in 1979 was scarcely higher than for the total U.S. Hispanic female population (Perez 1986, p. 10; Bernal 1982; Ferree 1979; Kurtines and Miranda 1980; Prieto 1987; Szapocznik, Scopetta, and Tillman 1978; Szapocznik and Fernandez 1988). Although both male and female Cuban immigrants may begin working in informal jobs in the enclave, men appear to be more capable of advancing out of those jobs, while women remain within them.

During the 1980s, as the number of female-headed households increased among Cubans, poverty rates also likely increased. In our discussion below of Cuban social capital, we will indicate how low incomes among females, however, create less poverty in the Miami Cuban community than in other U.S. Hispanic communities.

Those Cubans most likely to be poor are the elderly. Elderly Cubans receive more public assistance than other U.S. Hispanics and with over 80 percent having incomes of less than $5,000 a year in 1987, a greater proportion of the Miami Hispanic elderly are poor than elderly Miami whites or even elderly Miami African Americans (Pelaez and Rothman 1991). There are also simply more Cuban elderly than among other U.S. Hispanics. More than one-third of the Cuban population is 50 or older, and the average age of the Cuban-origin population is more than fifteen years higher than that of the total U.S. Hispanic population: 40.5 versus 25.5 (Perez 1992). In Miami, traditionally a retirement center for whites from the U.S. Northeast, more than one-third of the area's elderly population is Cuban (Dluhy and Krebs 1987).

Thus, although average Cuban income is relatively high, as are the number of Cuban-owned businesses, the typical Cuban is more likely to be working class. Moreover, many within the Cuban community are poor. Females earn low incomes as do new immigrants, and the Cuban elderly have higher poverty rates than Miami's African Americans. We now address how, in spite of these working-class and poverty-stricken members of the Cuban community, Cubans have not become welfare-dependent and have achieved more on the average than other U.S. Hispanics.

Three Forms of Cuban Capital

As indicated in the introduction, Cubans commonly assert that they are different, more hardworking and ingenious. Although not denying the presence of these positive characteristics, we maintain that the essential differences between Cubans and other U.S. Hispanics lie in three forms of capital—economic, political, and social. By capital, we mean available resources that can be invested or utilized to produce even more assets. After describing the three capital forms, we describe how they interact to construct Cuban ethnic solidarity, which bolsters their value.

Economic. Refugee communities usually contain a vertical slice of the sending society, a slice that includes not only workers but also professionals and entrepreneurs. The first wave of Cubans has been labeled the "Golden Exiles", the top of Cuban society who were most immediately threatened by a socialist revolution (Portes

1969). Some former Cuban government officials in the first wave brought personal savings and money embezzled from the Cuban treasury that capitalized small businesses in Miami (Forment 1989, p. 60). Many others had already established a footing in the United States, and when the revolution came they simply abandoned one of their residences for another across the Straits of Florida. Some had already moved their capital to the United States, depositing it in banks or investing in real estate (Perez-Stable and Uriarte 1990, p. 5). For others, their economic capital was more in the form of knowledge and connections. Before the revolution, a Cuban shoe manufacturer, for example, produced footwear for a major U.S. retail chain. He obtained his working capital from New York financial houses. After the revolution, the only change was that the manufacturing was done in Miami rather than Havana. The Cuban Revolution made him and many others exiles in a way that was different for upper-class Mexicans or Puerto Ricans. The revolution thus upwardly biased the socioeconomic profile of Miami's Cuban population. Even if they could not transfer their investments, their human capital—their knowledge and experience—came with them.[5]

Most, of course, could not instantly create a shoe factory, and many experienced a drop in socioeconomic standing. But they did usually find employers willing to give them work. Employers commonly prefer immigrant and refugee workers to the native-born. They allegedly work harder and complain less.[6] The early employers of Cubans in Miami were no exception. As one Miami African American asserted:

When they [Cubans] first came, white folks welcomed them; they welcomed them because, according to [the whites] we, the blacks, had forgotten our place. We had gotten very sassy and non-dependable and non-reliable; they found themselves having to deal with a new minority called Cubans and that was good for them because, once again, they had access to a cheaper pool of labor for the hotels, motels and restaurants.[7]

These Cubans, who were forced to work at low-wage jobs, thus were first integrated into the U.S. labor market in the same fashion as most Mexican immigrants and Puerto Ricans. But the two other forms of Cuban capital, political and social, meant that most Cubans did not stay long in these entry-level positions.

Political. Refugee communities frequently garner political capital because the very status of refugee reflects a political decision by the receiving state. In the United States, groups designated as refugees are offered special governmental assistance when they arrive that is not available to other immigrant flows (Loescher and Scanlan 1986; Zucker and Zucker 1987). Such was the case with the Cubans. The first wave of Cubans came in the midst of the cold war when the United States welcomed immigrants in general and those fleeing communism especially. The Cubans' arrival also coincided with the construction of "Great Society" programs, which provided extensive benefits to minority populations, including special programs for Cuban refugees. At the same time, the public sector promoted affirmative action to ensure ethnic and minority participation in employment.

The U.S. government created for the arriving Cubans an unprecedented direct and indirect assistance program, the Cuban Refugee Program, that spent nearly $1 billion between 1965 and 1976 (Pedraza-Bailey 1985, p. 41). The federal government provided transportation costs from Cuba, financial assistance to needy refugees and to state and local public agencies that provided services for refugees, and employment and professional training courses for refugees (see Table 4.2). During the 1960s, the IRS allowed Cubans to declare capital losses for properties in Cuba (Perez-Stable and Uriarte 1990, p. 6). Even in programs not especially designed for them, Cubans seemed to benefit. From 1968 to 1980, Hispanics (almost all Cubans) received 46.9 percent of all Small Business Administration loans in Dade County (Porter and Dunn 1984, p. 196).

Even more important was indirect assistance. Through the 1960s, the University of Miami reputedly had the largest CIA station in the world, outside of the organization's headquarters in Virginia. With perhaps as many as 12,000 Cubans in Miami on the CIA payroll at one point in the early 1960s, it was one of the largest employers in the state of Florida. It supported what was described as the third-largest navy in the world and more than fifty front businesses: CIA boat shops, CIA gun shops, CIA travel agencies, CIA detective agencies, and CIA real estate agencies. (Didion 1987, pp. 90–91; Rieff 1987, pp. 193–207; Rich 1974). Although it is uncertain whether these activities directly provided capital for what was to become the Cuban enclave,[8] this investment certainly served to provide the predominantly middle-class refugees of the mid and late 1960s with sufficient income to retool their skills.

These benefits, moreover, were not limited to those the federal government provided. The state of Florida passed laws that made it easier for Cuban professionals, especially medical doctors, to recertify themselves to practice in the United States. At the county level, in the late 1970s and early 1980s, 53 percent of minority contracts for Dade County's rapid transit system went to Hispanic firms. Dade

TABLE 4.2
Cuban Welfare Benefits

BENEFITS SPECIFICALLY FOR CUBAN REFUGEES

ECONOMIC
resettlement costs (transportation and basic maintenance)
CIA employment and front businesses
financial aid for unaccompanied children
IRS tax deductions for losses in Cuba

EDUCATION AND TRAINING
job training and assistance in finding jobs
college tuition loans
English language classes
vocational training
business education
varied adult education programs
bilingual education in public schools .
school operating expenses
Professional retraining and recertification for:
   Cuban physicians, nurses, lawyers, pharmacists,
   dentists, accountants, architects, engineers,
   veterinarians, and teachers

OTHERS
distribution of surplus food
health services
eased citizenship requirements

OTHER BENEFITS NOT NECESSARILY FOR CUBANS, BUT
UTILIZED EXTENSIVELY AND ADVANTAGEOUSLY BY THEM

Small Business Administration
Affirmative Action
   City of Miami and Dade County employment
Minority set-asides/targets
   City of Miami and Dade County contracts

Sources: Pedraza-Bailey 1985, Chapter 2, with the exception of IRS benefits, which are
mentioned in Pérez-Stable and Uriarte 1990:6.

County Schools led the nation in bilingual education by introducing it for the first wave of Cuban refugees in 1960. The Dade County Commission also designated the county officially bilingual in the mid-1970s.

Cubans in Miami had available especially for them language classes, vocational training, business education, and varied adult education programs. The University of Miami, along with others, trained, retooled, and recertified thousands of Cuban physicians, nurses, lawyers, pharmacists, dentists, accountants, architects, engineers, veterinarians, and teachers (Mohl 1990, p. 49).

In sum, the total benefits available to the Cuban community appear to surpass those available to any other U.S. minority group. About 75 percent of Cuban arrivals before 1974 directly received some kind of state-provided benefits (Pedraza-Bailey 1985, p. 40 based on J. Clark 1975, p. 116). The Cuban Refugee Program was especially generous, but on top of that state and local government granted special favors and Cubans qualified for minority status in affirmative action programs. The presence of entrepreneurs and professionals in the Cuban refugee flow provided a trained and experienced core of persons who knew how to access and use these privi-

FIGURE 4.2a

Comparative U.S. Latin Income Characteristics, 1980

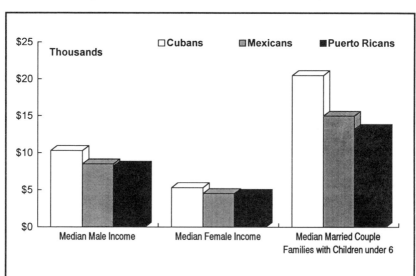

Source: Perez 1985, Tables 2, 4, & 9

leges. Cuban family structure further encouraged the maximum exploitation of these new resources.

Social. In terms of social capital, Cuban households have a number of social characteristics that became economic advantages in the United States. In income, Cubans do better than other U.S. Hispanic groups (Figure 4.2a). This is at least in part because of their family characteristics (Figure 4.2b). A smaller proportion of Cuban families have young children, a higher proportion have older adults (such as grandparents) resident in the household who can provide child care, proportionately more family members work, and, specifically, a higher proportion of married women work.[9]

The extent to which women work outside the home in the Cuban community is crucial to understanding the large number of workers in the Cuban household and the relatively high median family income of that population. Although Cuban females do not earn any more than other female Hispanics, their income is more likely to be

FIGURE 4.2b

Cuban Family Characteristics, 1980

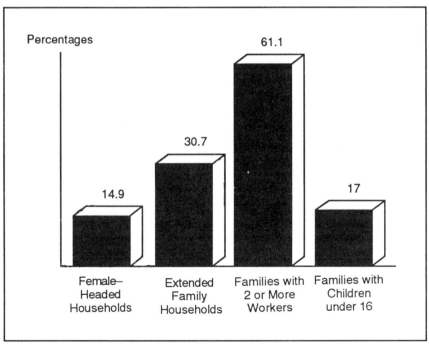

Extended Families = Persons > 65 yrs.
Source: U.S. Census 1980

only part of a family's income, thus producing a median income for married Cuban couples that is about one-third higher than that for other U.S. Hispanics. Thus, the strong family structure of Cubans[10] alleviates the low incomes of many females and the elderly. High rates of female employment in the Cuban community are not the result of transformations in the role of women, but rather a product of high aspirations regarding family income and social mobility (Prieto 1987; Ferree 1979). Among Cubans in the United States, therefore, a fairly traditional sex-role orientation coexists with high rates of female labor force participation (Perez 1986).

Much of this employment is in informal firms, but at the same time these firms are commonly family-operated firms that utilize particularistic hiring criteria, providing women with the culturally acceptable opportunity of working with family and friends. For the immigrant entrepreneurs, exclusive access to new arrivals is a source of low-wage labor and expanding consumer markets, and hiring co-ethnics facilitates greater control of the work force, minimizing worker opposition and unionization (Portes and Bach 1985, p. 203).

Community Solidarity

The use of Spanish in Miami frequently astounds newcomers. Not only is it more widespread than in other U.S. cities, but surprising people speak it. Spanish is spoken in Miami not just by those persons taking orders in restaurants but also by those giving the orders—both from the menu and from the cash register. It is not spoken solely by those washing the cars and cutting the grass, but by those having their cars washed and owning the houses that have too much grass. A prominent Miami Anglo stated in frustration during the 1988 debate on a state constitutional amendment to make English Florida's official language that "there are no more English radio stations". In reality, in Dade and Broward counties on the AM band there are twice as many English stations as Spanish ones, and on FM the ratio is nearly 7 to 1, but the perception is that Spanish has become dominant. Not only is Spanish spoken in diverse settings, but its usage is apparently increasing.

As Figure 4.3 demonstrates, in 1989 only 2.6 percent of Hispanics reported English to be the language most frequently spoken at home, down from 3.4 percent in 1980. More significantly, the same survey found that even at work the language most frequently spoken by Hispanics in South Florida is Spanish (42.2 percent), up from 36.6 percent in 1980. Moreover, the nightly newscast of one of the two Spanish-language television stations is watched by more viewers than any of the English-language newscasts.

FIGURE 4.3

Language Use by Latins in South Florida 1989

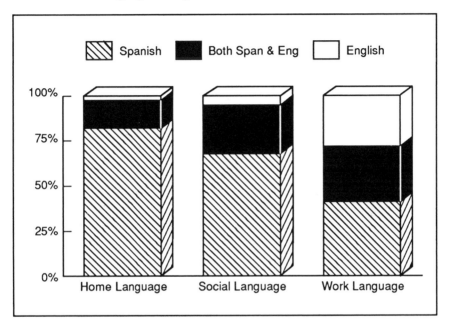

Source: Strategy Research Corporation, Eastern Ethnic Audit 1989

Rather than fading away, Spanish in Miami has become an important second language. Knowing Spanish is a positive skill in the job
market. With the plurality of the population being Hispanic and so
many being first-generation immigrants, employers recognize that a
good proportion of their market is Spanish-speaking and they commonly prefer bilingual employees. A 1989 study found 11 percent of
help-wanted advertisements in the *Miami Herald* referred to bilingualism as a qualification for employment. The figure may be an
underestimate because bilingualism may in some cases be a factor
in employment but not be listed as a qualification in a newspaper
job advertisement.

At worksites, language is the first social divider, then nationality,
and then race. When new workers arrive at a local apparel plant, the
first task during breaks is to determine whether the person speaks
Spanish, then her/his nationality, which is closely tied to the food
one eats. On one occasion a longtime Cuban American apparel
worker addressed a new employee she thought was Colombian,
"Oh, you're eating yellow rice. Colombians don't eat yellow rice.

We Cubans do." The new arrival replied, "Yes, but I'm married to a Cuban." "Oh, how nice!" responded the first woman. Thus, Spanish reflects wide and deep ethnic solidarity that often becomes more focused into a specifically national Cuban solidarity.

Cuban community solidarity has a number of functions: it produces a multiplier effect of Cubans' economic, political, and social capital; it ameliorates class exploitation within the Cuban community; and it masks both Cuban poverty and racism.

Cuban community solidarity produces a multiplier effect of the three forms of Cuban capital in a number of interdependent ways. First, it provides workers employment that requires no acculturation.[11] Not only does one not need to speak English, but also the workplace is politically and socially oriented more toward Cuba, or at least Cuban Miami's interpretation of Cuba. Moreover, in contrast to the work of Latins in other parts of the United States, Cuban enclave employment provides a Cuban boss and other Cuban community members who have economic power and influence. Cuban enclave employment is more often an apprenticeship than a dead-end job. Cuban employers frequently provide training to their Cuban workers and assistance in establishing their own independent business. Cuban garment workers become subcontractors, establishing an informal workshop in their home. Cuban construction workers become contractors, also working out of their homes. For financing, workers turned entrepreneurs can go to banks, sometimes owned by Cubans and certainly staffed by Cubans, where they are much more likely to find a sympathetic loan officer than in an Anglo bank. For markets, they rely on the Cuban community's loyalty, Cubans' preference for shopping at and buying from Cuban contractors and stores.

This economic solidarity integrally depends on Miami's peculiar Cuban politics. Forment has demonstrated how politics and profit became fused as right-wing exiles used their economic capital to establish themselves while enforcing political consensus within the Miami community by harassing, boycotting, and even terrorizing firms that were believed to be pro-Castro (Forment 1989, p. 47). Thus, an economic and social community emerged that was politically monolithic and possessed a level of self-reliance and public trust seldom found among minority communities. If one maintained the appropriate right-wing anti-Castro attitude, then entrepreneurs had access to low-wage, pliant labor and an expanding Cuban market, and workers were granted jobs that required no acculturation and yet offered opportunities and assistance for professional advancement. At the same time, Cubans' social capital provided women to work in the enclave for Cuban immigrant entrepreneurs, who legitimized harsh, informal working relationships by evoking ethnic solidarity.

This solidarity not only legitimizes class exploitation, but it also ameliorates it. Miami Cuban women, for example, recognize that the wages they receive are commonly extraordinarily low and the working conditions especially harsh. But seldom do they express a preference for working outside the enclave where conditions might be better. Rather, they view the severe working conditions as being at least partially balanced by ethnic solidarity. Not only can they speak their native language, but Cuban American employers are more likely to be flexible, to easily grant them time off for family or other personal matters. Women who do homework in the garment industry do not see themselves as being especially exploited, although garment homework is illegal, the hours are long, and the pay minimal. Instead, these women emphasize that the hours are flexible, that they can earn as much as they want, that they do not have to seek outside childcare. Moreover, they view the person with whom they subcontract as someone who can help them vault to the next stage, to establishing their own small factory. The ideology and hopes for self-employment within a context of paternalistic employee-employer relationships thus both mitigates the perception of exploitation and enhances community solidarity.[12] Community solidarity and class, and particularly gender, exploitation within the Cuban community thus have a paradoxical relationship. The enclave allows increased exploitation at the same time that it ameliorates exploitation by providing cultural advantages and the hope of self-improvement.

For many, self-improvement is elusive. According to the director of the Little Havana Community Center (LHCC), homelessness among the Cubans increased significantly through the late 1980s. Moreover, as discussed earlier, a high proportion of the Cuban elderly are below the poverty line. But the Cuban community's solidarity again ameliorates and masks this problem. First, family networks within the community alleviate poverty for many by helping many Cubans. As the LHCC director stated, "It has to be real bad for a Cuban to hit the street." In short, Cubans try to help one another. At the same time, not all Cubans get help when they need it. The expectation, however, is that Cubans can make it, so those in need of help commonly are afraid to ask for it. Again, the LHCC director: "I don't know if it's pride or what but it takes a lot for them to come to the shelters for food." As an example she mentioned an incident in October 1990 where twenty Cubans had been sent to Belle Glades to cut sugar cane by the Florida Employment Services. Within a few weeks of arriving, they had to return to Miami because violence had broken out between Cubans and Jamaicans. "And now we have to find a place for them. Seventeen of them are homeless."

Just as individual poverty-stricken Cubans have difficulty asking for help, Cuban leaders and the community in general have difficulty recognizing poverty as an important community problem. Elected Cuban officials and the Spanish-language media virtually never focus on poverty within the Cuban community as a problem. Although they do lobby and seek funds for organizations such as LHCC, that political activity is quiet and unobtrusive compared to the public attention to Castro's Cuba. Again, Cuban community solidarity produces a paradoxical effect. Poverty within the Cuban community is less widespread than in other U.S. Latin communities because economic success is more common and because family networks are more capable of assisting those in need. But when these resources are insufficient, those in need are less willing to seek assistance and the community is less willing to recognize and publicly address the problems of poverty within it.

The final function of Cuban community solidarity that we address is its ability to mask Cuban racism. Miami Cubans are primarily white and usually visually indistinguishable from Anglos. Miami Cubans also are firmly convinced that they are not racist. Whatever racial problems exist in Miami, they contend, result from the legacy of southern segregation and U.S. racism. They point out correctly that Cuba never had segregation laws and that blacks and whites intermixed more freely in Cuba than they do in the United States. This position, however, is maintained in Miami by reconstructing Cuban and Latin society as a peculiarly white society from which blacks are implicitly excluded. For example, one young black Cuban who grew up in New York and could pass for a black American recounted how in Miami he would often overhear white Cubans' racist remarks as they assumed that he was not Cuban and spoke no Spanish. Later on, when he would come forth and identify himself as a Cuban, he would repeatedly be told, "No, you can't be Cuban".

Correspondingly, Miami's black Cubans are virtually invisible. They live apart from the larger Cuban community. A black Cuban adolescent claimed that white Cubans get "pissed off" if she identifies herself as Cuban American. They would rather have her "pass as just black . . . period". A middle-aged black Cuban woman asserted that Cubans were more racist than white Americans. The woman moved into a mixed neighborhood where her white American neighbor did not seem bothered by having a black Cuban for a neighbor, but her next-door neighbor, a white Cuban, refused to speak to her.

White Cubans who had black friends in Cuba now ostracize them. One elderly black Cuban female used to visit a white Cuban family whom she had known for nearly fifteen years until she noticed a coldness toward her. A common friend, also white, told her that the old friend has declared, "I cannot continue to have this black woman coming over because my daughter's boy friend and his family are going to think that we are part black and I don't want the relationship to break up".

The Cuban community's solidarity, manifest most visibly in the use of the Spanish language, thus multiplies the effects of the three forms of Cuban capital while also having a paradoxical effect on both class exploitation and the presence of poverty within the Cuban community. Community solidarity both legitimizes exploitation and eases its effects by offering increased self-employment opportunities to some. It also moderates poverty through family networks while concealing it from the majority of the community, keeping it off the public agenda of community problems. Community solidarity also promotes a racist construction of the Cuban community excluding black Cubans. This racism also affects the community's relationship to Miami's African American community.

Competition with Other Groups

The other face of internal solidarity is external competition. Racial and ethnic strife has split no other U.S. city in the 1980s like it has Miami. Miami's African American community exploded three times during the decade. Each time the eruption was linked to the killing of a black by the Miami police, but also each time the question was raised whether Miami's black community was peculiarly suffering because of the successes of the Miami Cuban community.

In 1966, Martin Luther King had already noted Miami's emerging racial triangle and warned against pitting refugees against blacks in competition for jobs. Rather than concentrating on the political and economic support Cubans received from the local and federal government or on Cubans' internal economic and social capital, most of Miami's blacks and native white leaders, along with some academics (Mohl 1990; Porter and Dunn 1984; U.S. Commission on Civil Rights 1982), commonly presume that Cuban success has been at the expense of Miami's blacks. One black leader bluntly asserted, "It is a fact of life that Cubans displaced blacks."[13]

These views, however, are not entirely accurate. Although middle-class Cubans in the 1960s took whatever jobs were available and, in this sense, "displaced blacks", their stay in these jobs was relatively brief. Subjectively, the exiles did not see themselves com-

peting with the native minority, but simply making do until they
could return to Cuba. As those prospects became progressively dim,
many rapidly moved into self-employment in such areas as garment
contracting, housing improvements, and residential construction,
gradually creating the Cuban enclave described above.

The effects of this evolution were less to displace blacks than to
alter the local economy. Figure 4.4 indicates that the rising representation of the Hispanic (overwhelmingly Cuban) population in industries that commonly integrate new immigrants took place primarily
at the expense of native whites rather than blacks. Most telling is the
evolution of the hotel industry, which is commonly cited in Miami as
the core example of displacement. Although these figures must be
interpreted with caution because of changing census definitions,
they indicate that whites were the primary losers, at least as far as
employment in these sectors is concerned. The Cubans did double
their presence between 1970 and 1980—from 18 to 40 percent—but
the gain was entirely at the expense of white workers. Blacks actually

FIGURE 4.4

Hotel and Restaurant Employment and Ethnicity
Miami 1960, 1970 and 1980

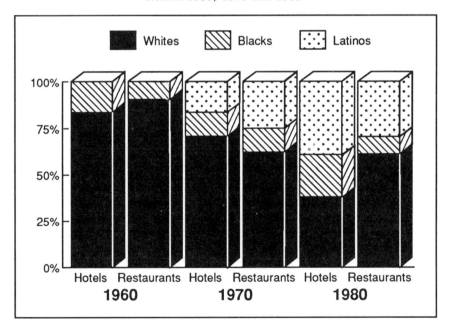

Sources: U.S. Censuses, Florida, 1960, 1970, and 1980

increased their representation in this industry from 14 to 23 percent in the same period.

Of the new jobs generated during the decade, blacks garnered about 20 percent, a figure commensurate with their proportion of the Miami population. They increased their representation in all the top occupational categories. Their proportion in the professions, for example, almost doubled, from 7 to 13 percent (see Figure 4.2). The Cuban presence did grow faster, but again it was at the relative expense of native white workers. Between 1970 and 1980, the Hispanics secured 65 percent of all new jobs, a figure significantly higher than their approximate 40 percent representation in the area's population, an aggregate gain that occurred entirely through reductions in the relative presence of native whites. Interestingly, while the overall number of whites in Dade County and the number of whites working as laborers declined during this period, the absolute number of whites working as executives or professionals did not decline. In other words, while both Hispanics and Blacks made both absolute and relative inroads into these highest occupations, they remained dominated by native U.S. whites.

There was no one-to-one substitution of blacks by Cubans in the labor market, nor a direct exploitation of one minority by the other. Rather, a new urban economy emerged in which the immigrants raced past the native black minority. A partial segmentation of the labor market occurred with a significant part, such as apparel, dominated by and seemingly reserved for Spanish-speakers, thus excluding native blacks and whites.

Nevertheless, the perception remains among many African and white Americans that Cubans are somehow responsible for black poverty in Miami. Cubans meanwhile reject this assertion, arguing that black Miami's problems existed long before they arrived. This rhetorical confrontation has produced political conflict within the city. In 1982, Overtown erupted after the acquittal of a Latin policeman who had fatally shot a black man at a video parlor. In 1984, the Puerto Rican–born mayor of Miami joined forces with two Cuban members of the City Commission to fire the popular black city manager, Howard Gary, sparking a recall petition aimed at the mayor. But the recall effort failed. Instead the city elected a Cuban American mayor in 1985 to go along with the Cuban American city manager who had replaced Howard Gary. The decade of the 1980s closed with Colombian-born police officer William Lozano's January shooting of a Caribbean-born black, Clement Lloyd, and a subsequent riot that occurred in front of the national press that had assembled in Miami for football's Super Bowl that weekend. The 1990s began similarly. African Americans were offended when local officials, led by Cubans, refused officially to welcome Nelson Mandela to Miami in his 1990 tour of the United States. Cubans responded by condemning Mandela for his praise of Fidel Castro. The three riots, punctuated by these other less violent confrontations, distinguished Miami among American cities. Nowhere else did African American alienation and frustration boil over so frequently. Nowhere else have African Americans felt so much at odds with and displaced by Latins. Although direct economic displacement appears to be a myth, Cubans have leaped over African Americans both economically and politically, and African Americans' frustrations and rage are quite tangible and real.

Conclusions

In many respects the Cubans are exceptional Hispanics in the United States—their average income is relatively high, and poverty rates and dependency on welfare is relatively low. Cuban immigrants have achieved economic and political success within the first generation, a dramatic exception to most immigrant communities' experiences, and they contributed importantly to the transformation of Miami's economy into the capital of the Caribbean. At a minimum, Miami Cubans demonstrate that there is nothing inherent in being a Spanish-speaking community or a recent immigrant community that produces general community poverty and welfare dependency. Nor does massive state-funded welfare necessarily produce a welfare dependency. In at least this one case, it has produced a successful ethnic enclave.

These accomplishments arose from three forms of capital. Economically, some Cubans brought capital with them from Cuba. More importantly, the migration flow contained a much higher percentage of professionals and businessmen who could relatively easily use their skills in the United States. Subsequent flows of working-class immigrants furnished low-wage, pliant labor to emerging enclave firms and created a community with a broadly diverse class structure. Socially, Cuban family structure permitted the most productive use of their economic capital by having relatively few children, placing women in the labor force, and maintaining three-generation families. Politically, no other Hispanic group has benefited so extensively from U.S. government aid, all the way from the White House down to the Miami school district. These three forms of capital have combined in a peculiar way to produce extraordinarily high ethnic solidarity that both ameliorates and masks class exploitation within the community, while providing a basis for ethnic political power.

While the Cuban community has prospered, Miami's African

American community feels left behind. In spite of many African Americans advancing into professional and executive positions since the arrival of Cubans, the majority remain poor and increasingly welfare-dependent. Equally important, in spite of the lack of evidence, many blame the Cubans for the relative failure of African Americans. Ethnic tensions in Miami are extreme, seething constantly and erupting periodically. The contrast between Miami's Cuban and African American communities discloses the coincidental fortuitousness of the Cuban success—immigration created by a cold war confrontation that produced an abundant welcome including massive state aid, settlement in a city geographically perfect and poised for a new role as a nexus to Latin America, a profile of immigrants that began with an early upward social and economic bias that was followed by controlled and limited waves of working-class immigrants, and internal right-wing hegemony that produced extraordinarily high community trust and internal cooperation for those who submitted to the dominant ideology. The absence of any one of these factors easily could have changed the entire profile of the community.

Thus, Miami's Cuban community appears to be the antithesis of Wilson's model of a permanent underclass. As such, it may confirm the model by demonstrating that class diversity and massive state assistance can produce a vibrant, viable ethnic community that obscures the deprivation of some of its members, the internal exploitation of others, and the political domination and suppression created by this instance of ethnic solidarity.

NOTES

1. See also Borjas 1982; Diaz 1980; Jorge and Moncarz 1980; Masud-Piloto 1988; Perez 1985, 1986; Portes and Bach 1985; Rogg and Cooney 1980. Cuban success has been attributed to different factors according to separate authors, including cultural and psychological variables, human capital, state support, and the peculiar nature of Miami's Cuban economic community (i.e., the ethnic enclave). Our own interpretation does not necessarily contradict these others, but we do deemphasize cultural and psychological variables.

2. Garreau 1981 refers to it as the capital of the Caribbean, and Levine 1985 as the capital of Latin America.

3. Incidentally, the Cuban-American members of Miami's power structure appear to have similar class, economic, and even sectoral interests to those of the local non-Cuban and elites in other cities. They are substantial businessmen or executives, especially those

concerned with real estate and development. See Stepick et al. 1990.

4. Grenier 1990 demonstrates that by the end of the 1980s Cubans in Miami were heavily represented in unions, especially those in industry and manufacturing.

5. See Peterson and Maidique 1986. Although they ostensibly argue that Cubans have a peculiarly entrepreneurial mentality, their data are equally if not more consistent with our hypothesis that structural factors and human capital are the crucial variables in creating successful Cuban American businessmen.

6. The literature in this area is immense. See, for example, Bonacich 1972, 1976; Castells 1975; Hechter 1977.

7. Field interview conducted by Alex Stepick and Patricia Fernandez-Kelly, January 1987.

8. Forment (1989) indicates that two of every three Miami Cuban entrepreneurs whom he interviewed asserted that some Cubans sold for a profit explosives and weaponry provided to them by the CIA. Unpublished data collected and analyzed by Robert Bach also indicate that at least some prominent Miami Cubans of the 1980s had their Miami entrepreneurial start in CIA firms. On the other hand, in extensive interviews conducted by Alejandro Portes among Miami Cuban leaders everyone denied the importance of the CIA in capitalizing Cuban enclave firms.

9. See Perez 1986 for an in-depth discussion of these points.

10. It must be mentioned that Cubans also have a relatively high divorce rate, which increased throughout the 1980s.

11. Portes and Bach (1985) and Portes and Jensen (1987). Sanders and Nee (1987) argue that the enclave only benefits entrepreneurs and not working-class enclave members.

12. For a more extensive discussion of this contrast, see Fernandez-Kelly and Garcia 1989.

13. Field interview conducted by Alex Stepick and Alejandro Portes, January 1987.

5

ECONOMIC RESTRUCTURING AND LATINO GROWTH IN HOUSTON

Nestor P. Rodriguez

Houston underwent considerable economic and social change in the 1980s. Much of the economic change resulted from a 1982–1987 recession in the Houston-area economy. Prior to the recession, the manufacturing of oil-related technology, the production of petrochemicals, and the construction of office towers set the tempo of the area's economy. After the recession, a more diversified industrial base (but still not free from oil) with a bigger service sector emerged as the economic structure of the area.

Immigration and the subsequent growth of new ethnic and racial communities were at the core of the area's substantial social change in the 1980s. As in other major metropolitan areas in the country, immigrants from throughout the world, but especially from Asia and Latin America, settled in large numbers in the Houston area during the 1980s. In the 1982–1987 period this immigration coincided with the out-migration of over 100,000 white Houstonians (Sallee and Dyer 1991), many of whom were casualties of the economic downturn. The settlement of Central Americans, Chinese, Vietnamese, and other immigrants created new communities in the city. These communities brought new languages and cultures and affected all major institutions (business, educational, health, recreational, etc.) in the area (see Rodriguez and Urrutía-Rojas 1991).

Large-scale Central American immigration in the 1980s diversified

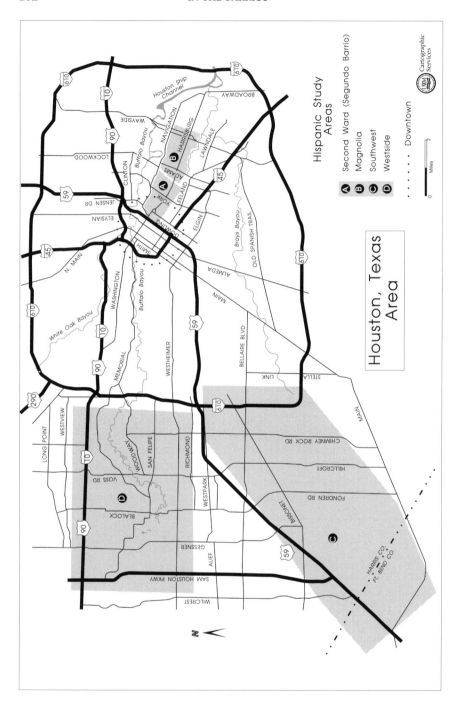

Houston, Texas Area

Hispanic Study Areas

A Second Ward (Segundo Barrio)
B Magnolia
C Southwest
D Westside

········· Downtown

TABLE 5.1

Latino Population Growth in Houston

	1970	1980	1990
Metropolitan:			
Latino	212,444	424,903	707,536
Total	1,985,031	2,905,353	3,301,937
City of Houston:			
Latino	149,727	281,331	450,483
Total	1,232,802	1,595,138	1,630,553

Source: U.S. Bureau of the Census, *Census of Population and Housing, Census Tracts, Houston, Texas, 1970, 1980;* U.S. Bureau of the Census, 1991, cited in the *Houston Chronicle,* February 8, 1991, p. 31A.

Houston's Latino population, which according to the 1980 census was 88.5 percent Mexican-origin.[1] The diversification was more than ethnic; it was a diversification of Latino settlement areas in the city as well. For the first time in the city's history, in the 1980s Latino communities emerged in the western half of the city, initially through the immigration of Central American refugees and immigrants.

The immigration of some 100,000 Central Americans into Houston in the 1980s was ethnically a new Latino experience but very much in keeping with the city's pattern of Latino growth. As Table 5.1 shows, Latino growth between 1960 and 1990 was substantially high. This is not a recent pattern either. Since the beginning of the present century, Latinos have grown in population size at rates that are two to three times higher than the city's overall growth rates (see Shelton et al. 1989). Large numbers of low-income Latinos are included in this growth. According to the 1980 census, 16 percent of all Latino families in Houston live in poverty (U.S. Bureau of the Census 1983, table P-21). Given the undercount of undocumented Latinos, who usually have higher low-income rates, the true percentage of Latinos in poverty was certainly higher.

To understand how Houston's recent economic recession and restructuring have affected the Latino communities it is important to understand the history of the city's older Latino communities.

Historical Background

Unlike other large urban areas in the Southwest, the history of Latino growth in Houston has occurred mainly in the twentieth century. Although there· is some speculation that Mexicans were used in the 1836 clearing of swamplands that became the city of Houston, the history of the city's Latino communities starts in the 1900–1910 period.[2] In this period Houston changed from an agriculturally dominant area to a center of oil and gas exploration and production. Latino growth in Houston started in the early 1900s in the form of Mexican-origin colonies. While they provided workers for growing industries in the area, the Mexican-origin colonies remained socially and culturally apart from the dominant institutional environment. The Mexican-origin residents referred to their communities as *colonias*. In the 1930s–1940s, partly related to the emergence of the second immigrant generation, the *colonias* underwent social and cultural changes that brought them closer to the dominant social system. As is explained in the next section, the growing incorporation into the dominant institutional environment transformed the *colonias* into barrios. The barrios represented a new structural relationship with the surrounding white institutional sectors. Although much of the *colonias'* social-cultural reproduction occurred outside the larger social system, the barrios' development (or underdevelopment) was heavily affected by relations to the dominant institutional environment.

The settlement of a Mexican-origin community in Houston at the turn of the century represented a unique development—it was the first Latino settlement in a large southern city. Houston was more than geographically southern; the city maintained Confederate traditions that included the structuring of race relations by Jim Crow laws. In contrast to other parts of Texas with a strong Mexican heritage, Houston's majority-minority relations were based primarily on relations between whites and blacks. At times affected by the violence of the Ku Klux Klan, these relations were as rigid as in other southern cities (Atlanta, Birmingham, Little Rock, etc.) and included widespread segregation and deep-rooted racism against blacks. In 1900 about 14,600 blacks lived in Houston, mainly in "Freedman's Town", a section of the city established by former slaves (see Shelton et al. 1989, p. 71).

Houston's first Latino neighborhood, the Second Ward (El Segundo Barrio), emerged in the 1910–1920 period in an area just southeast of downtown. European immigrant groups had originally settled in the area. In the 1910s Mexicans from communities in Texas and northern Mexico came to the Second Ward and found employment primarily in the nearby railroad yards of the Santa Fe Railroad. Indeed, some of the original Latino settlers of the Second Ward apparently located housing in abandoned railroad cars. The small *colonia* became a source of low-wage labor for other nascent industries besides the railroads. Some of the Mexican residents of the young *colonia* found low-grade service jobs in the central business districts, while other Mexican laborers found employment in the *colonias'* own ethnic businesses (Shelton et al. 1989, pp. 94–95).

Labor recruiters from San Antonio provided some of the first Mexican immigrant inhabitants of the Second Ward *colonia*. Many other working-class and business families came on their own, fleeing Mexican areas ravaged by revolution. Most of the jobs available for the Mexican newcomers were working on sewerage lines, the railroads, or in agricultural fields. Wages of less than a dollar an hour for ten–hour workdays were common among the Second Ward *colonia* workers.

By 1920 the *colonia* had evolved substantial social and cultural life. A Catholic church (Our Lady of Guadalupe), Spanish-language newspapers, ethnic businesses, and Mexican patriotic and mutual-aid societies helped form a sense of community in the Second Ward. Several leaders emerged to head social and cultural events among the mostly working-class inhabitants of the *colonia* (see De Leon 1989, chap. 1).

The year 1920 also witnessed the emergence of a second Mexican colony four miles southeast of the central business district and two miles southeast of the Second Ward. Attracted by the growing industries of the Houston Ship Channel, hundreds and later thousands of Texas Mexicans and Mexican immigrants settled in the Magnolia Park neighborhood of European settlers. The mostly low-wage Mexican settlers of the Magnolia *colonia* found a labor market more prosperous than what the earlier Second Ward residents had found. In Magnolia Mexican workers found low-wage jobs in ship-channel construction and in industries related to the ship-channel commerce (e.g., in cotton compresses, cement plants, and construction companies). Women found jobs in textile plants, factories, and stores. Wages remained low for the Magnolia Latino residents as most of them located lower-grade jobs outside the protection of labor and trade unions (Shelton et al. 1989, pp. 94–95).

When the Magnolia neighborhood was incorporated into the city of Houston in 1926, its Mexican-origin inhabitants were well on the way to developing a full-fledged community. In 1930 the *Houston Chronicle* reported that this community of "Little Mexico" had a business district of drugstores, restaurants, private offices, filling stations, grocery stores, bakeries, a Spanish talkie theater, barber shops, and furniture and dry goods stores. The Mexican business owners served a mostly Mexican clientele.[3]

The Immaculate Heart of Mary Catholic church also helped give the Magnolia *colonia* a sense of community. Established in 1926, the church served the large Mexican Catholic population not welcomed by whites at Magnolia's Immaculate Concept Catholic church. In addition, Protestant churches and a large number of community organizations and ethnic-related annual events helped to reproduce a Mexican society in the growing *colonia* at Magnolia Park.

In the 1920s representatives of the Mexican government regularly addressed the leaders and other members of the evolving Mexican communities in the city's east side, and also in the northside near the central business district. Some of the leaders in these communities had attended Mexican universities and maintained economic and political ties to the home country (see De Leon 1989, p. 31). With this Mexican orientation, leadership resources for the community development of the city's *colonias* remained outside the U.S. mainstream.

Even in the 1930s the Mexican neighborhoods, which now contained some 20,000 residents, "showed staying power", according to historian Arnoldo De Leon. But the period of the Great Depression also marked the beginning of a social and cultural transition for many residents in the *colonia* settlements (which in the 1930s had clearly spread to areas north and northwest of downtown). De Leon states:

> The development of culture and of barrio institutions continued to unfold and mainstream institutions further converted many. Social classes within the *colonia* became more apparent. A new generation of Mexican Americans appeared, proclaiming themselves as Americans instead of Mexican citizens (1989, p. 70).

The emergence of "Mexican Americans" introduced a new social-cultural category in the Mexican-origin neighborhoods. Mexican Americans generated a social force that moved the *colonias* in the direction of the mainstream. In doing so, they helped change the *colonias* into inner-city barrios.[4]

Yet, the U.S.–oriented values and goals of the "Mexican American generation" did not represent the total Mexican-origin population in the city's growing Latino barrios.[5] The Second Ward and Magnolia remained central settlement areas of new immigrants from Mexico. In fact, new immigrants accounted for a large percentage of the city's Latino growth. By the 1970s, as the Houston labor market entered a boom stage, new Mexican immigrants had developed settlement patterns outside the east-side barrios into the areas north and northwest of downtown.

Spatially the Houston Latino experience remained mainly an east-side phenomenon until the mid 1960s, with the exception of the few Latino neighborhoods north and northwest of downtown. This was part of the larger minority residential pattern of Houston. Until the mid-1960s most Latinos and blacks lived east of Main Street, which runs north to south and through the middle of downtown. West of Main Street lived mostly Anglo households of middle- and upper-income levels. Anglo working-class families were concentrated in a northern district several miles from downtown and in a couple of southern suburbs.

In terms of social class the east side Mexican-origin neighborhoods (the "East End") have remained working-class areas. The presence of significant numbers of unemployed or subemployed people, street-corner day-laborer pools, and low-wage work forces give the east side neighborhoods a lower-working-class atmosphere.

Transition: From Colonia to Inner-City Barrio

The transition of Houston's established Mexican-origin neighborhoods into inner-city barrios involved social, cultural, economic, and political changes. It was a restructuring of Mexican colonies into minority enclaves (barrios) in a larger white-dominated social system. This restructuring, which commenced with the appearance of the Mexican-American generation in the mid-1930s and continued into the 1950s, did not lead into a complete transformations of the Mexican-origin communities. Large numbers of newly arrived Mexican (and later Central American) immigrants helped keep segments of the communities' traditional culture in a continual process of reproduction.

Several developments were involved in the social transition from a Mexican *colonia* to an inner-city barrio. For example, as the *colonias* were incorporated into the city of Houston, they entered a larger system of municipal relations (police, health, transportation, etc.). Social organizations developed by members of the Mexican American generation that sought Anglo involvement helped shift social references and standards in the direction of the dominant society. Participation in major U.S. institutions also influenced this change. In the sports arena, for example, Mexican Americans returning home from military service during World War II were among the first to introduce baseball, and later football, in some of the developing barrios in the city.[6]

Linguistic change was a major cultural development contained in the transition from *colonia* to barrio. In the 1940s some prominent Mexican American leaders organized English training programs for barrio residents. Linguistic change enabled more participation in the larger culture. English-speaking ability, for example, meant that English-language newspapers, radio, and later television became major media sources in the barrios. Changes in the barrios' popular culture involved arenas such as cuisine and cinema (see De Leon 1989, chap. 4). Mexican Americans manifested a sense of U.S. national culture when they practiced U.S. versions of commemorative days, such as Halloween instead of *el día de los muertos*.

From their beginnings the Mexican-origin settlements in the Houston area had been part of the economic mainstream. They provided many workers for firms in the city's economy. Though Mexican workers often held inferior jobs, they were nevertheless employed in firms attached to the larger economy. In the *colonias'* ethnic enterprises Mexican workers provided goods and services that helped reproduce labor for the larger economy. What was an economic novelty in the transition from *colonia* to barrio status was mass consumerism in the white-dominated economy. Whereas the *colonia* residents had depended heavily on Mexican-owned enterprises in their settlements, the emerging Mexican American generation became an "American consumer". After World War II, it was primarily the immigrant population (especially recent arrivals) who as workers and consumers helped maintain the vitality of the barrios' ethnic enterprises.

Political change in the transition from *colonia* to barrio involved several stages. One stage was the turning away from political interests in Mexico to political concerns in the United States. In the early days of the *colonia*, residents had participated in political activities related to their homeland. Mexican officials carried messages between the *colonia* and the Mexican government. After World War II most of the political relationships between the *colonia* and the motherland ceased.

A second stage was the emergence of Mexican American political leadership. Since the 1910s community organizations and leaders addressed social problems and barriers facing the *colonias*, but several members of LULAC Council #60 took a new political direction in the 1930s when they allied with Anglo politicians both in Houston and in the state of Texas. Whereas earlier *colonia* leaders had turned to Mexican officials for political support, the Mexican Americans of Council #60 turned to native sources. In November 1940 the Latin Sons of Texas became the first Mexican American organization to endorse a slate of candidates in Houston. Working especially through the Democratic party, many Mexican American leaders and organizations supported Anglo candidates but had little success in placing Mexican Americans, or any Latino, in public office.[7]

A third stage in the political change was the decline of political life and leadership in the east side Mexican settlements. The out-migration of middle-income families no doubt affected this change, but perhaps an equally or more important impact was the shift of the political center of gravity from inside the Mexican settlements to institutions (e.g., city hall) in the larger society. Political behavior would no longer be organized through an indigenous culture but through the values and norms of an alien one. The barrio passed into an Anglo-dominated political sphere that had little room for the pressing Mexican-oriented issues that stimulated activism and leadership in the days of the *colonias*. Even in the early 1990s, the barrios' low level of political activity contrast sharply with the political enthusiasm they contained in the earlier part of the century. Indeed, in November 1990 several top Houston Latino leaders went on a hunger strike to motivate fellow Latino residents to register to vote.

The "dislocation" of the Mexican-origin settlements from *colonias* to barrios no doubt affected their present depressed community conditions. Many internal social and cultural sources of community stability and growth were lost in the restructuring of the settlements. Moreover, the quality of political leadership declined. In the 1910s–1930s Latino leaders emerged mostly through their relations to social and cultural organizations *within* the *colonia;* after World War II they emerged through relations to institutions *outside* the barrio. Once a center of a vibrant Mexican life, the Mexican settlements became enclaves of Mexican American and immigrant "minorities", who were generally among the least incorporated into the social and cultural mainstream.

Black communities also remained outside the mainstream and in several ways constituted a "city within a city" (Shelton et al. 1989, p. 75). The development of Latino communities actually paralleled the growth of black communities ("wards") in Houston. Given the city's stringent racial segregation, children in the black wards attended segregated schools. Some who graduated from the segregated high school went on to attend the city's black college, Texas Southern University. Like Latinos, blacks did not ascend to a measure of political power until well after World War II. As throughout the South, in the 1960s and 1970s blacks in Houston entered a period of revolt and protest to struggle against barriers of racism.

Economic Boom: 1970s and Early 1980s

The 1970s were "Houston's Golden Economic Age". It was the decade in which the Houston area matured as an industrial center in the world economy. In the 1960s and 1970s several multinational corporations established or expanded their energy-related operations in the greater Houston area, making the area a major source of technology and services for oil-, natural gas-, and petrochemical-producing regions throughout the world. This growth invigorated several other sectors of the Houston area's economy. Along with the development of new industrial complexes, the construction of office buildings and housing units skyrocketed. Eighty-five percent of the 485 office towers and buildings of more than 100,000 square feet that stood in the Houston area in the mid-1980s were constructed in the 1970s and the early 1980s. Housing construction also substantially increased the number of domicile units in the area between 1970 and 1980 (see Feagin 1988, chap. 7).

A dynamic labor-force growth paralleled the Houston area's economic expansion in the 1970s and early 1980s. In the manufacturing sector the number of workers increased from 145,600 in 1970 to 254,000 in 1982. In the nonmanufacturing sectors the number of workers increased from 500,700 to 1,329,400 between 1970 and 1982 (see Feagin 1988, p. 77). Overall, employment in the Houston area during the prosperous 1970s and early 1980s grew by 145 percent. The Houston labor force, which took over 100 years to reach 650,000 workers in 1970, almost doubled in size during the decade of the 1970s.

Expansion of the area's Latino labor force was equally dramatic. The number of Latinos in the Houston metropolitan area grew from 212,444 in 1970 to 424,903 in 1980, an increase of 100 percent.[8] The economic boom of the 1970s and early 1980s brought substantial prosperity to Latinos in the city's barrios and surrounding working-class suburbs.

With the absence of city zoning ordinances, a number of large manufacturing plants and other industrial complexes had located in the east side Mexican-origin barrios. Several thousand Mexican American workers found employment in the east-side industries and in the adjacent port facilities. Enjoying rising profits in the world oil economy, east-side corporate employers could pay workers relatively well, especially when pressured by labor unions. In some manufacturing plants, floor sweepers started at $8 an hour.[9] Mexican Americans in surrounding working-class suburbs (Rosenberg, Dear Park, etc.) commuted to jobs in the inner city or in nearby industrial complexes.

While Houston's economic boom brought jobs to Latinos, it did not bring large-scale labor-market mobility to these workers. As Table 5.2 shows, Latinos maintained an inferior labor-market position through the decade of the seventies. In 1980 a large majority of Latinos held manual jobs or low-paying sales and clerical positions. While overall 28.5 percent of Houston workers in 1980 held higher-paying white-collar jobs (professional, technical, and managerial),

TABLE 5.2

*Latino Occupational Distribution in the Houston Area,
1970 and 1980 (in percentages)*

	1970	1980
White-Collar		
Professional/		
technical/		
managerial	14.5	12.7
Sales/clerical	21.8	22.1
Blue-Collar		
Crafts	17.6	21.4
Operatives	17.7	12.1
Transport	4.3	5.2
Laborer	9.0	10.6
Farm Work	1.0	1.7
Service	14.4	14.3
Total	99.9	100.1

Source: U.S. Bureau of the Census, *Census of Population and Housing, Census Tracts, Houston, Texas, 1970* (Table P-8) and 1980 (Table P-21).

only 12 percent of Latino workers held such employment.[10] Given undercounts of undocumented, low-status Latino workers, it is safe to assume that the true percentage of Latinos in higher-paying white-collar positions was below 10 percent.

The attraction of the Houston area's economic boom for Latino immigrant labor, initially from Mexico and later from Central America, produced a seemingly contradictory impact on the area's Latino population. On the one hand, immigration expanded the area's Latino work force, which in turn increased wage income in the Latino communities. On the other hand, immigration, which consisted heavily of poor workers, increased the proportion of low-income workers (domestics, laborers, etc.) in the Latino communities. Of course, as workers and consumers the immigrants supported the growth of Mexican American and other Latino businesses in the Latino ethnic economy.

The explosive Latino growth in the city in the seventies swelled the established Mexican-origin barrios and expanded the Latino presence into other nearby neighborhoods (e.g., the Heights) and into suburbs. In the Heights, located in the northwest quadrant of the inner city, the Latino expansion created a zone of Latino transition. Mexican Americans and Mexican immigrants locating in the Heights introduced Spanish and Latino ethnic enterprises into the community's white, middle-income social structure. By the 1980s,

Latinos in the Heights had evolved a complete Latino community infrastructure that included ethnic churches, restaurants, cantinas, ethnic retail stores, and herbal and spiritual shops. The Latinization of the Heights neighborhoods also enhanced the growing attraction among white merchants for Latino customers. These merchants helped the community's Latino transition by displaying Latino decorations in their stores. Indeed, white-owned businesses display more Mexican and Central American flags than Latino-owned businesses. By the end of the seventies, several neighborhood areas outside, but still near, the city's east side had become zones of Latino transition. It was not until the early eighties that large-scale Central American immigration created zones of new Latino settlement in the city's west side. The creation of these new Latino settlement zones coincided with the Houston area's economic decline.

Economic Decline: 1983 to 1987

In the 1982–1983 period the Houston area entered a steep economic downturn that did not bottom out until 1987. When the price of oil in the world market dropped to $30 a barrel in 1983, oil-related industries collapsed in Houston and throughout many oil-producing regions of the world. The downturn ended eight decades of almost continuous economic growth in the Houston area and reached all sectors of the area's economy.

Having just finished a "Golden Age" of economic growth made the downturn all the more severe. Throughout the Houston area industrial complexes that had manufactured tools and equipment for oil exploration throughout the world stood idle. In Texas, as in other world regions, oil fields became graveyards of abandoned equipment worth millions of dollars. The construction of overseas oil refineries (in the Middle East, Asia, etc.) added to the economic decline in the Houston area. Gas drilling in Texas also dropped sharply during the economic decline (see Feagin 1988, pp. 96–105). Plant closings and production cutbacks in oil- and gas-related industries sent shock waves throughout the Houston area economy.

Industrial decline and unemployment crippled the Houston real estate market for business and residential structures. Overbuilding prior to the economic downturn also created problematic conditions that matured in the mid-1980s. In the early 1980s investors and developers in commercial real estate had increased office space by 100 percent and retail space by 60 percent. The consequences of this aggressive (over-)construction were felt in the mid-1980s. By 1984 the vacancy rates of Class A buildings in Houston were the highest of all major U.S. metropolitan areas. Some office buildings were completed in the mid-1980s only to remain virtually unoccupied.

The economic recession also hit the Houston residential housing market hard. Housing units became vacant as thousands of unemployed workers left the city or abandoned their mortgaged homes. Home foreclosures increased at a record-setting pace into 1987. Many of the residential vacancies were located in the city's west side, where real estate investors and developers had constructed large numbers of apartment complexes to house a growing white, middle-class population.

The economic downturn had a disastrous impact on the area's labor force. During the five years of economic decline, the Houston labor market lost a total of 200,000 jobs.[11] Many unemployed workers left the Houston area, while others stayed and took lower-paying jobs, waiting for prosperity to return. Still other workers entered a life of vagabondage, living under elevated freeways or in run-down buildings and houses abandoned during the recession.

Latino communities in Houston suffered greatly from the economic decline of 1983–1987. Thousands of Latinos who worked in the forty-nine manufacturing plants located in the east-side barrios were among the first casualties of the downturn, as manufacturers were the first to shut down when oil prices dropped in the world market. In the seventies and early eighties, for example, one manufacturer located in the barrio used 4500 workers in three shifts to maintain a large inventory of drill bits and other tools for oil fields throughout the world; after the oil economy collapsed, the manufacturer reduced its work force to a skeleton crew of 500 workers, who produced equipment only on demand. Other oil-tool manufacturers in the barrios laid off all their workers and locked the gates to their plants.[12]

The East-Side Barrios after the Economic Recovery

When the Houston economy improved in 1987, work conditions did not return to normal in the east-side barrios. Some industrial plants reopened but not to their previous capacities. Labor unions, weakened by worker layoffs, lost much of their power to negotiate with employers. Workers had to give in to employer demands for rollbacks of wages and vacation days. Menial jobs that used to start at $8 per hour now paid less than $5 an hour.[13] Bumper-to-bumper traffic that congested barrio streets during work-shift rotations in the days of prosperity did not return after the 1987 economic upturn.

The impact of the economic recession was evident throughout the east-side barrios. For-rent and for-sale signs, written in English and Spanish, went up "everywhere" as unemployed Latino workers and their families lost their homes or left the city. Rent signs reflected the pressing economic situation as they advertised rent reductions of as much as 50 percent. On the main avenues that crisscrossed the barrios, closed-down stores, eating places, and Spanish theaters indicated the economic stress.[14] Barrio nightclubs that had flourished during prosperity saw much of their working-class clientele disappear. The clubs also saw many immigrant women seeking economic survival as taxi dancers. Continuing immigration and the Houston area's economic upturn helped improve the barrios' economies in the late 1980s, but things did not return to the normality of the prerecession years.

Unemployment and underemployment remained a problem. A hungry labor market of big employers with high wages became a thing of the past. Many Latino workers left to look for work in other states, especially in Florida, Georgia, and New Jersey. Other Latino men and women found new, low-wage jobs in service industries. Some of these service jobs were in health-care and security services. A few Latinos used their savings to set up ethnic businesses. Many new-immigrant men formed labor pools on barrio street corners to seek work.

A Latina who grew up in the barrio of Magnolia and left between 1976 and 1984 summarizes the impact of the economic recession as follows:

> When I was growing up the industrial activity was the life stream of the barrio. The activities and noises of the union hiring halls, the ship channel, the shift changes, of freight trucks—all were the economic pulse of the barrio. We used to plan the time to drive to classes at the university around the rush-hour traffic at the plants and factories in the barrio. . . . I came back [in 1984] and found everything boarded up. I hear silence, the silence of boarded-up factories. The industrial activity that was the heart beat of the community is gone. . . . The Mercado building [a failed Mexican-style mall] has become a monument to the economic death of the barrio.[15]

Unemployed or earning insufficient wages, many Latinos in the east side sought assistance in social service programs in the barrios during the area's economic decline. Ripley House Neighborhood Center in the east side saw the number of Latinos seeking community assistance increase by over 200 a week in 1983. The community center provided health service, food, and other emergency assistance to unemployed Latinos and their families. According to the center's director, requests for food assistance doubled during the area's economic recession.[16] In the barrio of Magnolia a mission shelter for homeless men also saw a considerable increase of requests for assistance. Latino immigrants and whole families sought free clothing and meals from the mission. Although some Latino immigrants stayed at the mission, Mexican Americans who asked for help at the mission usually doubled up in nearby shacks.[17]

It is important to understand that the Houston area's economic downturn had different impacts for established residents and new immigrants in the east-side barrios. While a number of established Latino residents experienced economic disaster and left the city during the downturn, many others, including long-term immigrants, fell back on unemployment benefits and eventually returned to the labor force, albeit often to inferior jobs. The impact on new-immigrant workers was usually more severe. Being concentrated in secondary labor-market jobs, Mexican and Central American new-immigrant workers had no unemployment insurance to fall back on. Being undocumented, new immigrants could also not draw government-supported public assistance benefits. Thus, for new-immigrant workers and their families unemployment brought absolute poverty. To make matters worse, as the Houston economy improved in the late 1980s, the employers' sanction provision of the Immigration, Reform and Control Act (IRCA) passed in 1986 restricted the new immigrants' entry into the labor market. This situation was a major reason why Ripley House, churches, and other community organizations in the east-side barrios did not see a decline in the number of Latinos seeking clothing, food, and other types of public assistance in the late 1980s and early 1990s.

Excluded from many public assistance programs, undocumented immigrants by necessity must maintain a strong labor-force attachment. A 1986 survey of Central American immigrants in Houston, however, found an 18 percent unemployment rate among these newcomers (Rodriguez 1987, p. 18). Although an initial lack of labor-market familiarity among new immigrants accounts for part of this high unemployment rate, the contraction of the Houston labor market during the downturn also contributed to the Central Americans' unemployment. In addition to seeking food and shelter at community-sponsored agencies in barrios and other neighborhoods, the unemployed Central American (and Mexican) immigrants sought sustenance in households of relatives, friends, and other compatriots. As a last resort, many undocumented Latino workers and families left Houston to search for jobs in other cities (e.g., Boston, Chicago, and Washington, D.C.).

The formation of street-corner labor pools was one of the most visible signs of informal-economy expansion in the barrios during the downturn. Another sign of this expansion was the emergence of garage-sale type activity in houses, apartment projects, and vacant commercial lots. This makeshift economy provided low-priced clothing, used home appliances and other items for poor families, and cash monies for the informal vendors. It is safe to assume that the recession also affected the growth of the illegal economy in the barrios. Some Latinos, for example, sold or traded their food stamps to obtain non-food items. Unemployed immigrants sometimes became smugglers of other immigrants. No doubt high employment also affected the choices of some Latinos who saw the illegal drug trade as a resourceful economic alternative.

Restructuring and the New Latino Immigration

In this section we depart from the historical pattern of analysis in the previous sections and describe and analyze Latino immigration into Houston. For much of Houston's growth, Latino immigration has overwhelmingly meant Mexican immigration. In the 1980s, however, this Mexican-dominant, Latino immigration pattern changed as large numbers of Central Americans migrated to Houston from their troubled homelands.

Mexican immigration.   Houston's economic boom in the seventies acted as a huge magnet drawing Mexican workers into the area. Actually this attraction started in the mid-1960s, ending a Mexican immigration, low in the area, that had lasted for about a decade. While a few of the Mexican immigrants that poured into the Houston area in the seventies found jobs in large industrial plants, the largest numbers went to work in construction and service industries.

The record-breaking construction of office buildings, shopping centers, storage facilities, apartment projects, and suburban homes in the 1970s and early 1980s created an unsatisfiable demand for Mexican immigrant labor. Undocumented workers from rural and urban Mexico became a preferred labor force, especially among construction employers who paid low wages and offered poor working conditions. Many of these employers were Mexican Americans or long-term Mexican immigrants. The cyclical pattern of the construction industry afforded immigrant workers an advantage. They could return home during the construction low of the winter months. Only six hours away from Mexico by car or bus, this was an attractive opportunity for rural-origin Mexican immigrants to return home and work in their *ejidos* or other small farms. Later in the eighties, it became clear that for many Mexican immigrants in Houston "home" was becoming the United States.

Though initially much neglected by immigration researchers, the huge wave of undocumented Mexican immigration in the seventies included large numbers of women workers. Many of the women were single (never married, divorced, or separated) and migrated alone. In Houston Mexican immigrant women helped create a huge army of Latino immigrant-service workers. The immigrant women, and their male counterparts, penetrated all service industries with low wages and poor working conditions. The women workers especially found service jobs in restaurants, cafeterias, middle- and upper-income homes, and office-cleaning crews. Office-cleaning companies, some of which were national and international corporations, sought immigrant women workers as vigorously as construction firms sought male immigrant workers. The prosperity of both industries in the seventies and early eighties was strongly connected to the growth of low-wage, nonunionized Latino immigrant work forces (much to the dismay of unionized U.S. workers).

During the 1970s and 1980s, the growth of the Mexican immigrant population, concentrated in the city's east-side barrios, also enlarged the area's Mexican ethnic economy. This economy became another labor market for Mexican immigrant labor. In the barrios, restaurants, retail stores, theaters, supermarkets, and drinking places became major employers of Mexican immigrants. By the 1980s the large Mexican immigrant population created new employment niches, such as in check-cashing and money-order offices and in van lines transporting immigrants from barrios in Houston to barrios in Mexican cities and towns.

When the Houston economy entered a recession in the eighties, some Mexican immigrants returned to Mexico, while others migrated to other U.S. cities. Many, however, remained in Houston. With undocumented status, they suffered the worst of the area's economic hardship.

The end of the area's economic recession in 1987 brought mixed opportunities for Mexican immigrants in the Houston area. IRCA, the new immigration law, offered amnesty for those who had entered the United States prior to 1982. Over 90,000 Mexican immigrants stepped forward and requested legalization of their immigrant status in the Houston Immigration and Naturalization Service (INS) office.[18] Under the employer-sanctions provisions of the new immigration law, employers were fined for hiring undocumented workers, making amnesty an immigrant passport for "authorized" employment. On the other hand, for undocumented immigrants who entered the United States after 1981, IRCA became an additional barrier to finding work. Perhaps more than ever before, in the late 1980s undocumented immigrant workers in Houston were at the mercy of employers.

The failure of the construction industry to return to the prosperity of the seventies and early eighties created an additional restriction for immigrant Mexican labor. Construction companies had been a prime employer drawing Mexican immigrant workers into the Houston area. Although construction of new homes increased in the late eighties and early nineties, the overall construction industry came nowhere near the levels reached in the seventies and early eighties. The federal government's auctioning of a huge supply of real estate (4289 homes, 163 apartment complexes, and hundreds of commercial properties) obtained from failed savings and loan corporations helped keep new construction down in the area (Bivins 1990). With the continuing slump in construction, Mexican immigrant workers turned primarily to the service employment sector, which offered lower wages.

   Central American immigration. About 25,000 Central Americans applied for legalization through IRCA in the Houston INS office.[19] To an extent, the smaller number of Central American amnesty applicants, vis-à-vis Mexican applicants, indicated their later arrival in the Houston area. The majority of the estimated 100,000 Central Americans who settled in the Houston area immigrated after 1981, the cutoff year for amnesty. Several factors distinguished Central American immigration from the established Mexican immigration experience in the Houston area. First, Central American immigrants had substantial national and ethnic differentiation. These immigrants included Salvadorans, Guatemalans, Hondurans, Belizians, and Nicaraguans. Guatemalans and Hondurans included the ethnic and racial minorities of Mayans and Garifuna, respectively. Second, among Central American newcomers war and other political violence had played an important role in motivating migration to the United States. This motivation had not existed among Mexican immigrants since the days of the Mexican Revolution. Third, while thousands of Mexican immigrants came during the prosperity of the seventies and early eighties, the majority of the area's Central Americans arrived after the local economy entered a downturn in 1982–1983.

   Fourth, the majority of Central American newcomers settled in new Latino neighborhoods in the city's west side, miles away from the Mexican-immigrant settlement areas in the east-side barrios. Fifth, the refugee experience of many Central American immigrants gave rise to a sanctuary movement in the Houston area, a development that had not transpired with Mexican immigration. Finally, the coming of the Central Americans politicized immigration issues in ways that Mexican immigration had not. The undocumented Latino immigrant stopped being a Mexican "wetback" and became a Central American "refugee" fleeing death squads and other political violence, problems related by many to U.S. intervention in Central America.

Within a short time Central Americans evolved a substantial amount of community-building activities in the Houston area. In the large apartment complexes where they settled in the west side several miles from downtown, Central Americans organized baptisms, weddings, birthday parties, and other family celebrations that helped build a sense of community. Churches provided much support for events and activities that promoted community development among the diverse Central American groups. Members of refugee-support groups and other community organizations also provided many social and legal resources to aid the settlement of Central Americans. By the late 1980s, the west-side areas of Central American settlement contained many of the cultural institutions (ethnic churches, Latino clubs, soccer teams, etc.) found in the old east-side barrios.

Yet, the west-side Central American communities differed substantially from the east-side barrios because of the ethnic heterogeneity that came to characterize the city's west side in the 1980s. By the mid-1980s, Mexicans and several other immigrant groups had also settled in the west-side apartment projects where Central Americans resided. In contrast to residential conditions in the old barrios, in the west side, a Mexican or Central American tenant could have an Iranian, Ethiopian, Nigerian, Indian, or some other non-Latino immigrant nationality for a neighbor. The ethnic heterogeneity and the segmented social patterns that evolve with the spatial designs of large, multistory apartment projects no doubt are part of the reason why Latino immigrants have not developed barrio identities in their west-side residential areas.

Restructuring impact on Central American immigrants. Because Central Americans began their immigration into the Houston area just as the area's economy started to decline, they faced a significantly different employment opportunity structure than did the Mexican immigrants who came in the boom years of the seventies and early eighties. Central Americans settling in the city, especially in the west side, located mostly service jobs that paid from less than minimum wage ($3.35 per hour at the time) to about $4.00 an hour.[20]

In service industries, Central Americans were heavily concentrated in personal services and cleaning jobs. Household and office-cleaning work provided employment for many Central American women workers in the city's west side. Central American men found a wide range of service jobs (yard work, building maintenance and cleaning, car repair, etc.) and also formed street-corner labor pools to find work. Some of the Central American immigrants who took low-wage service jobs had left, because of life-threatening situations, skilled and professional jobs in their home country. For example, an electrical engineer from El Salvador found work as a laborer in a machine shop. A physician and his wife, a nurse, from Guatemala cleaned a laundromat.

Social networks became an especially effective means for immigrants to gain entry into the area's lean labor market in the mid-1980s. Through social networks based on kinship, friendship, or a common community of origin, immigrants located work for other immigrants and helped them adjust to their new workplaces. Some social networks located jobs with amazing results. One group of undocumented Mayan immigrants, for example, used social networks to find jobs for several hundred of its members during the eighties. Through their social networks the men penetrated a retail store chain as maintenance workers, while the women expanded into house-cleaning work in upper-middle-class, west-side neighborhoods. The Mayan social networks continue today to channel low-wage labor from villages and small towns in the western highlands of Guatemala to service jobs in the Houston area.

When the recession hit and office workers left the city, real estate capital in the large west-side apartment projects went into a severe crisis.[21] West-side apartment owners and managers initiated a restructuring strategy to save their apartment projects by replenishing their tenantries with new Latino immigrants, initially the undocumented Central Americans who were arriving in the early eighties. The apartment restructuring strategy to attract new Latino immigrant renters included reducing rents by as much as 50 percent, hiring bilingual apartment staff, offering English classes and Latino nightclubs on apartment grounds, and changing apartment names from English to Spanish. It was a bold strategy, that is, one seeking to attract thousands of poor Central American refugees and immigrants into white, middle-income apartment areas in the west side.

The apartment restructuring strategy succeeded as families and groups of Salvadorans, Guatemalans, Hondurans, and other Central Americans became concentrated in the large apartment complexes. Moreover, by 1987–1988 other low-income groups (especially Mexican immigrants and African Americans) were also locating in the west-side apartment projects.

From the start, the apartment restructuring strategy to replenish declining middle-income tenant populations with low-income Latino immigrants must have been planned as a temporary measure, useful only to wait out the recession. The low rents paid by the immigrants and the building deterioration caused by a transient and high-density immigrant renter population made the restructuring strategy unprofitable in the long term. Indeed, some apartment complexes with immigrant tenants closed down during the recession when building deterioration reached uninhabitable levels. Building deterioration in apartment projects where Latino immigrants lived indicated that apartment landlords were not investing rent incomes in building repairs. The late eighties brought the economic upturn that apartment owners awaited. In anticipation of the return of white-collar tenants, west-side apartment owners and managers implemented a second restructuring process. This process involved ridding apartments of low-income immigrant tenants and upgrading the units to attract returning middle-income renters.

Latino immigrants and other low-income tenants in the west-side apartment complexes saw the coming of the second restructuring strategy in measures such as hefty rent increases, the enforcement of previously ignored restrictions against families with children, the removal of bilingual apartment managerial staff, and the requirements of lengthy credit references to enter new units. Some apartment complexes simply closed down to undergo substantial renovation and reopened with new English names and rents that were $200 or more higher per month.

Central Americans and other Latino immigrants reacted in several ways to the new apartment restructuring strategy. Some immigrants doubled up in apartment units to share the new higher rents; others took in additional immigrant boarders in order to meet the new rents. Immigrants also moved out of the higher-rent apartment complexes. Some of these immigrants moved to inferior apartments with lower rents; others in households with women domestic workers moved into servant quarters at the homes where the women worked.

By the late 1980s and early 1990s, rent increases and the reduction of the apartment housing market (through the razing of some 6000 apartment units) also pressured newly arrived Latino immigrants, who gravitated to the new west-side immigrant settlement zones. Many of the recent immigrants were Central American youth (14- to 17-year-olds) who migrated unaccompanied by parents or other adults (see Rodriguez and Urrutía-Rojas 1990). Lacking work-authorization permits and unable to afford housing, some of these youths gathered into small groups to look for day jobs at street corners or to play ball in lots where apartments had been razed.

New Latino immigrant settlement in the western half of the city in the 1980s substantially increased the ethnic segmentation of the city's Latino population. Whereas in earlier decades intra-Latino ethnic division consisted mainly of the social separation between Mexican Americans and Mexican immigrants *within* established barrios,

in the 1980s the spatial separation between Mexican-origin neighborhoods in the eastern half of the city and Central American settlements in the western half became a prominent feature of the city's
Latino segmentation. In several social spheres (educational, recreational, residential, work, etc.), Mexican Americans and Mexican
and Central American newcomers maintain intergroup boundaries.
Yet these boundaries are not impermeable; interaction at the individual level, such as among co-workers and neighbors, creates linkages
among the groups. Latinos from different ethnic backgrounds have
also come together in the formation of several community organizations (e.g., task forces and ad hoc committees) that attempt to deal
with problems (job and educational discrimination, lack of health
services, etc.) affecting the city's Latino immigrant communities.

Conclusion

The history of Latino community development in Houston provides
useful case material from which to evaluate the appropriateness of
"underclass" concepts for understanding poverty conditions in
Latino communities. This section will address the underclass concepts of restructuring, concentration, and social isolation using the
Houston Latino experience.[22]

Restructuring.   The early history of the Houston east-side *colonia*
settlements shows the importance of understanding restructuring
processes in terms greater than economic ones. In the 1930s and
1940s segments of the emerging Mexican American generation promoted a cultural and political restructuring in the direction of the
dominant social system that substantially altered Mexican life in the
colonias. While this social change was sociologically inevitable and
eventually brought social and civil rights benefits for Latinos, nonetheless it did seem to diminish the quality of social life in these
Mexican settlements. Having lost some of the Mexican richness of
earlier days, the inner-city barrios that emerged in the 1940s and
1950s do not generate the same levels of social and cultural life described for the Mexican *colonias* in the first part of the century.[23] This
is also true of the barrios' political life. In east-side Latino neighborhoods where university-trained Mexican residents used to consult
with Mexican government officials and become involved with homeland politics, Latino leaders today wage hunger strikes to persuade
the neighborhoods' residents to register to vote. The transition from
colonias to barrios in Houston (which was repeated in many Southwest areas) and the subsequent emergence of minority group status
indicate that, at least in the Houston Latino case, it is important to

consider the role of race/ethnic relations in the growth of low-income, inner-city areas.

Restructuring strategies implemented by apartment owners and managers in Houston's massive west-side apartment industry during, and after, the area's recession also indicate the need to explore restructuring processes beyond the manufacturing sector and beyond the impact on the poor in their role as workers. As is described above, the apartment landlords' initial restructuring strategy provided Latino immigrants with an abundance of housing in the white, west-side area of the city. The growth of low-income Latino areas in the city's west side in the 1980s cannot be understood apart from this restructuring process in the apartment real estate sector.

The second apartment-restructuring strategy that sought to prepare apartment projects for the return of (white) middle-income tenants had a significant impact on the growth of inferior living conditions among Latinos in the west side. For many Latino immigrants the new high rents and other restrictive apartment conditions created the necessity of doubling up in apartment units or moving to lower-quality apartments in order to remain in the west-side job market. Thus, restructuring in the real estate sector produced pressures for poor Latinos just as real as those produced by restructuring in the industrial sectors.

Concentration.   In Houston's Latino settlements "concentration" involves not only increased concentration of the "most disadvantaged" but also of immigrants. An analysis of the relationship between concentration and the growth of low-income Latino areas must also take into account this dual residential presence. In Houston the established low-income Latino areas consist of long-term residents (Mexican Americans and established Latino immigrants) and new immigrants. Concentration results from different developments in the two populations. Among established residents, concentration builds as some, usually the younger generation, leave to start homes in more affluent areas. In the east-side barrios there is a practical need for this out-migration, because the presence of manufacturing plants and industrial warehouses make these areas a high risk for new-home investment. Here, then, concentration is related to the lack of zoning ordinances that would have prevented industrial plants from locating inside the east-side Latino neighborhoods (see Feagin 1988, pp. 156–161). Among new immigrants, most of whom arrive with low-income status, concentration results as established immigrant networks attract newcomers to immigrant sections in the low-income Latino areas.

Concentration plays useful functions for new immigrants in the old barrios. In these communities, concentration helps to generate an economy affordable to new immigrants. The presence of large numbers of immigrants promotes businesses, including informal ones, that provide low-cost housing, food, clothing, and recreation. This gives new immigrants a significant advantage to cope with their low-income status. The critical point here is that it is precisely concentration—immigrant concentration—that generates and ethnic economy that helps to sustain low-income newcomers in their initial entry into the city. In many of the city's low-income Latino areas, it is the emerging ethnic enterprises that are revitalizing neighborhoods that were devastated by the recession.

Given the historical association between low-income status and traditional culture among Latinos, concentration in the barrios also offers immigrants a cultural ambience most similar to the one left behind in their home countries. This is a significant convenience for new immigrants who have no prior experience with U.S. culture and a major advantage for rural-origin immigrants who lack experience in a modern-urban environment. For newly arrived immigrants, concentrations in low-income areas provide a familiar cultural setting of family, cuisine, and religious and recreational resources.

Concentrated areas of Latino poverty are often also heartlands of resourceful social networks for immigrants. Throughout Houston's low-income barrios is found a large array of social networks among immigrants from the same hometown or region. The social networks provide information about jobs, housing, and recreation, and about other things important in the lives of immigrants. The most developed immigrant social networks often extend to taverns, restaurants, and recreational places named after specific communities of origin in Mexico and Central America. Contacts made in these settings sometimes provide new immigrants the initial entry point into the city's labor market. Thus, as concentrations of low-income immigrants expand so do the social resources for new-immigrant settlement.

Finally, in the city's west-side case, concentration of low-income Latino areas evolved during Houston's economic downturn not because more affluent Latinos moved out but because large numbers of poor Latino immigrants moved in. This settlement, as described above, involved the collaboration of apartment landlords who sought to rebuild their depleted renter populations. Not only did this concentration of low-income Latinos enable some apartment owners to ride out the recession, but it also provided many west-side service employers with a large supply of labor. While the new zones of Latino immigrant settlement in the west side eventually became associated with illegal activities, they also blossomed as formidable community structures with active ethnic businesses, churches, sports teams, and other community organizations.

Social isolation.   At first glance it appears that the mass of immigrants in low-income Latino areas do experience a sort of "social isolation", more so than poor native Latinos who at least speak English. In their residential areas, immigrants form social and cultural enclaves and stay far from the English-speaking mainstream. At work the immigrants often labor in homogeneous immigrant work forces where contact with non-Latino employers is frequently conducted through Mexican American or established-immigrant intermediaries. In the east side, given the large size of the Latino neighborhoods and their spatial separation from other city areas, immigrants can, and sometimes do, completely avoid interaction with non-Latino settings. Yet, this social isolation, which is also characteristic of some native Latinos, is not detrimental, but functional and apparently highly positive.

In their social isolation from the mainstream, immigrants build or penetrate alternative Latino traditional institutions similar to the ones they left behind in their homelands and this happens in both Houston's east-side barrios and in the new west-side settlement zones. These institutions (family, religious, recreational, etc.) help produce and reproduce an immigrant community structure.

Thus, *initial* social isolation is a means to immigrant survival and eventual immigrant community development. Some of the most stable immigrant subpopulations in Houston's low-income Latino areas are the ones that maintained strong cohesion through social isolation from the mainstream. The city's two Mayan immigrant populations of over 1000 members each are good examples of this success. Both Mayan immigrant populations survived the recession with minimal job losses through their cohesion, which was enabled by social isolation not only from the mainstream but from other immigrant populations as well.

Low-income Latino areas in Houston differ significantly from the descriptions of inner-city poverty given by the underclass perspective. This is not to say that underclass-like conditions (joblessness, welfare dependency, serious crime, etc.) are not found in Houston's low-income Latino areas. Such conditions do exist in Houston in the barrios and in other low-income Latino areas of the city, but they exist mainly as social characteristics (among many others) and not as indicators of a social class—an underclass. Underclass conditions do not define the core of community structures in Houston's low-income Latino areas.

The industrial involvement in the east-side barrios, the switching to service jobs after the recession, the immigration of Latino men and women workers—all help to keep an economic life stream circulating in the city's Latino areas. As throughout the country, the city's Latino low-income areas contain significant numbers of lower-working-class members. Their numbers grew in the city's Latino areas during the 1983–1987 recession, but even then they failed to develop as the socially dislocated communities described by the underclass perspective.

NOTES

1. According to the 1980 census, Mexican-origin residents constituted 88.52 percent of Latinos in the city of Houston and 88.14 of Latinos in the overall metropolitan area. See U.S. Bureau of the Census (1983): Census Tracts, PHC80-2-184, table P-7.

2. See De Leon (1989, chap. 1). *Ethnicity in the Sunbelt* is currently the only book-length in-depth historical study of Latinos (Mexican Americans) in Houston. Those who pursue Latino studies in Houston no doubt will become indebted to this work.

3. The *Houston Chronicle* report is cited in De Leon (1989, p. 11).

4. In the 1940s Mexican-American leaders and organizations arose to deal with the many issues of civil rights affecting the city's Latinos. To be sure the civic-oriented League of United Latin American Citizens had opened a chapter in Magnolia (Council #60) as early as 1934. Many of the LULACers, including women in the Ladies LULAC Council No. 14, worked to encourage Latinos to pay their poll tax and vote, or to begin their process of naturalization. Battling barriers in education, politics, employment, and government, Latino leaders maintained a steady course toward the mainstream through the 1940s, 1950s, and into the 1960s (see Shelton et al. 1989, p. 95).

5. Several scholars (e.g., Rodolfo Alvarez, Richard A. Garcia, and Mario T. Garcia) use the term "Mexican American Generation" to refer to a new historical Mexican American cohort that emerged in the late 1920s and 1930s, bringing degrees of new values and orientations in Mexican American communities. See De Leon's *Ethnicity in the Sunbelt* (1989, p. xi); Alvarez (1973).

6. Personal interviews with Mr. A. B. Olmos, November 20, 1990, Houston, Texas, and Professor Milton Jamail (University of Texas at Austin), January 14, 1991.

7. The first major electoral success for a Mexican American in Houston occurred in 1972 with the election of David T. Lopez to a Houston school board. Elected to city controller in November 1975, Leonel Castillo became the first and only Latino to win a citywide election. In November 1979, Ben Reyes became the first and only Latino elected to the Houston City Council.

8. Source: U.S. Bureau of the Census, *Census of Population and Housing, Census Tracts*, Houston, Texas, 1970, 1983b.

9. Personal interview with Mr. W. R. Morris, Houston, Texas, December 16, 1990.
10. Source: U.S. Bureau of the Census, *Census of Population and Housing* (1983).
11. Smith (1989, p. 10); see also Feagin (1989, pp. 97–100).
12. Personal interview with Mr. W. R. Morris, Houston, Texas, December 12, 1990.
13. Ibid.
14. Personal interview with Raymundo Rodriguez, Houston, Texas, November 12, 1990.
15. Personal interview (December 18, 1990) with a Houston community organizer who prefers to remain unidentified.
16. Personal interview with Mr. Felix Fraga, Houston, Texas, December 10, 1990.
17. Personal interview with Mimi Hinnawi, Houston, Texas, January 14, 1991.
18. Information provided by the Houston office of the U.S. Immigration and Naturalization Service.
19. Information provided by the Houston office of the U.S. Immigration and Naturalization Service.
20. A survey conducted in 1986–1987 found that three-fourths of the Central American immigrants (male and female) interviewed in the city were employed in service occupations. The survey found a median hourly wage of $3.35 among all the Central American immigrants interviewed. See N. Rodriguez (1987, p. 19).
21. The west-side apartment complexes contained many of the 220,700 housing units that stood vacant in the city in 1985.
22. These concepts, of course, are central to the underclass perspective. See Wilson (1987).
23. See De Leon's *Ethnicity in the Sunbelt* (1989), chaps. 1–2. De Leon describes a rich and vigorous social community life in the early Mexican colonies in Houston that does not seem to be matched in today's barrios. My own observations suggest that it is the Latino immigrants (mainly Mexican) who are infusing the city's barrios with a new social and cultural liveliness. My point about a diminishing quality of life in the barrios refers mainly to social and cultural levels and certainly not to economic conditions.

6

THE QUEST FOR COMMUNITY: PUERTO RICANS IN CHICAGO

Felix M. Padilla

A S IN OTHER cities and regions of the United States, the Latino population in Chicago has increased dramatically over the last thirty years. While 110,000 Latinos were counted in Chicago in 1960 (2.8 percent of the total population), by 1980 their number was estimated at 422,063 (or 14 percent of the city's total population) (U.S. Census Bureau 1983). In the mid-1980s Chicago's Department of Planning estimated that by 1990 Latinos would number 615,513 (or 20.3 percent of the city's total population). The same report also projected an additional 5 percent increase in population growth among Latinos by the year 2000, boosting the total to 763,080 (City of Chicago, Department of Planning, 1984).

These official figures are conservative. (*The Hispanic Alamanac* predicts the Latino population in Chicago for the year 2000 will grow to 1 million.) Yet they clearly show that Chicago is a leading urban center of Latino life and culture in the United States. Mexican Americans and Puerto Ricans represent the two largest Latino groups living in Chicago (64 percent and 22 percent, respectively). Cuban Americans, Guatemalans, Salvadorans, Colombians, and other Latin American immigrants constitute the rest.

The rapid growth of the Latino population in Chicago over the last three decades has inspired and reinforced various community-building efforts. Latinos have invested a great deal of time, energy,

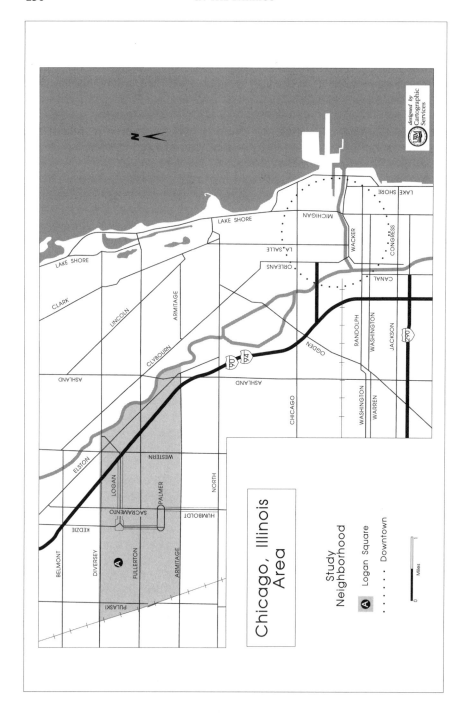

Chicago, Illinois Area

Study Neighborhood

Logan Square

· · · · · · Downtown

and resources in developing their own ethnic neighborhoods (barrios)—areas within which they aim to better serve their own social, cultural, and economic needs and interests. In 1990, nearly three-fourths of Latinos lived in just ten of the city's officially defined seventy-seven community areas, and 52 percent were concentrated in just five of those areas. Most of these areas, or sections in them, have gradually developed into Latino communities. They are known by both residents and outsiders as "Latino neighborhoods".

South Chicago, Pilsen/Little Village, Back of the Yards, and Near West Side, located on the south side, are the historic and contemporary leading Mexican American barrios. In 1980, 95 percent of the residents of Pilsen and Little Village were Latino, 92 percent of whom were Mexican. Latinos comprised 30 percent of South Chicago's residents in 1980, and 89 percent of the Latinos there were Mexican. West Town, Humboldt Park, and Logan Square, on the near northwest side, have been the city's Puerto Rican barrios over the years, though these neighborhoods have acquired a culturally diverse Latino character with the arrival in the late 1980s of masses of Mexican immigrants and Mexican Americans from other parts of the city, as well as of a substantial number of Cubans and other Latin American newcomers (entering during the 1970s and 1980s). Altogether, these three communities represent the largest Latino area in the city.

Community-building efforts among Latinos were undertaken at the same time that Chicago experienced a series of major economic changes that left many working-class individuals and families without traditional avenues for earning a living and organizing their lives. Latinos established their barrios while experiencing the virtual disappearance of factory jobs from the city's economy and the growth of the service economy, with its emphasis on work that requires high levels of education and/or training. At the same time, the Chicago public school system—the social institution charged with preparing present and future generations of working-class young people for the new economic order—has deteriorated. Further, during this period of economic restructuring, Latino barrios were becoming crowded with drug-dealing, business-oriented youth gangs—perhaps the most visible sign of the irrelevance of the new economic order for a significant segment of the city's population.

This chapter focuses on the impact of economic restructuring and other forces of social change on the efforts of Puerto Ricans to establish themselves during the 1970s and 1980s within Logan Square, a community that is mixed both ethnically and in social class. The specific questions addressed are: What particular economic and social changes were taking place in the city of Chicago and in Logan

Square that paralleled the efforts by Puerto Ricans to install themselves as part of this community? How have these changes affected Puerto Ricans in Logan Square? How have Puerto Ricans tried to come to terms with these changes? How have city officials, community social service providers, and other residents responded to schemes developed by Puerto Ricans in response to these changes, and, in particular, to new actors in the informal economy like drug-dealing youth gangs?

Puerto Ricans in Chicago

Although Puerto Rican immigration to Chicago can be traced to the late 1940s, it was during the 1950s that it began to reach massive proportions. By the decade's end, 32,371 Puerto Ricans lived in the city. By 1969, the number had more than doubled, to 78,963 residents.

Like other ethnic and racial groups before them, since their arrival in Chicago Puerto Ricans have labored to establish a distinctive community. They worked hard to carve out a geographic area wherein their cultural traditions could be transmitted, maintained, and reinforced. It was a giant challenge for a predominantly rural, agricultural people who did not speak the language of the host society; yet Puerto Ricans managed to establish several barrios in different areas of the city. Initially these barrios were small enclaves located in both African American and white areas of the city. Interracial conflict and urban renewal in south and west side areas and gentrification in north side communities during the 1960s and 1970s led to the massive removal or displacement of Puerto Ricans (Padilla 1987). As a result, a Puerto Rican ethnic concentration emerged in several north side communities that had been sparsely settled by Puerto Ricans previously. The best known is Division Street, several miles northwest of downtown Chicago, or the Loop.

Division Street is made up of two officially defined "community areas", West Town and Humboldt Park. Puerto Ricans arrived there en masse almost simultaneously. In fact, the pull of Division Street was so strong that by 1970 42 percent of the city's Puerto Rican population resided there.

The majority of Puerto Rican workers in Chicago are employed in poorly paid, menial, dead-end jobs. Initially most newcomers worked in the restaurant industry—as busboys, sweepers, kitchen help, waiters, and the like. Others were employed in business firms as messengers and delivery men; some in stockrooms and packaging areas of stores. Still others labored as janitors (Padilla 1947). The 1960 census showed that the majority of Puerto Rican workers were placed in three categories—all low-skilled: "operatives and kindred" (45.7 percent), "laborers" (13.7 percent), and "service workers" (11.7 percent). Only 1.6 percent of all Puerto Rican workers had professional, white-collar occupations.

During the 1970s, the employment situation of Puerto Rican workers remained fairly constant, as it did for most Latino workers. A report commissioned by the Latino Institute, a citywide advocacy, research, and training organization, indicated that in 1970 the majority of Latino workers were employed as operatives and laborers in entry-level jobs. "Latino concentration in these jobs was far above levels in other large cities and the nation. Less than 8 percent of Chicago's Latinos were in the professional and managerial categories. There was a heavy concentration in manufacturing . . . and very few concentrations in growing job categories. . . . Less than 2 percent of Latinos in Chicago had government jobs" (Orfield 1983, p. 16).

The economic position of Latinos in 1980 was dismal, yet the report indicated that "there were no economically devastated, all-poor [Latino] communities" (Orfield 1983, p. 18):

> At $15,630, Latino median family income in the City was 30 percent lower than the white median and 12 percent greater than the black median. Twenty-four percent of Latinos, 32 percent of blacks, and 11 percent of whites in the City were impoverished. While black families in Chicago were more likely than Latinos to earn less than $10,000 per year, they were also more likely to earn over $35,000. Thirty percent of Latino families had 1979 incomes below $10,000, compared with 38 percent of blacks and 16 percent of whites; whereas, 8 percent of Latino families, 11 percent of black families, and 21 percent of white families had incomes over $35,000 (Orfield 1983, p. 18).

Puerto Ricans in Logan Square: "Suburbia"—First Contact

Logan Square, a community directly north of the historic Puerto Rican Division Street neighborhood, is one of the largest Latino communities in Chicago. The majority of its residents are Latinos. According to the 1980 census, 43,829 people were counted as being of Spanish origin, out of which 23,792 were Puerto Ricans, 14,961 Mexicans, and 1,590 Cubans. But for a very long time, this neighborhood was essentially the home of working-class, foreign-born, and native European ethnics. Census reports show that considerable numbers of Swedes, Norwegians, Germans, Scandinavians, Russian

Jews, and Poles lived in this community at different times. Out of a total population of 114,174 in 1930, 33.5 percent were Polish, 16.7 percent German, 12.4 percent Norwegian, 9.9 percent Russian Jewish, and 4.4 percent Swedish. The figures changed very little over the next ten years. By 1960, when the total population of the community was officially counted at 94,799, only 723 were non-whites. In the same year, Poles were the most numerous, constituting over 40 percent of all residents, followed only by Germans at a little over 12 percent. As late as 1970, the census described this area as a predominantly white community: only 15,765 of the 88,555 residents were Latinos.

From the outset, Puerto Ricans settling in Logan Square moved into predominantly white areas of the community. Rather than concentrating in any one or a few areas of Logan Square, they lived among long-standing white residents. These "Spanish-speaking immigrants" were viewed with much suspicion. There was a perception that Puerto Ricans were moving into Logan Square to overrun the neighborhood as their own. As a result, racial and ethnic conflict ensued among the various groups. There were many racial/ethnic conflicts, most involving young people. These incidents of friction took place in schools and in certain neighborhood streets where youngsters tended to congregate and hang out (Padilla 1992).

Yet, the view Puerto Ricans held of Logan Square was highly positive. They often referred to this neighborhood as "Suburbia" (pronounced sooboorbia); living there was perceived as a measure of social prosperity and improvement. Puerto Rican parents believed they had found in Suburbia a serene and tranquil neighborhood, a place with safe streets and good public schools. In their minds, this was the kind of area they had longed to move to, a neighborhood suitable for raising children.[1]

Anyone who takes a casual walk through some of Suburbia's streets today can understand why Puerto Rican and other Latino families rated the community so highly twenty years ago. Suburbia's housing is unquestionably splendid, of high quality and style. Logan Square is one of the original "boulevard communities" of Chicago, and some of its housing is characteristic of this unique system. The boulevards were the choice sites for prosperous merchants and entrepreneurs, who built magnificent mansion residences in the city. Like a green necklace of open space sparkling with trees, monuments, fountains, parks, and landscaped squares, these wide, continuous, landscaped thoroughfares (modeled after the grand Parisian boulevards) pass through some thirty-four Chicago communities and cover a total of twenty-eight miles. A recent report by the city's Department of Planning suggests that the city's boulevard system "should be as closely linked with the name 'Chicago' as Central Park is to New York, the hills to Hollywood, or our own lakefront and skyline to Chicago" (City of Chicago 1989:5).

Lining Suburbia's two boulevards and major square are "late-Victorian and Queen Anne–style mansions bedecked with towers, turrets, classical columns, bays, stained glass and balustrades" (Chicago House Hunt Book 1989, p. 50). The most popular residence is the two-flat graystone with three bedrooms and one bath. A housing-building boom during the late 1920s established Suburbia as a "rental area", with most of its residential units contained in two- and three-flat graystones and a small proportion (less than 20 percent) in apartment buildings of ten or more units. Suburbia's housing make-up has changed very little over time. In 1940, 75.1 percent of the housing was tenant-occupied. Census reports for the twenty-year period between 1950 and 1970 showed essentially the same numbers. The count for 1980 was 65.1 percent. Overall, Suburbia has sustained itself as a hub for tenant families and individuals. Indeed, the majority of Puerto Rican residents in Suburbia are renters.

The sharp increase in the price of housing experienced in most American cities during the 1980s escalated the price of housing in Suburbia. By the spring of 1990, two- and three-flat properties on the boulevards and square were selling for between $200,000 and $350,000. On side streets, two-flats were going for $100,000 to $200,000 (Padilla 1992). Until recent times, most of Suburbia's housing was relatively inexpensive and affordable. In 1960, for example, the median value for owner-occupied units was $13,700. Twenty years later the census reports showed a moderate increase, to a median value of $30,460, roughly one-third less than the city average.

A Working-Class and Professional Community

Suburbia's healthy economic profile reflected the overall economic situation of Chicago. The "city with big shoulders" became a popular slogan to describe Chicago as it developed a reputation as the economic fortress of the Midwest and one of the leading industrial and manufacturing centers of the nation. For most of its long ascendancy, Chicago offered job opportunities to hundreds of thousands of new arrivals in its wide-ranging manufacturing sector. Beginning in the latter part of the nineteenth century and continuing for over fifty years, the burgeoning steel mills, freight warehouses, meat-packing plants, mail-order establishments, building construction, clothing shops, breweries, distilleries, and a host of complementary units that serviced factories or utilized their by-products were the leading centers of employment in the city of Chicago. The jobs that Puerto Rican residents of Suburbia were able to secure over time contributed to their high opinion of the area. Puerto Ricans coming to Suburbia joined a community of working-class people. Throughout the 1970s and 1980s many professional workers, many of whom were Puerto Rican or Latino, moved into the area. Attracted by its close proximity to work and reputable housing stock, most purchased and rehabilitated some of the best housing in Suburbia.

Chicago's manufacturing economy was greatly aided by its key location on Lake Michigan and its development as the center of a regional and, later, national railroad system—both of which combined to make Chicago one of the primary hubs of transportation in the country. Population growth, and the large surplus of labor it entailed, contributed enormously to the development and maintenance of Chicago's industrial economy. Like that of other industrial cities, Chicago's factory system depended on a continually available "reserve army" of workers—workers who could be mobilized during periods of economic expansion and laid off during declines without serious social disruption. In fact, this reserve army of workers could help control those inside the factory gates. And, indeed, Chicago received its massive share of workers: the city was second only to New York, "the Great Metropolis", in economic and population growth.

To find employment in Chicago's manufacturing economy, Puerto Rican residents of Logan Square (and elsewhere in the city) simply needed to demonstrate a willingness to work. Poor education, lack of special training, or limited English were not obstacles to entering the work force at this time. In effect, the rapidly expanding industrial urban economy, with an abundance of entry-level jobs and few requisites, could not say no to prospective laborers. In 1940, when the median school years completed for Suburbia's residents was 8.2, the unemployment rate for a labor force of 53,174 was a little over 5 percent. And by 1960, when the median school years completed had increased moderately to 9.1, the unemployment rate had dropped to 4.2 percent.

During this period, manufacturing employment was the means of connecting workers to the expanding industrial urban economy, situating themselves to take advantage of emerging opportunities. Although industrial labor was highly exploitative (e.g., workers worked long hours in unsanitary and dangerous conditions for low wages), it offered a ray of hope. The common perspective shared by workers at this time was that, if not they themselves, at least their children and grandchildren would be the benefactors of their participation in the industrial order. Workers were socialized to be patient, to have faith in the future. Almost willingly, they became "sacrificial victims" for the next generation.

By 1980, when Puerto Ricans and other Latinos had come to make up over half of Suburbia's population, the major changes that had started unfolding several decades before were affecting all segments of the larger society. These changes—most critically the decline in the manufacturing sector—transformed the social order and presented new challenges. The working class and the poor were the most severely affected; individuals and families, historically limited in resources, were left to invent appropriate ways of dealing with the new social circumstances.

Economic restructuring had a major effect on the lives of Puerto Ricans and other Latinos. Since the end of World War II, the manufacturing base of Chicago (and other central cities like New York, Pittsburgh, Philadelphia, Cleveland, and Detroit, which had built up a century earlier) shifted increasingly toward one made up of service occupations. The changes meant that the original industrial urban centers would now be based on service and the collection, storage, and dissemination of information (knowledge) rather than on the production of products or goods. Industrial work, until the 1960s the backbone of the American economy, was relegated to secondary importance as manufacturing firms moved out of Chicago or simply closed down. Employment growth was now in offices, banking, legal services, insurance, retailing, health care, education, custodial work, hotel and restaurant work, security, and transportation.

As manufacturing plants relocated outside the central cities, white middle-class families moved to the suburbs. Fusfeld and Bates point out that the general movement of people to suburban areas "has been highly selective. It has disproportionately been the young, employed, and white populations of central cities that have resettled in suburban peripheries, leaving the old, unemployed, and black inhabitants behind" (1984, p. 93).

During the period 1970–1980, the white population of Chicago declined by almost 700,000. By 1980, Chicago's total population was 57 percent minority residents, and it was predicted that this figure would rise by 10 percent by the early part of the next century. In Suburbia, which had been experiencing decline at a steady pace since the 1930s (e.g., between 1950 and 1960, 22,000 people left the community), the number of residents in 1980 was below 85,000, less than 75 percent of the peak figure half a century earlier. Construction of a major highway in the early 1960s along the north boundary of the community contributed in part to the population decline; as did the general "white flight" noted above.

Despite the sharp decline in white middle-class residents, Logan

Square did not disintegrate and flounder. The massive influx of Latinos helped to maintain Logan Square as a fairly stable community. Latinos from other areas of the city, as well as new immigrants, poured into Suburbia during the 1970s and 1980s. Of the city's seventy-seven community areas only three were more populous than Suburbia in 1980. By 1980 Latinos came to represent the majority of the residents in nineteen of the community's twenty-nine census tracts—in two census tracts they constituted over 70 percentile of the residents, and in seven over 60. For many Latinos, Logan Square was an area of "second settlement", the place where the more upwardly mobile began to gravitate. The new immigrants contributed significantly to the stability of the neighborhood. One major function they fulfilled was to generate new sources of demand for ethnic goods and services, prompting local Latino business to meet their cultural needs.

As Chicago's manufacturing relocated and populations shifted, it became clear to city planners and government officials that the future economic health of the city would be tied to its role within the new service economy. Already by the late 1950s, Chicago city planners had concluded that the city's economy should emphasize specialized methods of production, distribution, and marketing (City of Chicago, Department of Planning 1958). A joint report by the business community and newly elected Mayor Richard J. Daley predicted that as manufacturing continued to gravitate to outlying, previously vacant land, Chicago's economic future would rest primarily on its service industry base. Particular emphasis was laid on buttressing the Central Business District (CBD), located downtown in the Loop; the CBD was expected to be the growth sector of the city's economy. The report recommended that the city improve access to the Loop and encourage office space construction to maintain and accentuate Chicago's position as a regional financial and administrative headquarters.

In response to the overall city restructuring, pro-growth coalitions of downtown businessmen, planners, newspaper editors, construction unions, real estate interests, and others engaged in efforts to retain the remaining white middle class and attract some of those who left. These groups believed that Chicago could not remain economically and socially viable if it became overwhelmingly populated by the African American, Latino, and impoverished *surplus labor*. The planners argued that Chicago would not be able to rejuvenate its economy without a strong, stable professional class, the leading component of the service economy. From this perspective, most of the policies designed to improve social and economic conditions in the city were to benefit significantly and disproportionally the white middle class of the city and its suburbs since a segment did in fact remain attached to the city's economy through the daily commute to work in the Loop.

The Effect of Economic Restructuring on Puerto Ricans in Suburbia

Chicago lost more than 300,000 manufacturing jobs between 1948 and 1977, with the most pronounced losses occurring after 1967—the period when racial minorities were coming to dominate the city's population (Berry et al. 1976). The removal of these jobs from the city's economy meant an acute depreciation of labor-force participation for workers in this sector. While the unemployment rate in Suburbia in 1960 stood at 3.6 percent, by 1980 it had tripled to 9.4 percent. In the two census tracts in which Puerto Ricans represented the majority of the population, the rate of unemployment exceeded 20 percent; in another it was more than 15 percent. A 1970 official estimate of the percentage of people living under the poverty level in Suburbia was 10 percent; by 1980 it had risen to 18.7 percent. In virtually every census tract where Puerto Ricans formed the majority of the community's population or the largest percentage of Latinos, their poverty level was higher than everyone else's. There were two tracts in which the rate of poverty reached nearly 30 percent.

Despite the change to a service-oriented economy, for a large number of Suburbia's Puerto Rican workers, manufacturing continued to be how they earned their living. Of the 34,383 persons counted as employed in 1980, 42.7 percent held jobs in the manufacturing sector. In those census tracts where Puerto Ricans and other Latinos represent the overwhelming majority of the population, employment in manufacturing industries was higher than for the whole community. The rate of participation in manufacturing employment for Puerto Ricans in eight tracts where they represented at least 60 percent of the population exceeded 60 percent. Of the city's seventy-seven community areas, only two others had a larger proportion of workers employed in manufacturing; one was Division Street.

The continuing concentration of Puerto Ricans in manufacturing work may have to do with their willingness to commute long distances to work. The 1980 census shows that out of a total of 32,976 workers age 16 and over in Suburbia, a third spent 30 to 40 minutes commuting to work. For another sixth, the distance to work took 45 to 60 minutes. This suggests that most of the manufacturing jobs held by Puerto Rican and other workers from Suburbia are located outside the community. This restricts those who can secure work or remain employed over long periods of time. That is, work-trip origins and destinations increasingly reduce the chances of poor racial and ethnic workers to find and remain in permanent employment. Berry and his colleagues indicate that resistance to commuting on the part of these groups "is due partly to their lower rates of car-ownership and to their lower earnings. Only half of Chicago area's black households and two-thirds of the Spanish households own cars, compared to four-fifths of white workers. Black and Spanish workers earn on the average only two-thirds as much as white workers" (Berry et al. 1976, p. 32).

As manufacturing jobs disappeared from the city's economy, employment in the more permanent, high-salaried occupations of the new service sector went to those with high levels of education and/or training. This left minority residents out because of the historic denial of educational equality. The significant role played by education and training within the service sector is explicitly described by Hicklin and Wintermute:

Service industry occupations generally fall into one of three levels based on their educational requirements and earning potential. At the top level are those occupations that require at least a college education. These offer the higher wages and the most security and include managers and professionals. The middle level consists of occupations that may require some college and offer middle level wages. Included in this level are some sales and marketing occupations and upper level clerical workers (e.g., office managers and executive secretaries). At the bottom are those occupations which require, at most, a high school degree. These occupations offer very low wages and little opportunity for advancement. They include service occupations such as janitors, security guards, and personal service workers, sales jobs such as cashiers, and clerical jobs such as typists, general clerks and messengers (Hicklin and Wintermute 1989, pp. ii–iii).

Relying on the system of public education to establish the academic foundation with which to pursue the educational credentials necessary for "good jobs" in the service economy is a handicap for Puerto Ricans and other low-income residents of Chicago. Described in 1988 by William Bennett, then Secretary of Education, as the "worst education system of the nation", the Chicago public school system has ineffectively serviced its poor racial and ethnic minority students. As the *Chicago Tribune* reported in an article on one elementary school observed over a six-month period:

The report from Goudy Elementary School classrooms, which are representative of the system, was stark and poignant. Such schools . . . are hardly more than daytime warehouses for inferior students, taught by disillusioned and inadequate teachers, presided over by a bloated, leaderless bureaucracy, and constantly undercut by a selfish, single-minded teachers' union that has somehow captured and intimidated the political power structure of both city and state governments. The outlook for improvement is not hopeful . . . mainly because public school students in Chicago are increasingly the children of the poor, the black and the Hispanic—a constituency without a champion in the corridors of executive and legislative power. To many politicians, public school systems such as Chicago's are a symbol of urban decay beyond help, a bottomless pit of incompetence and a waste of both tax dollars and political capital (*Chicago Tribune* 1988, pp. x–xi).

Puerto Rican youngsters from Suburbia, largely concentrated in two of the city's high schools, have encountered these problems. Official rates for early school-leavers indicate no real problems in this area, but the reality is that at one school, the dropout rate is believed to be at least 40 percent, while at the other, it exceeds 45 percent.

Group Resistance

Rightly, Puerto Ricans do not perceive the service sector as a vehicle for their upward mobility, emancipation, or empowerment. Rather, they tend to perceive the service economy as a curse whose cost in lost factory jobs is heavy, inflicting great pain as underemployment and poverty come to stand at the center of their everyday reality. In most cases, service industries offer these groups low-wage unstable employment. In effect, the shift from manufacturing to services has resulted in the creation of a "two-tier society, by providing a small number of highly skilled and high paying jobs and a much larger number of low-skilled, low-paying, part-time and unstable jobs, with no apparent internal career ladders permitting upward mobility. The 'middle', comprised of the sort of well-paid unskilled and semiskilled jobs formerly provided by unionized manufacturing plants, was disappearing, along with middle-class incomes, middle-class life styles" (Hicklin and Wintermute 1989, p. 1).

Puerto Ricans and other Latino residents of Logan Square have not passively accepted instability, insecurity, and other negative effects of marginal participation in the service economy. They have resisted, escaped, or sought ways to shift the crushing weight of the existing social order. As the majority population of the community, Puerto Ricans, Mexican Americans, and Cubans have sought to develop a good part of Suburbia into a "Latino ethnic neighborhood", wherein some long-standing community institutions and structures have been changed and some new ones created to advance the interests of Latino people. As the Latino residents in Suburbia have come to represent a critical mass, they have supported initiatives catering to their distinctive ethnic experiences and needs. As a result, Suburbia has become one of the most recent hotbeds of Latino organizational activity in the city.

Education

In recognition of the leading role played by education in the service economy and the schools' historic neglect of Puerto Rican and other Latino children, several community initiatives sought to promote and improve the academic levels of Suburbia's students. One of the first was developed by Aspira, Inc., of Illinois, a community-based organization incorporated in 1969 to help build youth leadership in the Puerto Rican community. (The word *Aspira* means "to aspire", and students who participate in the program and activities of the organization are called "Aspirantes.") Preparation of students for college has always been Aspira's cornerstone. The organization asserts that competent and productive community leaders need the special skills and insights only a college education can provide. Aspira seeks to identify and work with what have come to be defined as "educable Latino youth", who are served through a program of counseling, guidance, tutoring, and high school clubs. As they participate, Aspirantes are instructed by staff members, particularly by club organizers and counselors, in the history of their culture. It is expected that students' personal and professional lives will be meaningfully enhanced by a better understanding of themselves and their community.

Throughout the 1980s, Aspira's central office was located in Suburbia, enabling youngsters from the community to have access to its various services and programs. One measure of Aspira's success is the number of community leaders who were early members of the organization. Former and present members are quick to point out that many of the community's leaders are former Aspirantes.

As an associate member of the Network for Youth Services (NYS), a coalition of Latino organizations that banded together to promote collaboration and to use their resources to serve Latino youth more efficiently, Aspira worked with other organizations to create a school program for some of Suburbia's youngsters who had dropped out of school. Presently known as the Aspira Alternative High School, the program was started in the mid-1980s as a state-accredited academic institution. A high school curriculum is offered primarily to Latino female and male students (most of whom are Puerto Rican), from 16 to 21 years of age. According to school officials, most of the male students are former gang members (although it is common knowledge that most are still active), while the majority of the female students are teen-age mothers. The Aspira Alternative High School is designed to serve sixty students with a faculty of five to six teachers, a counselor, and a principal. There is no formal recruitment of students; most learn about the school through word of mouth. It is difficult to get accepted into the program, primarily because there is a long waiting list.

Clearly, the problems with this community's conventional schools are chronic. The complex set of educational problems facing Latino students in Suburbia sparked the creation of another alternative high school program by the local Boys and Girls Club about the same time the Aspira Alternative High School program was built. Established in 1948 to serve the youth of Suburbia, beginning in the 1980s the club has been directed by two second-generation Puerto Rican young men, who have given the various programs of the club a more academic orientation, trying to make them coincide with the backgrounds and interests of Latino youngsters.

In 1988 the Boys and Girls Club put into place its alternative high school program, which serves the same type of student as Aspira's Alternative High School. The Boys and Girls Club's program enrolls forty students instead of sixty, as at Aspira. One major difference between the two schools is that the Boys and Girls Club's program is essentially built around one teacher, who serves as the instructor for most of the subjects in the curriculum. She also coordinates class offerings by teachers from the students' traditional home school who come to the Boys and Girls Club twice a week to offer these classes. Student placement is made primarily by the home high school counselor. In essence, the alternative high school is commissioned to serve as a "dropout center" for students unable to make it through the regular school program.

Housing

During this period of structural transformation, a great deal of community-based organizational work in Suburbia has been devoted to housing. Leading efforts have been undertaken by the Hispanic Housing Development Corporation (HHDC), established in 1975 to ensure that the city's Latino populations and communities are awarded their proportional shares of public housing funds, estimated in 1970 to have been near 1 percent. The specific purpose of the HHDC "is to develop and manage affordable, quality housing for low to moderate income families and elderly within Chicago's

Latino communities. Hispanic Housing also seeks to expand employment and training opportunities for Latinos in the fields of real estate development, property management, construction and marketing" (Hispanic Housing Development Corporation 1989, p. 1).

The first development project of Hispanic Housing consisted of the rehabilitation of a 160-family apartment complex in Suburbia. The total cost of the project, completed in 1980, was estimated at over $6 million. Two years later, HHDC rehabilitated a 196-family apartment complex at a cost of over $12 million, its second project in Suburbia. All rents are subsidized by the federal government. In all, the Hispanic Housing Development Corporation has been responsible for $50 million in housing development in Latino communities throughout the city, over half of it in Suburbia.

HHDC has also generated employment opportunities and developed estate-job skills by creating a property management division in 1983 to oversee operations. The management entity is primarily responsible for the maintenance of the development corporation's properties. Since its inception, this unit has been self-sufficient, levying fees from tenants and using these to finance administrative and operating costs. To date, the property management division is responsible for a total of 557 units in twenty-seven separate buildings.

Small Businesses

Following the lead of earlier ethnic groups in Suburbia, some Latinos have attempted to change their economic conditions by going into business. Two streets, which had formed the shopping centers of the neighborhood in the past, were joined by another directly south, expanding the commercial heart of the community. Lining these streets is a wide variety of stores and shops, demonstrating that a good part of Suburbia's commercial district is now dominated by the Latino culture. Puerto Rican, Mexican American, and Cuban food stores, restaurants, and jewelry stores are some of the leading business establishments in Suburbia. Many advertisements, posters, billboards, and neon signs in the community are in Spanish or are bilingual. Restaurants advertise *comidas criollas* (authentic indigenous cuisine). Grocery stores specialize in tropical fruits like mangos, platanos, coconuts, guavas, and tamarindo, and vegetables like *batatas* (white sweet potatoes), yucas, yautia, and llame. Puerto Rico, Mexico, and Cuba are often included in the business names, as in "El Banco Popular de Puerto Rico". Flags of the native countries are prominently displayed in shop windows. During election years, posters for Latino candidates are also found on many windows. Wall murals in the district depict aspects of Latino culture.

The rapid growth of the Latino population in Suburbia during the 1970s created a "Latino market", and Latino entrepreneurs rapidly responded to this market. The community's special needs and preferences could be best served by those who knew it intimately, that is, by members of the Latino community itself. With the ability to furnish Latino cultural products and services, entrepreneurs were quick to find a niche in their ethnic community. This business activity in Suburbia involved a direct connection with ethnic group homelands and/or cultures and knowledge of tastes and buying preferences—qualities unlikely to be shared by larger, non-Latino competitors.

Latinos have had special problems caused by the strains of settlement and adjustment to the larger society, aggravated by their distance from conventional service institutions. Consequently, the business of specializing in problems of adjustment and participation in the larger society was one early avenue of Latino economic activity. Latino-owned travel agencies, law firms, realtors, and accountants became common in Suburbia's commercial environment. Such businesses frequently perform functions far beyond the basic provision of legal aid or travel information and reservations. Trust is an important component of these services, and the need for trust pulls the newcomer toward a business owned by a Latino. Latino people prefer personal relationships over impersonal, formal procedures, a predisposition that increases the clientele of businesses specializing in adjustment problems.

One major consequence of the concentration of Latino businesses in Suburbia is the promotion of ethnic identity through cultural dominance of the area. The size of the Latino ethnic market provides room for specialists whose services would otherwise not be much in demand, while customer traffic strengthens the group's dominance of the community.

The Informal Economy

For some Latino residents of Suburbia, the informal economy has become a practical alternative to marginal status in the service sector. Unregulated income-generated activities, which often avoid state regulations that prevail in Suburbia's informal economy, include number-selling (*la bolita*), home work (e.g., baby-sitting, food preparation and sales, sewing, jewelry, and cosmetics), and street peddling, among others. The majority of people involved in the informal economy are poor, people who are desperately in need of subsistence for their families. Low wages and lack of benefits in the larger economy have pushed them to informal economic activities. However, some people employed in the informal economy are not poor or marginal, but have regular jobs and moonlight in the evenings or weekends. These include plumbers, electricians, car repairmen, and secretaries. In effect, informal economic processes cut across the whole social structure. Both the poor and the professionals are active participants. Some of these individuals generate incomes above the level of workers in the formal economy.

It is the gang-sponsored drug dealing that stands out as the most visible informal business operating throughout Suburbia. Nearly a dozen gangs and/or sections of the same gang deal drugs in the community. Gangs have divided Suburbia into various open markets or turfs, each controlled by a different group. At times the same gang may hold absolute dominance over several turfs. Certainly, drug dealing can be found in most street blocks, corners, and school-yards of Suburbia. Increased alarm over the spread of drug dealing and related crime in Suburbia and elsewhere in the city has led to many government and local neighborhood initiatives to eliminate informal economic enterprises. Taking cues from the federal "War on Drugs", policymakers have adopted an attitude of hysteria and hate toward drug users and dealers, particularly gang members. Since the early 1970s, every plan has been built around one central idea: to punish more severely those drug dealers who were appre-hended and convicted. Legislation, policy, and programs have all aimed to "remove these drug criminals" from society by imposing longer mandatory prison sentences. In addition, these "criminal drug laws" have been relentlessly enforced without regard for legal and human rights or thought to the burden of criminal records for young people.

Several special anti-drug and -gang enforcement units and pro-grams were developed in Chicago to fight the drug war at the grass-roots level. These various efforts targeted communities like Suburbia that had developed reputations as major drug distribution, market-ing and use areas. Both the ideology and financing of these programs carried through the vision of the federal, state, and city governments of how best to deal with these young people, who are often viewed as representing the "public enemy".

The Metropolitan Enforcement Groups (MEG) was an undercover or secret police force, whose members came from existing law en-forcement agencies (including local police and sheriff officers, and the Illinois Bureau of Investigation). MEG members did not wear uniforms, drove sporty cars, and tried to blend into high schools and colleges and universities, settings believed to be havens for drug dealing and use. In their daily spying operations, members of MEG used gear like video cameras, 35-millimeter binocular cameras, and portable radios. Information was also secured through paid informants and undercover drug buys. All of this action was intended to enhance the rate of arrest and conviction among users and dealers.

A narcotics conspiracy squad, a collaboration between the Chicago Police Department and the U.S. Attorney's Office, Drug Enforcement Administration, and Internal Revenue Service, was another major unit formed to fight street-level drug dealing in Chicago's neighborhoods. The task force was to target "narcotics gangs" of five or more dealers operating on a daily basis. The plan called for the apprehension and prosecution of dealers under the federal continuing criminal enterprise statutes, which carry minimum sentences of ten years and maximums of life imprisonment. The city also stepped up the recruitment and training of racial and ethnic minority agents to move against African American and Latino drug distribution centers in the city that had been relatively untouched by white officers because of cultural and language differences. Just as Latino agents became some of the best weapons in the ongoing war against drug cartels in Latin America, racial and ethnic minority agents could infiltrate drug gangs in their own communities.

In the face of government and police inability to end the power drug dealers had wielded for so long, citizens' watch groups were organized and thrown into the drug war. These groups were made up of angry neighborhood parents, who mobilized to fight the drug dealers who had gone after their children and had taken over the neighborhood. These parents were convinced that their neighborhood would not be cleaned up until the residents themselves stood up and took charge; so they did and are still doing.

To stop drug dealers, these groups emphasize identification and then harassment of drug dealers. This is followed by reports to law enforcement agencies. In Suburbia and Division Street, representatives of over twenty community-based organizations formed a council to organize neighborhood residents to combat drug dealing and use and associated gang violence. The council started a letter-writing campaign, published newspaper articles, reports, and ads, and spoke on radio and television programs to convince parents to become involved in cracking down on drug dealers and users. These efforts helped establish formal parent groups and neighborhood block patrols that watched neighbors' homes, telephoning neighbors to keep them informed of crimes in the community, showing up in court to support victims, and pressuring police to enforce curfews for youth. "WE CALL POLICE" and "BLOCK WATCH" stickers were displayed on windows and doors of houses and buildings throughout these areas.

It is difficult to determine the outcome of these different initiatives. One thing is sure, however: city police officers, neighborhood parents, and other adults are now pitted against gang members and those youngsters believed to be drug users and pushers. It has become a war between good and evil in which gang members, dealers, and users of drugs represent evil.

Conclusion

An enduring characteristic of Puerto Ricans in Chicago has been their ability to adjust and survive economic hardship. This ability was severely put to the test in Suburbia, where the goal of community residents was to gain economic and social stability. Puerto Ricans came to live in Suburbia, a neighborhood of second settlement, believing that they were going to position themselves for access to better housing. It was in Suburbia that Puerto Rican children were finally going to receive a "good education" and use this education to improve their own economic conditions. These views and aspirations unfolded as Chicago was undergoing a major economic transformation, substantially reducing traditional employment opportunities. Hardship was reinforced by the rising cost of housing, an impotent public school system, and a drug war that forced many adults to organize a system of neighborhood surveillance. Thus, the Puerto Rican people's struggle to establish themselves in Suburbia represents another uphill fight, a direct continuation of their fifty-year history in Chicago of trying to make it in the absence of essential resources.

In spite of these inhibiting conditions, Puerto Ricans did not give up. Some Puerto Rican residents of Suburbia decided to commute to jobs located in suburban areas or in distant city neighborhoods. Some managed to graduate from high school and college and become professionals. For others, the Latino ethnic market offered business opportunities. Just as significant, community-based organizations were created to serve that group of residents in Suburbia who are shut out completely from work opportunities, who cannot afford the high rents presently charged, and who are not served by the public schools.

NOTES

1. Puerto Ricans who became residents of Suburbia were unwilling to identify themselves with "those people from Division Street", for they believed the mass media, civic government, and others attributed to Division Street those stereotypic characteristics conventionally bestowed on slum areas and dwellers. To avoid this typecast, Suburbia's Puerto Ricans, some of whom had lived in Division Street, privately denied any affiliation with it.

7

HISTORICAL POVERTY, RESTRUCTURING EFFECTS, AND INTEGRATIVE TIES: MEXICAN AMERICAN NEIGHBORHOODS IN A PERIPHERAL SUNBELT ECONOMY

Phillip B. Gonzales

SINCE THE mid-1970s, the term "underclass" has been used in a variety of ways to characterize those most severely affected by poverty in the United States. William J. Wilson used it in his structural explanation of severe inner-city conditions (Wilson 1987, 1990).[1] Mexican Americans have always been beset by serious poverty and recently have also been affected by national trends in poverty formation, such as a rise in female-headed households. Some researchers have thus asked if Wilson's analysis of ghetto poverty is appropriate to the conditions of Mexican American poverty.

Those researchers who use statistical aggregate data tend to reject the comparison. Based on gross socioeconomic correlates, they conclude that Mexican Americans are better off than blacks (cf. Cuciti and James 1990; James 1988; Ricketts and Sawhill 1988). Although statistical comparisons between Mexican Americans and blacks have empirical value, as a test of Wilson's theories this kind of work has its problems.

First, it misreads Wilson as if he were generalizing about the condition of minority poverty throughout the country. Wilson (1990) has since clarified that *The Truly Disadvantaged* is a regional study

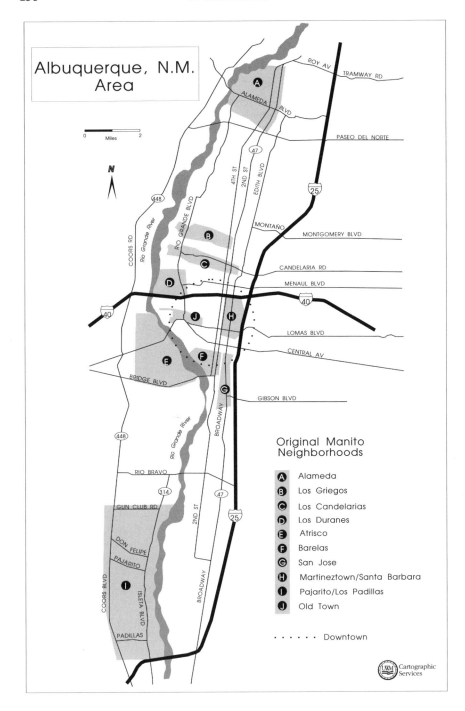

Albuquerque, N.M.
Area

0   Miles   2

N

Original Manito
Neighborhoods

Ⓐ   Alameda
Ⓑ   Los Griegos
Ⓒ   Los Candelarias
Ⓓ   Los Duranes
Ⓔ   Atrisco
Ⓕ   Barelas
Ⓖ   San Jose
Ⓗ   Martineztown/Santa Barbara
Ⓘ   Pajarito/Los Padillas
Ⓙ   Old Town

· · · · · · Downtown

UNM Cartographic
Services

concerned with inner-city ghettos in Midwestern and Eastern cities that, Wilson says, account for 10 percent of the increase in poverty in the last twenty years. It may be beside the point to carry out statistical comparisons outside of the regional context within which Wilson's analysis is focused.

Second, the exclusive use of aggregate statistical data is not in accord with Wilson's method. Wilson uses statistical information to advance what is at heart a qualitative and historical argument. By the mid-1970s, according to Wilson, the heavy industry that had traditionally employed black males either closed down or moved away from the very cities that had drawn hundreds of thousands of southern blacks after World War II. At the same time public programs and market forces opened up opportunity for the black middle class. As its own lot improved, the black middle class left the inner-city neighborhoods, thereby severing the "vertical integration" that its businesses, organizations, and leadership provided to the lower classes. The resulting "concentration effect" was to leave the inner-city residents in deteriorating ghettos bereft of mobility channels. Catastrophic social dislocation followed: extreme joblessness among males, teen-age pregnancies and illegitimate births, female-headed families dependent on welfare, and serious crime.

If this scenario is the model, it is not profitable to read Wilson as a base line for determining which group is not damaged. Not that this particular comparison is not valuable; it is just that Wilson provides a sense of the "shape" of poverty in the inner cities of the Midwest and East for a distinct racial group. To be more directly comparable, our search should be for configurations of poverty that are formed out of the historical relationship between Mexican American neighborhoods and their particular contexts. Thus the issue of vertical integration becomes generally more important in terms of integrative ties and organized resources that once aided survival for the impoverished. From a historical and structural standpoint, Wilson's model suggests that integrative institutions existed in the era prior to economic restructuring. If the onset of economic restructuring is a marker after which the character of poverty in the Midwest and East began to change, the question for other regions should be to what extent social change disrupts traditional integrative ties. To carry out the analysis according to this version of Wilson, we need to (a) specify the historical conditions of poverty in a locality; (b) determine the extent to which the legacies of those conditions persist, including integrative ties; and (c) search for any other changes in the historical foundations of poverty that might correlate with economic restructuring.

Of course, economic restructuring means something quite different in the Southwest, where Mexican Americans are mainly distributed. "Sunbelt development" means that the regional economy expands and the national economy recenters itself in the southern tier states. This implies positive consequences such as added jobs and a greater chance for minorities to create an "informal sector" within a more dynamic economic milieu. But how does this square with increasing Mexican American poverty? According to Moore, "Hispanics in the Sunbelt boom areas may well profit only indirectly from the region's boom. Thus, comparatively few Hispanics have the training necessary to enter new industries at a high wage level, and many of the growth industries that do employ Hispanics are low wage with weak unionization" (Moore 1988, p. 4). In fact, many may not profit at all from a Sunbelt boom, especially if they are already at the bottom of the class structure.

Sunbelt development notwithstanding, the Southwest has never been as economically homogeneous as older sections of the country. Moore points out that the greater Southwest is made up of "subregional economies" (1988; see also Lamphere et al. 1993), such as the "border subeconomy" with strong immigrant and/or market connections to Central and Latin American countries. The diversity of the Sunbelt economy means that poverty is significantly conditioned by local contexts; development has been an uneven process. What this chapter will examine is a subregional economy that has always been peripheral to but still within the broad trend of Sunbelt development in the Southwest.

The Southwest has not been immune to national poverty trends. If that margin of worsened economic condition has had any organizational consequences in the life of the poor, we should be able to "see" (Moore 1988) the new processes of poverty formation at the community level. Does recent poverty mean a further deterioration of preexisting conditions, including a weakening of integrative ties, or does it signify more concentrated consequences on top of the historical conditions of poverty?

Rather than "underclass," I shall employ the term "restructuring effects" to mean a temporal dimension in the reproduction of poverty. Such a strategy enables us to ask what the recent trend of poverty increase means for Mexican Americans in a particular locale, and what has been added to the foundation of poverty laid down in the community generations ago. This question is largely unaddressed by aggregate analysis. Restructuring effects, then, refers not to specific people and their behaviors, but to conditions in neighborhoods that affect people's lives.

A final consideration is the fact that each ethnic grouping has unique features that make their own contributions to the shaping of community and poverty. Migration from Mexico is the most striking element of the Mexican American experience, but there are others, such as the generational effects on culture, which must be also reckoned when approaching particular settings. Based on Wilson's distinction between the historical foundations of poverty and the more recent social dislocations associated with economic restructuring, the aim of this chapter is to specify the sociohistorical bases of ethnic poverty in one historically Mexican American city. This entails examination of the older barrios and neighborhoods where Mexican Americans have long resided.

In addition, an overarching canvass of Albuquerque, New Mexico, reveals newer sections of poverty in areas away from traditional "Hispano" neighborhoods, zones that have arisen during the period of economic restructuring. The specific characteristics of the poverty in these pockets appear to be operating along the lines of Wilson's "concentration effects"—an area that is poorer, having few if any integrative ties, characterized by severe social dislocations, involving more transients including Mexican Americans, immigrants from Mexico, and other poor minorities.

The chapter concludes by considering the theoretical implications of the pattern found in the Albuquerque context.

The Setting: A Peripheral Economy

Albuquerque, New Mexico, is a medium-sized city, with a population of 480,000. Thirty-seven percent of the Albuquerque SMSA (the bulk of Bernalillo County) is Mexican American (U.S. Bureau of the Census 1991b). Mexican Americans, however, comprise 53 percent of those living in poverty and 60 percent of family household members living in poverty (City of Albuquerque 1989).[2]

The process maintaining this ethnic stratification must be seen against the backdrop of the city's historic economic marginality. Albuquerque is the largest city in New Mexico, but in a national perspective it is clearly peripheral. Neither major industry nor agriculture has ever supported its economy, nor has the city attained importance as a financial center.

Prior to Sunbelt development, Albuquerque went through four modern economic periods. The first was dominated by the railroad, which arrived in 1879, transforming Albuquerque from an obscure frontier outpost to the state's commercial center. Until 1941 the railroad was the city's largest and highest-paying employer (City of Albuquerque 1970).

The second phase was initiated by World War II:

> Like its Sunbelt contemporaries Tucson and Phoenix, Albuquerque
> on the eve of [World War II] was basically what it had been since
> the railroad brought it into being in 1880: little more than a small
> town that attracted tourists and health seekers and served as a
> trading and distribution center for a limited hinterland. World War
> II and the cold war that followed, however, led to the establish-
> ment and rapid expansion of Kirtland Air Force Base and Sandia
> and Manzano bases, which specialized in special weapons devel-
> opment and atomic research. By the mid-1950s the military and
> military-related activities so common in the region had replaced
> the declining Santa Fe Railroad as the city's most important source
> of economic growth (Rabinowitz 1983, p. 256).

The war boom caused Albuquerque/Bernalillo County to grow rapidly from 69,391 in 1940 to 145,673 in 1950 (Rabinowitz 1983, p. 256).

The third era emerged out of a relative postwar prosperity. The
weapons labs and military bases spurred an expansion in defense
and nuclear-related manufacturing. The number of people employed
in manufacturing increased more than sixfold between 1940 and
1960. However, since Albuquerque's total population continued to
mushroom (up to 262,700 in 1960; Rabinowitz 1983), manufacturing's
importance remained slight. Employment in the 1960s remained concentrated in government institutions (federal, state, and local), tourism, services, and construction, with manufacturing employing only
9 percent of the work force (Lamphere et al. 1993).

The final economic period coincides with national economic restructuring. Since the 1970s, the most significant development in
the Albuquerque economy has been a new era of manufacturing.
Manufacturing employment in Albuquerque doubled in the 1970s
and early 1980s as 300 new plants were established. Value-added
manufacturing tripled in real terms (Lamphere et al. 1993). Albuquerque's rate of manufacturing growth surpassed that of El Paso
and Phoenix. However, the two major kinds of manufacturing during this period were apparel and electronics, both of which hired
mostly women and paid between $4 and $7 per hour. As a result,
the impressive absolute growth in manufacturing meant something
other than affluence.

Despite the growth of industrial employment in the state as a
whole, New Mexico remained a poor state. In fact, the industrialization that occurred after 1960 did much less for New Mexico's standing relative to other states than the war and the immediate postwar
defense boom. By 1959 the median family income in New Mexico

had reached 95 percent of the national average. By 1979 it had dropped back to 85 percent. Nor was there any evidence that manufacturing wages in New Mexico were, as a whole, converging toward the national average. Average production-worker wages in New Mexico reached their peak relative to the national average (92 percent) in 1955. In 1982, they had increased from 1970 levels but were still less than 80 percent of the national average (Lamphere et al. 1993). For a Sunbelt city, Albuquerque did little for its unemployed. During the recession of 1983, for example, Albuquerque's unemployment rate was 9.1 percent compared to the national average of 10.2 percent (Lamphere et al. 1993).

In sum, Albuquerque never generated sufficient wealth to be called a real center of economic development in the Southwest. In New Mexico, government is the largest employment sector, 26 percent versus 15 percent nationally (New Mexico Department of Labor 1989). In Albuquerque, the public school system is the largest employer, followed by the Sandia Weapons Laboratory. Albuquerque's marginal economy has set the context for the organization of Mexican American neighborhoods and poverty.

Foundations of Neighborhood and Poverty

Dealing with important sociological issues and "Mexican Americans" is rarely easy because of the heightened diversity that the category "Mexican American" encompasses. It is analytically useful to keep three subgroups in mind, each of which has had a major generational impact on the Mexican American community in Albuquerque. First is the *Manito* (Edmunson 1957), a colloquial term that refers to descendants of the Spanish and Mexican colonists who settled the area before Albuquerque became a part of the United States. Second is the group I call (for clarity only) Chicano inmigrants, that is, Mexican Americans moving to Albuquerque from other parts of New Mexico and the Southwest. Third are the *Mexicanos*, people settling in Albuquerque directly from Mexico. I apply these names only to stand for three distinct experiences of incorporation into the Albuquerque metro area in the twentieth century. Whether members representing two or all three groups maintain themselves distinctly in the community, or whether they merge socially among themselves, are empirical questions not addressed here. However, each represents a dimension within the broader ethnic category of "Mexican American".[3]

Manito incorporation, 1897–1947. *Manito* denotes a distinct cultural strain rooted in New Mexico's history. In the *Manito* experience, substantial portions of indigenous New Mexican communities were brought into an expanding urban system, a community-building process distinct from migration or immigration. In Albuquerque, the process of annexing *Manito* neighborhoods preceded later overlays of Mexican American community and poverty.

The Hispanic presence in New Mexico is old, dating back to the Spanish colonial settlement of the area in the seventeenth and eighteenth centuries. Original Albuquerque, that section of the city now known as Old Town, was founded by New Mexico's provincial governor in 1706. Through the Mexican period and after the United States took forcible ownership of the Southwest in 1848, Albuquerque was a township at the center of a string of villages along the Rio Grande River, which bisects rectangular New Mexico as it runs from north to south. Just north of Albuquerque were the settlements of Los Griegos, Alameda, Los Candelarias, and Los Duranes, in an area that would come to be known as Albuquerque's North Valley. To the east lay Martinez-Santa Barbara. To the south lay the villages of Barelas, San Jose, Atrisco, Pajarito, and Los Padillas, which would eventually become the South Valley.

Albuquerque existed as a predominantly *Manito* agrarian community. The seat of covered wagon trade, it was important to *Manito* elites of the Rio *abajo*, or lower Rio Grande, group of settlements (Atencio 1985). When the railroad came to Albuquerque in 1879, it by-passed the Albuquerque plaza a couple of miles to the east. At this point, the New Mexico Townsite Co., an auxiliary of the Santa Fe Railroad, immediately founded Albuquerque "New Town" along the tracks (Neel 1928). An exclusive class of Anglo-American businessmen, merchants, and lawyers undertook the planning and construction of modern Albuquerque.

New Albuquerque was incorporated as a town in 1885 and as a city in 1891 in complete separation from *Manito Albuquerque* (City of Albuquerque 1968). As the city developed, New Town became a commercial center and Anglo Americans established their own residential neighborhoods and subdivisions around it (Klein 1974; City of Albuquerque 1988, 1976a). The scheme of the relation between *Manito* and Anglo districts between 1880 and 1948 can be summed up as "center segregation." Expanding in size, the leading Anglo middle class moved farther east on higher ground toward the Sandia Mountains to establish what is popularly known as "the Heights" (due east of Atrisco) (Cassel 1956). By design, the Anglo leaders steered Albuquerque's economic development as well as their residences away from the older Mexican areas of "the Valley". Throughout this period, most Anglo development neglected the *Manito* Valley and its village environs (Simmons 1982; Atencio 1985).[4] But enough Anglos remained in the Valley for its rural atmosphere, dairying, and truck farming to make a long-term difference in neighborhood structuring (Sargeant and Davis 1986; Atencio 1985).

According to the ethnohistorical evidence, much of what was a native *Manito* society in the Valley portions of Bernalillo county survived up through the 1930s. The villages, most having been established as Mexican colonial land grants to families of humble settlers, continued the traditional irrigation system (*acequia*) that obligated each household to contribute labor. In religion, villagers followed native Catholic practices and belief, including the clandestine *penitente* brotherhood of flagellants. Spanish remained the dominant language in these communities. Mutual aid societies provided important economic resources, such as affordable burial insurance, and served to integrate community leaders with the working people (Atencio 1985). These villages were under what has been termed the *patron* system, a form of community leadership in which a dominant figure of wealth and authority commanded votes and other support (Fisher 1976; Waggoner 1941; Sargeant and Davis 1986; Atencio 1985).

A substantial continuity of native institutions ran through the 1930s. However, traditional subsistence farming died. Federal and state regulatory commissions appropriated control of the river's flow by enforcing laws of water allotment and assessing taxes that did not accord with old irrigation methods. The area lacked the natural resources for large-scale growing, and Anglos monopolized what little market-oriented farming was possible. By the 1930s, *Manitos* were dependent on wage labor. Most of the available jobs were outside the villages in sawmills, dairies, and meat-packing plants, and as sheepherders. Throughout the depression and into the 1940s, a high portion of *Manitos* came under public assistance, for both work and social services (Waggoner [1941] reporting a remarkably high 53 percent for San Jose). The Anglo-dominated union tended to lock *Manitos* out of the better railroad jobs. As long as the villages remained outside the city limits, primitive living conditions without basic streets and sewers prevailed. The villages lacked commercial enterprises, and the people were dependent on New Town businesses for basic provisions. This entire fifty-year process saw the urban impoverishment of a traditionally agrarian folk in their own homeland (Fisher 1976; Waggoner 1941; Chambers et al. 1975; Duran 1983).

As other *Manito* villages throughout rural New Mexico went into economic decline during the Depression, the young people moved out to seek employment elsewhere, including Albuquerque (Atencio 1985). Walter at the time observed severe overpopulation and the difficulty of accommodating newcomers into a weak wage economy.

As he wrote concerning the San Jose district, "[I]n a village which is eighty-five percent Spanish speaking, living standards are extremely low and appear to be falling steadily. . . . Family income, in many cases, is less than $300 per year, and practically every family receives a part or all of its income from direct or work relief. The social structure itself is put under a severe strain, and divorce and desertion, practically unknown in the rural village life of the people, are beginning to mount steadily" (Walter 1939, p. 156).

A fledgling *Manito* middle class did arise. Excluded from business, it turned to the professions—law, education, journalism, and politics. Many of its members assimilated by way of Anglo intermarriage. But it was also integrated into the community, many of its members living among the working and lower classes and advocating for their interests on such issues as education and political representation (Atencio 1985; Gonzales 1985). On the *Mexicano* front, one result of the peripheral nature of the economy was that in the first half of the twentieth century, less than 3 percent of those who settled in the United States from Mexico did so in New Mexico (Hernandez-Alvarez 1966). The *Mexicanos* who did arrive at this time largely became acculturated into the *Manito* cultural fabric. However, this process was subtle, for during this time a strong *Manito* version of the Spanish heritage publicly emphasized a Spanish colonial legacy and deemphasized, and sometimes rejected and suppressed, *Mexicano* identification.[5]

Chicano in-migration, 1941–1960. The expansion of Albuquerque's employment base by the war and by the service economy drew thousands of Chicano migrants from other parts of New Mexico and the Southwest and some people from Mexico. The influx swelled population in the *Manito* village areas (Waggoner 1941; F. C. Moore 1947). The in-migrants moved onto vacant land between the original village sites. Also, as middle-class Anglos improved their lot and relocated to the Heights' newer subdivisions, their old neighborhoods were taken over by working- and lower-class Chicano families (City of Albuquerque 1987b). These population trends dispersed Mexican Americans and their attendant poverty throughout the Valley and extended the boundaries of the older neighborhoods. Many of the newcomers would not have the same attachments to a village community as the older native residents.[6]

The Mexican American districts in the Valley remained outside Albuquerque's city limits throughout the war. After the war, Albuquerque, like other Sunbelt cities, undertook an aggressive annexation policy, partly in anticipation of the 1950 census. In 1948, Albuquerque annexed Barelas, and began in 1949 to take in the *Manito* communities of Old Town, San Jose, Los Duranes, Martineztown/

Santa Barbara, and Los Griegos (Vogel 1967; City of Albuquerque 1968, 1987b). The establishment of the city/county service structure brought the predominantly *Manito* areas of Alameda, Los Padillas, and South Barelas within Albuquerque's sphere of influence.

The Mexican American districts underwent some infrastructural differentiation in the expanding 1940s. The more isolated ones experienced serious social disorganization. Divorce, marital separation, family desertion, chronically ill husbands, and illegitimate children were all observed in the San Jose district during this decade (Waggoner 1941; Sjoberg 1947; Cassel 1956).[7] Meanwhile, the three erstwhile villages closest to the center of dominant Albuquerque—North Barelas, Martineztown, and Old Town—turned into typical Southwest urban barrios. From the 1940s to the end of the 1950s, North Barelas and Martineztown flourished as what one local report calls Albuquerque's urban villages. "One of the factors which made [Martineztown-Santa Barbara] such a stable and closely knit community," it states, "is the mixture of residential dwellings with small businesses" (City of Albuquerque 1976b). North Barelas bordered the zone of the railroad shops and lay close to downtown, enabling it to develop an important ethnic small-business center. Tending to attract the distinct *Manito* middle class, North Barelas contained significant vertical integration involving churches, a merchant class, and traditional service organizations, like the League of United Latin American Citizens (LULAC), which were composed primarily of professionals (Cassel 1956). Culturally, commercial recreation in North Barelas and Martineztown served the entertainment needs of residents from other neighborhood districts that remained largely rural in character (Waggoner 1941; Robbins 1980).

Chicano in-migration augmented the *Manito* culture complex. As native institutions such as the *penitentes* disappeared, they were supplanted by more general twentieth-century Mexican American forms. The lower-class *pachuco*, or "zoot-suit", style, for example, was imported from El Paso and Los Angeles (see Cassel 1956). Urbanization, including acculturating mechanisms like public education, reduced but did not eradicate much of the indigenous culture. By the 1960s the Valley area reflected the "remnants" of the original *Manito* culture and way of life (Cline and Wolf 1967; see also Sjoberg 1947).

Chicano expansion since the 1960s. Since the 1960s, the Mexican American population has continued to disperse throughout the city and county. With the high native birth rate and continued in-migration from throughout the Southwest, patterns of residence varied. New bedroom communities sprang up on the west side of the river opposite the Anglo Heights, where working-class and middle-class neighborhoods adjoin each other. Middle-class Mexican American families are sprinkled throughout the Heights, while working-class Chicanos have moved into some older areas in the Heights, replacing lower-middle-class Anglos. Still, most of the poor Mexican Americans continue to reside in the North and South valleys.

Recent Mexicano arrival. While it is difficult to tell precisely, it appears that the rate of *Mexicano* settlement in Albuquerque has not increased dramatically since the 1950s. According to one study, 4.2 percent of *Mexicanos* with established U.S. residence in 1979 were in New Mexico (Portes and Bach 1985). In another report, 1 percent of all applications for legal residence under the terms of the 1986 Immigration Reform Act were made in New Mexico (Schick and Schick 1991). Heer (1990, pp. 57–58) found 2 percent of all undocumented Mexicans in the United States in 1980 residing in New Mexico. The Mexican consul informally estimated for the author that the number of legal *Mexicanos* in the Albuquerque area is 10–12,000, and the illegal 15,000.

The character of the *Mexicano* presence in Albuquerque, however, appears different from previous eras. Before, *Mexicanos* quietly blended into the local scene. Now, they appear to express themselves more freely, for example, in a visible *Norteno* style. They have instituted Mexican family customs such as the *quinceanera,* a cultural and quasi religious ceremony in which a young woman is formally introduced to society of the occasion of her fifteenth birthday (see, e.g., *Albuquerque Journal,* October 14, 1990), which had not been seen until recently. To some extent, they maintain their identification. As an example, community social service workers and high school teachers observe some teen-age gangs and cliques that are predominantly Chicano and others that are mostly *Mexicano.* In fact, a "Mexicanization" of Albuquerque is detectable; thus, for example, the "Spanish Heritage" theme of the New Mexico State Fair includes heavy doses of entertainment from Mexico. At the neighborhood level, *Mexicano* distinctiveness is sustained by the circular character of Mexican migration.

Traditional Integrative Ties Amidst Incremental Change

Albuquerque's economy has undergone discontinuity, but its twentieth-century effect on the Mexican American community and poverty has been incremental (cf. Evans 1993). New forms of community organization have emerged out of previous ones as external elements have been added on to preexisting conditions. A clear illustration is the continued viability of the Atrisco Land Grant, first awarded to a family of *Manito* settlers by King Charles II of Spain in

1692. Located just across the river from original Albuquerque, the grant was reduced to 46,000 acres in the nineteenth century and no longer provides subsistence, as it once did. Today its *Manito* heirs operate it as a real estate corporation,[8] testimony to a historical evolution possible only in the context of a marginal economy.

As Albuquerque expanded in the first half of the twentieth century, links to village life were substantially weakened but not torn asunder. Because Albuquerque has been economically peripheral, its lower-class structure includes integrative ties that originated in the early part of the century. Three such ties that have survived economic restructuring are a tradition of home ownership, *Manito* politics, and Anglo residence in Mexican American districts.

Housing. Displacement from the land as a result of the Americanization of the Southwest is a major theme in *Manito* history. Loss of land, sometimes through fraudulent means or tax delinquency (Chavez 1948), diminished *Manito* village communities in the Albuquerque area. (The story of Alameda is an example of the complete Anglo takeover of choice *Manito* real estate.) *Manitos* retained land mainly because their communities lay outside the city limits in areas not desired by Anglos. In a context of ethnic residential segregation, the ownership of homes by *Manito* descendants provided an important resource for poorer people needing to rent. In addition, the vacant rural areas were available for purchase. *Manitos* coming in from other parts of New Mexico settled whole new neighborhoods near the older village sites (Atencio 1985).

In her 1941 community study, Waggoner noted "a high degree of stability in the population of San Jose at the same time that a high degree of migration into the district [was] taking place" (1941, p. 42). Moore's follow-up study five years later found that "Home ownership had increased to 64.6 percent of the total number of families as had the number who were renting which was found to be 32.3%" (Moore 1947, p. 100). Waggoner noted that at the time some 61 percent of the residents in San Jose lived in houses that had been in the family from five to thirty years and more (Waggoner 1941). Moore noted five years later that 46.3 percent of the people who moved to San Jose did so in order to buy a house (Moore 1947). Thus, not only did native *Manitos* inherit title to traditionally held lands, but Mexican American arrivals from elsewhere could buy property in the unannexed portions of the Valley.

The photos and descriptions in a series of community studies and master's theses in the Albuquerque area from the 1940s to the 1960s show humble dwellings—small owner-built adobe-and-wood structures without much sleeping room and no indoor plumbing, reliant on wood for fuel and fronting unpaved streets (Waggoner 1941;

Moore 1947; Cassel 1956). "In fact," according to Sjoberg, "the greater part of San Jose could be considered a blighted area; some of this area could be considered a slum by accepted standards" (1947, p. 18). As late as 1966, one report said that Martineztown had an appearance "not unlike that of a Mexican border town—the dust of the roads blending with that of the yards" while many of the houses had "out-buildings and . . . latrines" (Vincent 1966, pp. 9–10).

The independence of the *Manito* villagers was being very steadily eroded, including their ability to hold onto native lands (Walter 1939). Still, the process was incremental. Many of the homes described from the 1940s on were, after all, occupant-owned homes. Sjoberg (1947) noted that the "furnishing of living quarters is one field in which we find that aid is provided by children and relatives to those on relief." Thus, of eighty-one Mexican American welfare clients studied by Sjoberg in San Jose, twenty-two owned their own homes, two were in the process of buying, ten lived in houses provided for them by their children, and another twenty-six lived with relatives in one house (1947).

Today, the city of Albuquerque reports that the Mexican American Valley areas show higher poverty rates than the rest of the city, and yet they continue to be marked by residential stability. In the South Valley, 49 percent of the population in 1980 lived in the same house they had five years earlier, compared to 47 percent of the total population of the metropolitan area. Among Mexican Americans, "stability rates were substantially higher at more than 54%. In the South San Jose neighborhood [one of the older *Manito* areas] which had the largest concentration of poor children under five in the area, nearly 71% of the population resided in the same house they had lived in five years earlier" (City of Albuquerque 1989, p. 8). In the North Valley, where 67 percent of all families are Mexican American, as are 83 percent of all families below the poverty level, the housing report was much the same: "North Valley neighborhoods . . . exhibit relatively high degrees of residential stability. Indeed, more than 59% of all residents of the area in 1980 reported living in the same house in which they had lived five years before" (City of Albuquerque 1989). The city points out that this overall rate was surpassed in several of the older Mexican American neighborhoods.

These reports show the important part housing availability has played in the socioeconomic structure of poverty in Albuquerque. The peripheral pace of Sunbelt development here has meant a depressed housing market relatively manageable for lower-income people. As one community profile points out, at 63 percent, the ratio of Mexican American owner-occupied homes almost equals the Anglo ratio of 65 percent (City of Albuquerque 1987a). Moreover, the highest concentration of Mexican American owner-occupied housing lies in the historically *Manito* Valley areas of the city (City of Albuquerque 1987a).

Since these early studies, it has become far more difficult for low- and very-low-income people to build their own houses. Inflation has caused them to devote over 30 percent of their income to household maintenance, and in some older *Manito* districts such as Barelas the proportion of renters exceeds that of owners (City of Albuquerque 1976e). Still, in the peripheral economy that characterizes the Albuquerque SMSA, 26 percent of all for-sale units built since 1980 were affordable to those at the lower end of the income spectrum (Southwest Land Research 1989). Moreover, home ownership has been aided by the city's HUD-sponsored home-rehabilitation program. Since 1976, over 1200 full rehab and over 400 partial rehab loans as well as 81 Section 312 home-buyer loans were awarded to income-qualified residents (City of Albuquerque 1991a).

Relative residential stability leads to a heightened sense of neighborhood identification among the residents of San Jose, Barelas, Old Town, Martineztown, Duranes, Los Griegos, and the old *Manito* districts outside the city limits (Atencio 1985; City of Albuquerque 1989; Robbins 1980). The clearest public evidence of neighborhood integration is the traditional yearly religious fiestas in devotion to the patron saint of each of these formerly subsistence villages (Vincent 1966).

Albuquerque Mexican Americans highly value home ownership, perhaps as a sign of self-reliance. This is reinforced by a sense of traditional *Manito* communalism—friends, relatives, and neighbors gather to build a house. Construction is a major job field for Spanish-surnamed males: among a list of 300 Hispanic-owned businesses certified by the city of Albuquerque (1991b), over one-third are construction or construction-related. Not only do many carpenters and laborers build their own places, but they also "moonlight" by constructing or repairing the homes of family members, neighbors, and informal referrals. Just how widespread this is needs further study, but it appears to be extensive.

These traditional housing patterns also benefit *Mexicanos*. Those who settle in the barrios, and most do, rent from Chicanos and *Manitos* who provide decent housing at affordable rents. In these locations, *Mexicanos* are freer to set up both informal and formal economic enterprises. Leading the author on a tour through Martineztown, a Chicano community service worker pointed out *Mexicano* mechanics in backyard garages and one instance of a Chicano providing his property for a *Mexicano chicharroneria* (meat-processing plant). At the outer edges of the county, in virtual sand dunes, a few *Mexicanos* had pooled resources to buy property and set up junkyards, an adobe-making plant, and a roofing company.

Political integration. A second legacy stems from the greater "vertical integration" that once existed between the professional and lower classes of Mexican Americans. Owing originally to those pockets not dominated by Anglo economics or politics, the Spanish-surnamed in New Mexico have skillfully, consistently, and effectively participated in electoral politics (Cline and Wolff 1967). Around Albuquerque in the early twentieth century, "Anglos held tightly to the reins of authority inside the city limits, but outside, [*Manitos*] dominated the Bernalillo County government" (Simmons 1982). As the city annexed the county village districts in the Valley, it incorporated *Manito* politics as well (Sjoberg 1947). From the beginning, *Manito* politicians were conscious of their own interests as opposed to those of the "Anglo Heights" (Cline and Wolf 1967).

Together, Zinn (1976) and Sjoberg (1947) sketch a historical model for the organization of grass-roots power in the Valley districts. After the arrival of the railroad and the loss of economic autonomy in the villages, power was vested in the *patrones,* who maintained community loyalty by using their relative wealth and political influence, and mediated between the Anglo and *Manito* societies (on the *patrones,* see also Simmons 1982; Fisher 1976; Moore 1947; Atencio 1985). Sjoberg observed that "the politician"—the local elected official, especially the justice of the peace—took over from the *patron* by the late 1940s. In the 1960s and early 1970s, activist paraprofessionals who administered community action programs rose to prominence. (It appears that the Mexican American community responded well to the "maximum feasible participation" goals of the 1960s poverty programs, thereby enhancing neighborhood stability if not cohesion [Vincent 1966; Anderson 1991].) In the 1970s, Zinn noted a shift in primary leadership taking place from community action organizers to Democratic party workers including office holders.

Today, the party apparatus is a structural feature of the Valley communities reflected in the high level of Spanish-surnamed representatives at state, county, and municipal levels. Every Valley district in the state house of representatives is represented by a Spanish-surnamed legislator. The Democratic party organizes effectively at the precinct level, and what Cline and Wolf observed in 1967 is still largely true: "Democratic party leaders rely on the hard core *Manito* workers and their families to pile up a substantial vote for the ticket in Bernalillo County which casts slightly over a fourth of the total state vote" (1967, p. 11). The careers of precinct (and often elected) officials tend to be organically rooted in their ethnic communities where their leadership roles are known by all (Dewitt 1978).

As a result of this political integration, Democratic party workers dominate the staffs and administrations of community social service agencies. This particular arrangement in the Valley stems from pre-annexation days when the county provided many social services to the indigent (Moore 1947). According to one Anglo city human services official, *Manito* political involvement means a greater cultural sensitivity, and therefore more effective delivery of social services to the people (Gonzales 1990).[9]

Anglo Co-Residence. It would be misleading to suggest that Mexican American neighborhoods in Albuquerque are strictly segregated. The 1990 census tract counts show that most of the traditional districts within the city limits have Mexican American majorities and significant Anglo minorities. For example, 66 percent of the residents in Los Griegos are classified as Hispanic origin, while 30 percent are non-Hispanic White; 60 percent of Duranes is Hispanic origin, and 37 percent non-Hispanic White. The Mexican American ratio appears greater in areas augmented by Chicano migration into Albuquerque, and yet Anglos remain present. East Atrisco, for example, has 76 percent Hispanic origin and 19 percent non-Hispanic White; the Sawmill district off Old Town has 73 percent Hispanic origin and 24 percent non-Hispanic White (Middle Rio Grande Council of Governments of New Mexico 1991).

Much of the presence of Anglos in the Valley districts is recent, the result of gentrification. But there is also a historical Anglo legacy in these areas (Sjoberg 1947; Cassel 1956; Chavez 1948). In some cases an Anglo minority stood aloof from the original villages (Sargeant and Davis 1986; Atencio 1985); in other cases, as in Old Town and North Barelas, the neighborhood abutted newer neighborhoods Anglos had built at the edges of downtown. This particular proximity is unlike the classic community segregation that characterized relations between Anglos and Mexican Americans in Texas and southern New Mexico.

The presence of Anglos and middle-class Mexican Americans in traditional Albuquerque barrios reflects the preservation of a rural way of life or ambience. Los Duranes, for example, has been described as a "largely working-class Hispanic neighborhood" which is also "home to retirees, young professionals and artists" (Rodriguez 1991). In a press "trends" description of Los Duranes, "Shiny tin roofs have sprung up next to sagging adobes, and newcomers are moving in next door to people whose families have been here for three generations or more". But Duranes also includes clearly impoverished streets, dilapidated houses, evidence of widespread drug use and other indicators of lower-class social disorganization (Anderson 1991).

As Massey (1990) argues, ethnic segregation in itself tends to concentrate underclass or disorganizational effects among the poor. A sense of how these can be offset by residential integration is suggested in Albuquerque. One important consequence of the presence of middle-class Anglos in predominantly Mexican American neighborhoods is the organization of neighborhood associations, such as Albuquerque's Downtown Neighborhood Association. This organization in the oldest Anglo residential district in the city organizes anticrime watches, campaigns for the preservation of historic buildings, monitors zoning changes to stave off business encroachment, distributes a neighborhood newsletter, raises funds for parks, and sponsors block holidays.

The treasurer of the Downtown Neighborhood Association told the author that despite recruitment efforts Mexican American residents have declined to participate in the organization because it is "white". A Mexican American activist in the neighborhood claims that the association has an ethnically exclusive and elitist agenda set by professional Anglos that is not sensitive to the working-class interests of Mexican American residents. Despite the sharp social and cultural boundaries apparent between the two groups (see Anderson 1991), their tension in itself is an aspect of neighborhood awareness. In any event, the Mexican American spokesperson concedes that all have gained from many of the association's successes, such as keeping out unsavory businesses and establishing parkways.

In this district middle-class Anglo homes adjoin working-class Mexican American neighborhoods. The same kind of relationship is not so evident in other areas, like Barelas and San Jose, which have very few Anglo middle-class residents. These neighborhoods, however, are characterized by a greater degree of Mexican American political integration.

Restructuring Effects

A study on poverty and the socioeconomic status of various neighborhood districts in Albuquerque reports on the city's poverty over the last twenty years and its intensification in the 1980s. It states, "Between 1980 and 1987, the number of households at or below 50% of median income had grown at a rate which was nearly 60% faster than all households in the city. This segment increased its proportion of all households from 22% to 27% over that seven year period" (City of Albuquerque 1989, p. 5). Given the disproportionate levels of poverty among Mexican Americans and other minorities, it is clear they have borne the brunt of this trend toward increasing poverty among families.

Many of the factors associated with increased with increased poverty in Albuquerque reveal serious social dislocation for Mexican Americans. Of children in poverty, 62 percent are Mexican American; further, 84 percent of the Mexican American poor live in families. Households in the low-income group are much more likely to consist of families with children than was the case in 1980, with large increases among female-headed families with children. The Mexican American birth rate is higher (half of all live births in 1987), while the ratio of mothers receiving prenatal care is lower than average (13.9 percent). Also, child abuse appears on the increase, half of it involving victims under the age of 6. There is a particularly sharp increase in the number of young children with parents under 24 years old (City of Albuquerque 1989).

Part of the increase in poverty has occurred in the Valley barrios despite the integrative ties just identified in those neighborhoods. The pressures evidence themselves variously. Gentrification has encroached on the older *Manito* heritage sites, in some cases all but obliterating the original community, Los Candelaria, for example. In inner-city areas, business development, particularly light industry such as warehousing and construction yards, has intruded into residential life (City of Albuquerque 1976b). Since the 1970s, the city of Albuquerque's sector development studies on the Valley barrios consistently report housing that is "substandard", "in poor condition", "inadequate", and "deteriorating" (City of Albuquerque 1988; 1987b; 1976a; 1976; 1976c; 1976d; 1970). Higher than average crime rates have affected those neighborhoods as integrative ties have loosened in recent years (City of Albuquerque 1987b).

In addition to the impact of increased poverty on the historical foundations of poverty in Albuquerque during the period of economic restructuring or Sunbelt development, Albuquerque in the last twenty years has seen the emergence of a new poverty pocket away from the old Valley strongholds in a formerly Anglo middle-class section of the Heights. The 1989 city study gives a graphic portrait of poverty in the Heights: "While much of the Valley remains poor, over the last two decades new concentrated areas of high poverty have gradually emerged in older areas of the Heights where the aging housing stock and newer, low-cost multi-family housing has attracted a large proportion of the rapidly growing low-income population." The report also observes, "In contrast to the . . . Valley areas, with their strong ties of family and culture rooted in consciousness of a continuous history extending to the early 18th century, [this] area of the City . . . was not developed until the 1950s [as an Anglo subdivision]" (City of Albuquerque 1989, p. 9).

Compared to the Manito Valley areas, the Heights is poorer than the barrios. The area is "currently in the process of transition from a stable, lower-middle class Anglo . . . residential community to an ethnically diverse area of extreme poverty". During the 1980s, 16.2 percent of the family households had incomes below the federal poverty level. As the city points out, "Of these approximately 32% were headed by single women with children under school age. A total of 3,174 children under five years old lived in the area, of whom 1,144 live in families below the poverty level (36%)." In 1980, the area had the highest concentration of poor children under age 5 of any area served by the city's Department of Human Services. Currently, the Central/Southeast area has a larger proportion of families—14 percent—receiving public assistance. Moreover, "School lunch program data suggest that the problems of child poverty have increased sharply over the past seven years" (City of Albuquerque 1989, pp. 9–11). At the three elementary schools serving the area, one reported that 94 percent of its pupils qualified for free lunch, the second 74 percent, and the third 73 percent. The area had "the dubious distinction of containing the elementary school with the largest number of pupils eligible for free lunch as well as the school with the highest percentage of its enrollment eligible for such assistance." The city of Albuquerque believes that since the 1980 census the overall poverty rate worsened considerably (City of Albuquerque 1989, pp. 9–11).

Housing factors in the Heights differ from the Valley. The Heights poverty pocket has the highest density housing and lower home-ownership rates of any area within the Albuquerque metropolitan area. As the Anglo owners moved on to better single-family housing farther east and north, their Central/Southeast homes became multi-family rental units. The quality of this housing is indicated by the fact that rents there fell to well below the City average, attracting ever increasing numbers of low income households and furthering the rapid transition of the area. Accordingly, neighborhoods are less stable. "In contrast to the Valley areas," the City of Albuquerque (1989, p. 29) states, "where half or more of the households in 1980 lived in the same house they had five years before, only about one-third (36%) of families in the East Central area reported similar stability. This ratio has undoubtedly declined further with the continuing shift from homeownership to rental housing in the area." Moreover, "unlike Valley areas, no informal or semi-formal neighborhood institutions including friendships and neighboring groups, churches, and neighborhood associations exist in the East Central target area" (City of Albuquerque 1989, p. 29), and the area does not have a traditional sense of political integration.

The ethnic composition of the Central/Southeast Heights is distinctive. Actually, Mexican Americans there "constitute only 30% of all families in the area and only 38% of the families below poverty. Although Hispanic children make up a substantial proportion of all poor children, at only about 47% of children in poverty, their percentage is sharply below that found in [the Valley] as a whole." Other low-income people in the area include young Anglo transients, the city's largest concentrations of poor Native Americans, a small but growing Southeast Asian population, and a significant concentration of black families.

As a result, the city states, "In sharp contrast to the Valley areas with their strong bilingual cultural milieu, only about a quarter of all persons over 18 years old in the East Central area reported using a language other than English in the home." Even among the area's Mexican Americans, the ties to native culture appear weakened. Only about 75 percent of those over 18 reported using a language other than English in the home, compared to nearly 90 percent in the valley areas. The percentage of the Hispanic population not speaking English, or not speaking it well, was also significantly lower at 6 percent compared to 11 percent in the valley areas.

Finally, as the city states, "One neighborhood within the [Heights area of poverty], locally referred to as 'the war zone,' has extensive problems with open prostitution, violent crime, transience, and steadily increasing poverty" (City of Albuquerque 1989, p. 19).

The organization of poverty is decidedly different in the Heights than in the Valley barrios. The Heights lacks the kind of neighborhood resources that have produced at least some measure of stability and opportunity in the Valley. Unlike the Valley, the Heights is not predominantly Mexican American; rather it is an area to which a large portion of the Mexican American population, both Chicano and *Mexicano*, have migrated.

The Heights poverty area represents a harsh reality that has arisen in tandem with Sunbelt development in the Southwest; however, the connection to economic restructuring is indirect. The families here came to Albuquerque as part of the larger trend of migration to Sunbelt centers in the Southwest, or to seek jobs specifically in Albuquerque's manufacturing sector. Sunbelt manufacturing employs primarily Chicanas on the production line, most of whom have been in the Albuquerque labor market for some time (Zavella 1987; Lamphere et al. 1993). For most newcomers, however, the local version of Sunbelt industrialization has proved inadequate to the needs of families and the proportional employment of Mexican American males.

Conclusion: Theoretical Implications

Inspired by Wilson's analysis of the ghetto, this chapter finds historical poverty in Albuquerque conditioned by layers of neighborhood evolvement. Under economic marginality, poverty and society have changed incrementally, less subject to the wholesale shifts in community organization that have impacted minority groups in economically central regions of the United States. Sunbelt development hit Albuquerque as the latest in a wave of broad restructuring trends that prove significant for initiating subtrends but are hardly revolutionary in their impact.

Broadening Wilson's concept of vertical integration, research on Latino communities can look for the structures of integrative ties and the impact that economic restructuring has had on them. The structure of integration in Albuquerque is founded on legacies. Residential stability, to the extent that it remains, anchors the indigent in an encompassing sense of community. Political integration can form a part of such community feeling, but its effects have more centrally to do with the organization of social services. Indirect effects are possible, as illustrated in Albuquerque by the role of Anglo residents in predominantly Latino areas. Theoretically, the structures of integration can assume infinite shapes throughout the land.

Economic change can erode the structure of legacies. Dislocations can impact older communities and their strong ties of ethnic culture and family relations. Assaulting traditional neighborhoods are increasing poverty among families, drug and alcohol problems, crime, gentrification, changing development patterns resulting in the loss of primary jobs to fringe areas, and other threats to a historic stability. Another part of town can experience the same effects but without any structure of integration to speak of, as most residents lack a strong sense of neighborhood identity, familiarity, or belonging. These zones can be bereft of formal service providers, an effective neighborhood association, and other integrative ties.

Recognizing the distinction between the older legacies of poverty and newer conditions of neighborhood deterioration is facilitated by Wilson's key insight regarding the way that poverty itself was altered as a primary result of momentous economic change.

NOTES

Special thanks to Felix Torres, Michael Passi, Arturo Sandoval, Victor Arrey, Cecilio Garcia Camarillo, and Carolyn Anderson for their aid in the research for this chapter; also to Joan Moore, Raquel Rivera Pinderhughes, Mercer Sullivan,

Guillermo Grenier, Felix Padilla, and Patricia Zavella for their responses to earlier drafts.

1. Wilson also disagrees with the argument that severe poverty is attributable primarily to an intensification of historical racism, discrimination, and the social domination of African Americans by Anglo society. Historically determined poverty may have set the stage for present conditions, Wilson argues, but the current black underclass has structural roots and reinforcements (Wilson 1987).

2. Minorities together constitute about 43 percent of Albuquerque's total population, others being Native Americans (3 percent), African Americans (3 percent), and Asians (1 percent). Minorities make up 64 percent of those living below poverty and 72 percent of family household members living in poverty (City of Albuquerque 1989).

3. My use of these labels is distinct from the classic and complex issue of what terms the people themselves have utilized for purposes of self-identification and why. For one attempt to clarify the twentieth-century usage of ethnic nomenclatures in New Mexico, see Gonzales (1993).

4. "Albuquerque's civic boosters and real-estate promoters, if they paid any attention to the outlying villages at all, must have regarded them as an embarrassment, for neither their poverty nor their rustic architectural style helped in creating the image of a modern and typical American city" (Simmons 1982, p. 338).

5. Quite successful senior New Mexicans speak about the *surumato* disparagement that was applied to them and their families by citizen *Manitos* (e.g., Cobos 1972).

6. The distinction is apparent in a comparison of Rudolfo Anaya's first two novels. *Bless Me Ultima* (1972) is the story of a young boy completely enfolded in the culture of his northern New Mexico village prior to World War II. *Heart of Aztlan* (1976) reflects the same person as a later youth in the alienating Albuquerque barrio of Barelas.

7. But F. C. Moore (1947) reports a protest by San Jose residents in 1946 to the city's annexation proposal, suggesting high neighborhood identification in a poor area.

8. The commercialization of the Atrisco Land Grant (Westland Corporation) is opposed by a dissident faction wishing to see the grant returned to traditional uses for heirs (see, e.g., Anaya 1990).

9. A politically organized social service system is not without its problems. According to one social service expert, recent charges of corruption in the delivery of medical services to the poor reflect a parochial ethnic patronage system where rational administration is needed (Gonzales 1990).

8

PERSISTENT POVERTY, CRIME, AND DRUGS: U.S.–MEXICAN BORDER REGION

Avelardo Valdez

T HE HIGHEST indicators of poverty in the United States are along the Rio Grande Valley in Texas. The scarcity of institutional resources and economic development, relative to other areas of the state, is attributed to the fact that this area is identified as a Mexican American region. Social mobility is, nonetheless, possible for a small proportion of Mexican Americans whose class interests often conflict with the majority of this population. The interests of these Mexican Americans usually coincide with those of the dominant Anglos. As a result, most Mexican Americans occupy a subordinate status based on ethnicity and class. Recent economic changes have exacerbated social differences among Mexican Americans, solidifying the dominant position of the middle class and the subordinate position of the working-poor.

This study focuses on the impact of this economic transformation on Mexican Americans in Laredo, Texas, who comprise 90 percent of the population. The research explores how sectors of Laredo's poor have adapted alternative social strategies to survive economically. It also examines how the presence of the international border, combined with high poverty rates, generates disproportionate levels of illicit behavior, particularly related to drugs.

Wilson and others argue that during the last two decades an underclass has formed among urban blacks as a result of national economic restructuring (Wilson 1987; Harrington 1984). The un-

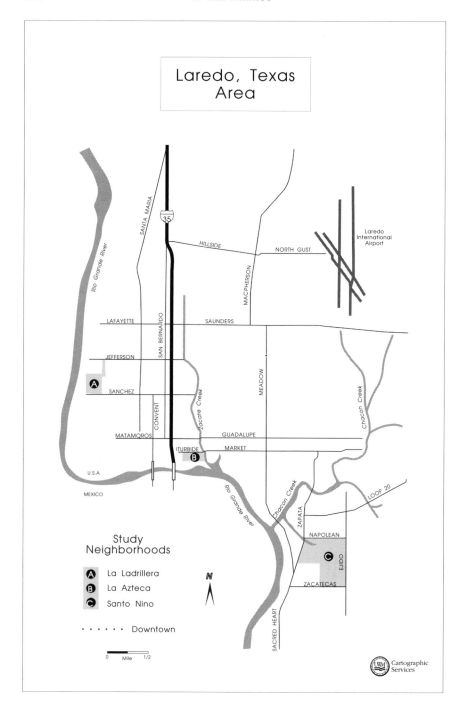

Laredo, Texas
Area

Study
Neighborhoods

Ⓐ La Ladrillera
Ⓑ La Azteca
Ⓒ Santo Nino

· · · · · · Downtown

0   Mile   1/2

Cartographic
Services

derclass is associated with chronic poverty, joblessness, residential segregation, and the breakdown of community institutions. Among the most significant impacts of these economic changes was the disappearance of a stable wage-based economy in urban areas. As a result, many economic activities in black ghettos were now generated outside the formal wage market (Wilson 1985). This included increased governmental dependency and criminal activities centered on the ghetto's illegal economy. Although the discourse on the underclass often alludes to this underground economy, few studies have focused on it, particularly as it concerns the Mexican American community (Moore 1989).

This chapter will explore whether the underclass model applies to Mexican Americans. The research describes the evolution of the U.S.–Texas border regional economy over the last two decades, analyzing Laredo's contemporary economy and poverty among Mexican Americans. The study then discusses the pervasiveness of crime, linked to the region's illicit economy, and its impact on three neighborhoods in this predominately Mexican American community.

Laredo: Portrait of a U.S.–Mexico Border City

Laredo is a major commercial and retail link between the Mexican state of Tamaulipas and Texas. The city's primary economic activities are international transportation, manufacturing, and retail trade. Laredo's major transportation artery is Interstate 35, which leads 150 miles north to San Antonio and the rest of the United States. Laredo's shopping mall and upscale restaurants and popular night spots are also located along or adjacent to this highway. The interstate is flanked by fast-food restaurants, motels, international auto insurance companies, money exchange houses, gas stations, tire stores, and other businesses catering to U.S. and Mexican tourists.

The interstate leads directly to the new international bridge crossing into Nuevo Laredo, Tamaulipas. The older bridge is several blocks to the west. Most of the businesses catering to Mexican shoppers, American and Mexican tourists, and travelers are near the older bridge. There is a constant flow of pedestrians, automobiles, trucks, and commercial busses here, for just across this bridge is the heart of downtown Nuevo Laredo.

Laredo's downtown is north of the old bridge, centered around a plaza bustling with shoppers, schoolchildren, office workers, peddlers, undocumented Mexicans, Nuevo Laredo shoppers, elderly pensioners, and other residents from both cities. Laredo's city busses reach all parts of the city from this plaza. The city's new municipal building, county courthouse, county jail, financial institutions, hotels, and other services and businesses are located here.

Northwest of the central city lies a huge railyard where the National Railroad of Mexico and the Missouri Pacific lines meet. Much of U.S.–Mexico trade is shipped through here. The tracks lead south to a railroad bridge that crosses into Mexico. Surrounding the railyard are acres of parked semitrailers used to transport goods. Semitrailers are also seen on the interstate access roads entering Laredo from the north, where a concentration of import/export brokers and warehouses cater to the maquiladora industry.

East of downtown Laredo is a warehouse and manufacturing district served by rail lines and trucking firms. Highway 83 runs southeast through this area to Zapata, Texas. This highway, as it runs from downtown through south Laredo, is an important retail corridor for local residents, lined with auto-parts stores, grocery stores, restaurants, nightclubs, and other businesses. The homes in this part of the city are predominantly single-family houses on large lots in older subdivisions off the main highway. Neighborhood roads and streets are mostly unpaved and without sidewalks. Many residents are migrant farm workers who travel to the Midwest during the summer and reside here in the winter.

The disproportionate percentage of families in poverty is reflected in the dispersion of the poor through all areas of Laredo. The poorest neighborhoods are adjacent to the central business district, transportation and shipping facilities, and the Rio Grande River. In these neighborhoods small clapboard houses sit on single lots. Many of the streets are unpaved, and are hot and dusty during the summer. Inadequate drainage causes flooding in many of these neighborhoods during the rains. Barrios such as El Azteca, El Cuarto, Canta Ranas, and Los Colonias, are highly enclosed neighborhoods, with long-term multigenerational residents, that have developed distinctive identities. There are other still poorer neighborhoods on the outskirts of the city called *colonias*, newer areas best described as poor subdivisions lacking many essential services.

There are sections of Laredo that are associated with the wealthy. The city's traditional upper class tends to reside in the near northwest side of the city. This area, south of Martin High School, is filled with large homes on perfectly manicured lawns with thick foliage. The streets are all paved and have sidewalks. Many of these houses are built in a Spanish-stucco style and surrounded by large walls. Newer middle-class subdivisions lie on the far north side and in an area surrounding the city's airport. These subdivisions are home to many middle-level managers recently moved to Laredo as well as lower-middle-class residents native to this region.

Mexican Americans are found throughout the class structure. As in other south Texas border cities there is a small Mexican American upper class of bankers, ranchers, and professionals. A larger middle class has also developed. It consists of small businessmen, teachers, lawyers, health workers, semiprofessionals, public employees, and politicians. Additionally there is a working class that is employed in civil service, blue-collar jobs, and retail and clerical work. The majority of Laredo residents, nonetheless, are poor and only marginally integrated into the local economy, primarily as unskilled workers.

Nuevo Laredo residents, as is true of other Mexicans living along the border, have a special legal status that allows them limited access to U.S. border areas. This allows Mexican residents to shop, visit, and conduct business in U.S. border regions. The free flow of Mexican residents into Laredo is typical of other U.S. border cities. Many Mexicans along the border, however, abuse this privilege by working, which is prohibited by U.S. immigration laws. Some estimates conclude that 20 percent of Laredo's work force is comprised of Mexicans who commute daily or weekly into the city. These workers often are employed at salaries and under conditions unacceptable to Mexican Americans. The presence of Mexican workers in Laredo and other border cities contributes to the low salary structures, high unemployment levels, and poverty of these regions.

The predominance of persons of Mexican origin throughout the class structure and Laredo's proximity to Mexico create a homogeneous cultural milieu. Although English is the official language, Spanish is the dominant language of the city. Mexican Americans are found in all levels of business, government, education, mass media, and religion. Many Mexican Americans from throughout the class structure, who are natives of Laredo, claim never to have experienced ethnic prejudice and/or discrimination in this community. Poverty and inequality for most Mexican Americans in Laredo appears to be more the result of class differences than ethnic or racial prejudice.

The Development of the Texas Border Region Economy and the U.S.–Mexican Populations

The economy of the Texas border region was based on agriculture and ranching during the late nineteenth and early twentieth centuries. In most places, society was stratified in a castelike system, with Mexicans at the bottom of the hierarchy, Anglos owning the ranches and farms, and Mexicans working as ranch hands and farm workers (Montejano 1987).

The exceptions to this pattern were found in border cities such as El Paso, Laredo, and Brownsville, which function as commercial regional centers for Texas and Mexico. An elite class of Mexican merchants developed there that interacted with Anglos on a more egalitarian basis. As these cities diversified economically, there emerged a more fully developed class structure among the Mexican-origin population than is found in other parts of the Texas border region and the Southwest.

Major economic changes occurred throughout the border region in the post–World War II period. This area witnessed the internationalization of production and the exchange of populations between Mexico and the United States (Fernandez 1989). During the last twenty-five years binational economic federal programs have intensified the economic interdependency of these two regions. The Texas border counties experienced more rapid economic growth than the national and state averages (Miller 1983). The Mexican border states of Tamaulipas, Nuevo Leon, and Coahuila experienced even greater economic expansion, particularly after the passage of the Border Industrialization program (BIP). Started in 1965, this joint U.S.–Mexican program allowed the U.S. manufacturers to assemble goods in Mexico that would be taxed only on their increased value on their return to the United States. Employment expanded with industrialization on both sides of the border, which also generated a sharp upturn in trade, financial, and real estate activity, and significant Mexican business investment and property development.

The benefits of economic growth were unequally distributed in Mexico and the United States. The maquiladora industry, the result of the BIP, did not solve Mexico's chronic employment, underemployment, and economic development problems. Many critics argue that in fact the BIP exacerbated and prolonged Mexico's economic crisis (Fernandez 1989; Hanson 1981). For instance, the maquiladora industry attracted thousands of workers (mostly female) and their families to Mexican border cities. Many earned a peso equivalent of $7.50 a day, hardly enough to support their families. The infrastructures of these cities were unable to support the onslaught of people lured by the promise of jobs in the maquiladora industry. Many workers were forced to live in sprawling slums without basic services like running water, drainage, and electricity. The major beneficiaries were the Mexican business elite, who were able to take advantage of these opportunities.

The benefits of economic growth for Mexican Americans along the Texas border were also marginal because their status improved little during this period. The Texas border region as a result of the BIP experienced increases in manufacturing and retail trade, while these sectors, particularly manufacturing, were reduced in other areas of the state. Despite this economic growth and increase in the labor force during the 1970s compared to the statewide growth, unemployment was higher in this region than the state and national averages. Median family income for this region, as well, remained relatively lower than the state average—by about two-thirds (M. J. Miller 1983). Although poverty rates in the border region were reduced from 45 percent to approximately 33 percent from 1970 to 1980, they remained the highest in the state.

Many of the new jobs in Texas created by the BIP were absorbed by Mexican commuters and U.S. blue-collar workers from outside the border region. Many of the unskilled blue-collar positions went to workers who had acquired previous experience and training for these jobs in other areas. Mexican commuters, both legal and illegal, were hired in positions throughout the labor force in lower-status blue-collar jobs. These were the same jobs sought by lower-status Mexican Americans who refused to work at the salaries and under the same conditions as the Mexicans. Competition from both outside groups worsened and perpetuated the low status of the Mexican American populations in this region.

Economic Reconstruction along the U.S.–Mexico Border: The Case of Laredo, Texas

The border separates Laredo from Nuevo Laredo, Tamaulipas, in Northern Mexico. These two cities have populations of 113,000 and 500,000, respectively. Together the cities have played a traditionally dominant role in the region's economy (south Texas and northern Mexico), particularly in the retail and service trade and as an export/import center. The economic interdependence of these two cities has resulted in a series of regional booms and busts over the past fifty years (Martinez, 1983b). Prior to the 1970s Laredo's economy was based on ranching, tourism, retail trade, and international trade. A large portion of its Mexican American population migrated to work as temporary agricultural workers in other areas of the United States. More recently, Laredo's economy has benefited from the maquiladora industry, with non-Mexican-owned companies assembling and producing products in Mexico yet maintaining administrative control in the United States and other countries.

The economic boom: 1970 and 1982. During the 1970s and early 1980s Laredo experienced an economic boom. The economy was based primarily on ranching, oil and gas, retail trade, and international trade. Laredo served as a major point of U.S.–Mexico commercial trade because it was located on one of the most direct routes between these two regions. A daily average of 151 railroad freight cars entered Laredo in 1978 (Hanson 1981). The city during this period had one of the highest retail sales per resident in the nation (Harrell and Fischer 1985), based primarily on purchases made by Mexican residents. Furthermore the Mexican middle class invested their inflationary pesos in businesses and real estate on the U.S. border. Between 1970 and 1980 Laredo's population grew from about 70,000 to 90,000 as its labor force swelled by 75 percent. Poverty declined from 45 to 35 percent (Miller 1983). This growth offset the loss in 1972 of a military base that was Laredo's single largest employer.

As Laredo retailers expanded their businesses by two- and three-fold, the city became northern Mexico's primary shopping center. Prices for housing, land, and other property rose. Economic prosperity, however, was unequally distributed within the population. According to Miller (1983):

> The boom, tied to an unstable false economy, certainly generated tremendous affluence for some and temporarily augmented the ranks of the small Laredo middle class. The vast majority of residents, however, gained little. The boom brought jobs, but as always, competition for them with Mexican commuters was stiff and wage levels remained low. Moreover, persistently low incomes coupled with greatly inflated cost of living, doubtless for many had a depressing affect on their quality of life.

As a result Laredo's economic prosperity during this period did little to change the status of the poor in this community.

The post-1982 period. In 1982, the Mexican government lowered the value of the peso by 80 percent and Laredo's economic boom was shaken. The economic impact of the first devaluation in February (which increased the rate of exchange from 25 to 52 pesos to the dollar) was mainly limited to retailers dependent on Mexican consumers. The August devaluation (raising the rate to 70 pesos to the dollar), however, had devastating effects on the entire border economy. Devaluation terminated Mexican investment and cut back the international brokerage and transportation industry in the region. The third devaluation, in December 1982, intensified the depression, and was followed by business closings, job losses, and significant reductions in other sectors of a local economy largely dependent on the Mexican market.

Unemployment and underemployment along the international border increased throughout the eighties. In the early 1980s Laredo's unemployment rate stood at 10 percent, and in 1983 the unemployment rate increased to 25 percent, which represented 11,000 workers. From 1984 to 1988 unemployment levels fluctuated between 16 and 13 percent, about double the overall rate in Texas. Not until 1989 and 1990 did unemployment level off, at approximately 10 percent.

The leveling-off of the unemployment rate was a result of the overall increase in Laredo's labor force in 1989–1990. The number of nonagricultural wage and salaried employees rose from 40,800 to 42,700 between 1988 and 1989. Employment also climbed 8 percent in wholesale and retail trade, and 5 percent in total manufacturing. Finance, insurance, real estate, and government employment, however, saw a decrease in jobs (Texas Employment Commission 1990).

Official unemployment rates in Laredo, however, are understated because they do not include persons who have ceased to look for work and other legal residents who are not considered. These official statistics also do not include unemployed Mexicans from Nuevo Laredo. Thousands of these jobless Mexicans, who face high unemployment and extreme inflation in their country, commute to Laredo in search of work. This unemployed sector, estimated as high as 40 percent of Nuevo Laredo's population, exacerbates the social and economic problems experienced by Laredo residents.

The Maquiladora Industry: Laredo's Contemporary Economy

Laredo's contemporary economy continues to serve a Mexican market, but has moved to one based primarily on international manufacturing, export, and trade. This economy is largely dependent on maquiladoras, which are non-Mexican owned factories and assembly plants located primarily along the border. The Mexican government provides the maquiladora industry with substantial duty and tariff advantages. Most U.S. companies involved in maquiladoras have established labor-intensive twin plants along the U.S.–Mexico border. These firms are involved in cloth and fabric production, leather production, clay products, electronic and electrical equipment, and transportation equipment. Rising labor costs in the United States make the relatively cheap labor in Mexican border communities attractive to U.S. manufacturers. These companies have the best of both worlds with low-cost, quality production in Mexico and well-developed markets in the United States.

In 1987, the total number of maquiladora plants along the border increased by nearly 28 percent from the previous year to 1259 plants. By September 1988, the number of plants had increased by another 16 percent to 1459 plants (Montoya and Noyola 1989). In July 1989, there were 70 maquiladora factories in Nuevo Laredo employing 14,991 workers. This was an increase from 39 plants and 8769 workers in December 1987 (McRay 1989).

Many have argued that the plants in Mexico should enhance the socioeconomic status of U.S. residents along the Mexican border (Sanders 1986). However, the growth of the maquiladora industry has not had a significant impact on the economic status of this population, particularly that of Mexican Americans in Laredo. This industry has done little, overall, to develop Laredo and other Texas border communities economically. Most maquiladora factories adjacent to Laredo, for instance, purchase their primary raw materials from non-Texas suppliers, and industrial supplies and services from non-border cities.

Laredo has benefited from the maquiladora industry mainly through income spent by maquiladora workers in the service trade sector and increased business to transportation and warehousing firms. In service trades Mexican Americans often find themselves competing with Mexican nationals, particularly at the entry-level positions. Mexican Americans were hired to some extent at blue-collar positions in the transportation and warehouse industry. However, many of the managerial positions generated by this industry went to persons from outside south Texas. Native Mexican-origin persons in Laredo were in the main not hired for these jobs, owing to their lack of education and/or job experience and in some cases discrimination.

Persistent Poverty

Although poverty levels fluctuated during the 1980s, by 1989 they had reached levels consistent with those of the previous decades. Laredo's economic transformation favored upper-class and middle-class Mexican Americans and skilled managers and professionals from outside south Texas. These were the persons who had the skills and capital to take advantage of the opportunities offered by these economic changes. The majority of Laredo's Mexican Americans, however, continued to survive at economically low-subsistence levels.

In 1990, 37 percent (52,635) of the total population of Laredo (Webb County) lived below the official poverty line as compared to 34.5 percent (31,291) in 1980. The poverty rate in Laredo runs more than double that of Texas and triple that of the United States. In 1980, 30 percent of families were impoverished compared to 39 percent in 1970. Despite the decrease of families living in poverty from 1970 to 1980, the rate was still 100 to 200 percent higher than the state or the nation. Laredo also has a disproportionate share of female-headed households: in 1980, 19 percent of all families in Laredo were female-headed compared to 12 percent and 11 percent in Texas and the United States, respectively.

During the 1980s poverty levels again reached those of the early 1970s. In this decade the instances of teen pregnancies steadily increased (from 23 percent of all births in 1983 to 28 percent in 1986). The demand on public and private assistance programs rose after the devaluation crisis of 1982. In 1990, 2300 families were on federal Aid to Families with Dependent Children (AFDC) for a total of 5172 children. More than 2500 households were added to the food-stamp rolls between January 1981 and December 1983. Although applications for the next four years were below 1983 levels, they rose to 4212 in 1988; this was the second-highest number of food-stamp applications since 1983. Over one-third of Laredo's entire population was on food stamps at one time or another during this period (see Table 8.1).

Poverty levels are reinforced by low levels of human capital skills. The median years of school completed in 1970 and 1980 in Laredo were 7.6 and 9.5, respectively, figures far below state and national averages during this same period. In 1980, only 32 percent of Laredo's population had graduated from high school compared to 62 percent in Texas and 67 percent in the United States. Laredo also has a disproportionate percentage of foreign-born—22 percent in 1980 compared to 6 percent for the rest of the nation. The majority of these were Mexican nationals, but these figures do not include the undocumented Mexicans living in this city. This large immigrant population influences language and other ethnic variables. In Laredo, for instance, 94 percent of all persons age 5 years or older speak a language other than English.

Poverty has had a devastating effect on the psychic well-being of

TABLE 8.1

*Number of New Applications for Food Stamps and Total Caseload,
1983–1989*

Year	New Applications	Total Case Load
1983	5676	36,306
1984	3996	37,363
1985	3652	35,955
1986	4068	36,084
1987	3816	36,879
1988	4212	37,494

Source: Texas Department of Human Resources, 1989.

residents as well. According to Laredo social service workers, case-loads have continued to increase over the last few years. Many clients exhibited anxiety and stress disorders. Children's referrals have doubled, with slight increases in the number of people applying for mental disability under the federal Supplemental Security Income (SSI) program.

Crime Indicators, Drug Violations, and Drug-Related Murders

Persistent poverty among large segments of Laredo's population generates various adaptation patterns as the poor find innovative means to subsist economically. This may include government assistance programs, self-employment with undeclared income, and/or illicit behavior, particularly related to drugs in the 1980s.

Borders politically divide economic markets by restricting the exchange of goods, services, and people between two nations. This situation structurally creates conditions conducive to illicit commerce and contraband. The large discrepancy in economic status between the United States and Mexico reinforces the opportunity structures for these types of illegal activities.

In Laredo, as in many other U.S.–Mexico border communities, contraband retail trade is a major economic activity, often involving legitimate business and commercial sectors. Stock in trade includes stolen vehicles, guns, and the traffic of undocumented immigrants. Laredo is a city with extensive trafficking in drugs, primarily marijuana, heroin, and cocaine. The exact proportion of the population involved in some illicit activity in Laredo is difficult to determine, but compared to non-border communities the proportion is certainly high. The extensiveness of these illicit activities, moreover, creates a climate and culture of permissiveness toward this type of behavior.

The official crime rate in Laredo in 1984 was 68 (crimes per 10,000 inhabitants) and had increased to 89 by 1988. Between 1987 and 1988 crime increased 21.7 percent, a growth concentrated in aggravated assault (57 percent), robbery (47 percent), narcotics violations (46 percent), murder (36 percent), and auto theft (33 percent). According to the Laredo Police Department, increases in crime were largely related to drug activity. For instance, 85 percent of burglaries are estimated to be drug-related. The most significant increase was in the category of theft under $50, which consist mostly of shoplifting cases that are associated with drug addicts.

The Uniform Crime Report data on Webb County show that overall drug violations increased 46 percent from 1987 to 1988 (see Table

8.2). These data indicate that violations related to possession of illegal substances increased overall by 60 percent and marijuana possession by 79 percent.[1]

Use and marketing of drugs and contrabanding of illegal aliens across the U.S./Mexican border are linked in the Laredo area. In 1988 there was a slight decrease, compared to 1987, in alien apprehension. As alien smuggling decreased, however, narcotics smuggling increased. The Border Patrol reports the total value of drugs confiscated increased 60 percent (U.S. Border Patrol 1989). Marijuana was the primary drug seized, followed by cocaine and heroin. During the month of June, 1989, agents of the Laredo Sector of the Border Patrol made thirty-two marijuana seizures totaling 4273 pounds, valued at $3,418,770. This is an increase of more than 300 percent over the same month in 1988 (983.19 pounds of marijuana valued at $788,525).

The substantial increase of narcotic seizures by the Laredo Sector of the Border Patrol has been accompanied by a decline in the apprehension of undocumented aliens. This trend began after the passage of the U.S. Immigration Reform and Control Act of 1986. Increased patrolling of the border made alien smuggling more risky and less profitable. Many of the smugglers, called coyotes, began to concentrate their efforts on the contrabanding of illegal drugs. According to data provided by the Laredo Border Patrol, there is in fact an inverse relation between marijuana seizures (and other drugs) and the apprehension of aliens, particularly after 1986. Whether the smugglers actually switched from undocumented aliens to trafficking drugs, as indicated by Border Patrol officials, is still open for discussion.[2]

Clearly, more drug traffickers are being apprehended in south

TABLE 8.2

Webb County Substance Abuse, 1987–1988

Offenses	1987	1988	Change
All Drugs			
Offenses	324	474	+46%
Possession			
All Drugs	293	469	+60%
Marijuana	244	436	+79%
Traffic			
All Drugs	31	5	−83%
Marijuana	28	5	−78%

Source: Texas Department of Public Safety 1988.

Texas. Law enforcement officials claim that Texas, along with New Mexico, Arizona, and California, is becoming the preferred route for smuggling drugs into the United States. Some estimate that about 40 percent of all drugs smuggled into the United States pass through south Texas (U.S. Border Patrol 1989). In the Laredo sector, the Border Patrol seized more drugs in fiscal year 1989 than in the previous four years combined. Similarly, the DEA's Multi Agency Task Force reported that during the first year of its existence (1988) they arrested 132 persons and confiscated drugs valued at $18,500,419 (Laredo Police Department 1988).

Drug-trafficking activities are a causal factor in the majority of murders from 1985 to 1989. Although most murders in the Laredo area are not officially designated as drug-related, most persons familiar with the circumstances involved disagree. Based on discussions with different sources, Table 8.3 indicates the actual number of reported murders and those that were drug-related from 1985 to 1989. These data indicate that in a four-and-a-half-year period, sixty-eight persons were murdered in Laredo; 61 percent (forty-two persons) of these murders were drug-related.

Increased levels of crime in Laredo are also related to the population's disproportionate substance-abuse problems, particularly related to its intravenous drug (IVD) users. Estimates of the number of intravenous drug users in Laredo vary. Use of the National Insti-

TABLE 8.3

City of Laredo Murders, 1985–1989

Year	Number of Murders	Drug-Related
Murders		
1985	15	12 (80%)
1986	21	12 (57%)
1987	11	6 (56%)
1988	14	6 (43%)
1989 (June)	7	6 (85%)
Total	68	42 (61%)

Webb County Murders, 1988

Year	Number of Murders	Drug-Related
Murders		
1988	5	4 (80%)

Source: *Laredo Morning Times*, Police Department, and others.

tute of Drug Abuse's (NIDA) method of estimating drug prevalence during a six-month period results in an estimate of 4530 persons in Webb county who use intravenous drugs (Balli 1989). Others have estimated that the population involved in IVD use is as high as 12,000. A reasonable estimate, based on the cumulative data in this analysis, would be approximately 5000 to 6000 IVD users in the Laredo area out of a total population of 113,000.

The social pathology generated by these IVD addicts and users reverberates throughout the community, particularly affecting the users' immediate families, friends, and neighborhoods. For instance, many arrests for shoplifting, burglary, and auto theft are in neighborhoods with a high proportion of addicts. As previously mentioned, these offenses are closely associated with intravenous drug users.

The Impact of Poverty and Crime: Three Distinct Neighborhoods

By focusing on three specific low-income neighborhoods, this section analyzes how social, economic, and ecological factors facilitate the development and continuation of illicit activities. Most of these data were gathered from field observation and interviews.

The pervasive poverty of Laredo means that low-income residential areas are found throughout the city. In this type of environment, impoverished families experience various forms of disorganization. As a result, the poor often engage in innovative behavior as a means to adapt to the social and economic conditions they confront. Many Laredo residents turn to drugs and alcohol as an escape from reality. Others take advantage of the opportunity presented by the international border to engage in various types of illicit activities.

La Azteca. La Azteca, located on the Rio Grande River east of the new international bridge and west of the power plant, is one of the oldest barrios in Laredo. Most of its residents are elderly first-generation Mexican Americans, recent Mexican immigrants, and young Mexican American families. Many who live here are Mexican nationals with relatives in the residential area located immediately on the opposite bank of the river in Nuevo Laredo. The barrio covers about ten square blocks, consisting of densely built single-family clapboard homes and a labyrinth of narrow unpaved streets that often end in cul-de-sacs. Many of these structures are weather-beaten wooden shacks that seem ready to fall over from age and neglect. The majority of the homes are owner-occupied, but the residents are too poor to invest in repairs. Other properties in the area are owned by speculators who patiently await development of this area.

The major characteristic of the Azteca is its accessibility to Nuevo Laredo, particularly its sister community, La Victoria, across the river. The shallowness of the Rio Grande, and Azteca's proximity to downtown Laredo, provides an ideal environment for contrabanding. Once across the border, individuals can hide in the dense foliage on the islands that separate the two banks of the Rio Grande, then find cover in the Azteca neighborhood, and finally slip unnoticed into the streets of downtown Laredo. The location is so convenient that many Mexicans living in Nuevo Laredo with day jobs in Laredo use this crossing daily.

Many residents of Azteca are involved in smuggling undocumented immigrants into the United States. Homes in the neighborhood are used as safe houses to hide aliens until safe transport can be arranged. One afternoon I saw a young man about 15 years old appear at the top of a flight of steps leading to the river. As he spotted us, he hesitated a few minutes and looked over the rest of the street. He disappeared down the steps and reappeared seconds later, followed by a woman, two teen-agers, and a small child. The group slowly worked their way down the street, the young man going ahead to check things out and wave the group forward. He was acting as the group's "coyote", or guide. A car was likely waiting down the street to take them to downtown Laredo, a five-minute ride. For these services, each person would probably be charged $20 to $50.

The coyotes are allowed to conduct their business through the barrio as long as Azteca residents receive portions of the fee or benefit in some manner. Smuggling activities are coordinated by both Mexicans and Mexican Americans. The Mexicans bring people across the river, and Azteca residents guide them through the barrio and into downtown Laredo. The young coyote we saw with the group of Mexicans is known to Azteca residents and operates with their permission. Other forms of illicit activities in the Azteca area include smuggling goods such as guns, electrical appliances, and other retail merchandise.

Much of the illicit drug activity in La Azteca centers around a group of young men between the ages of 17 and 25, most of whom are intravenous drug users addicted to heroin. These individuals are in the early stages of the drug-use life cycle typical of Laredo's male IVD population. Many of these young men begin drinking beer, smoking marijuana, sniffing glue, and taking pills in their early teens. They often come from broken families, where there is little parental supervision. They have been raised in poor neighborhoods, socially and geographically isolated in some of the worst barrios in Laredo. Schools and other public institutions are not perceived as challenging viable alternatives. Most of them are unemployed high school dropouts, their identity centered around cliques of family and neighborhood peers.

In the Azteca many of the addicts support their addiction by illicit activities facilitated by the neighborhood's strategic geographic location. As in other communities along the Rio Grande, many of Azteca's young IVD users secure resources by transporting Mexicans and Central Americans. One 19-year-old IVD user is living with his parents:

> He shoots up once or twice a week. He makes his money for drugs by stealing and transporting aliens from this side of the river to the downtown area. He gets paid $30 for each person.

This activity has a fast yield and does not take a lot of organization. Young IVD users in La Azteca are familiar with the patterns of the Border Patrol and have developed a system to minimize risks.

Dealing in drugs is another source of income for many young users. Throughout these low-income neighborhoods dealers bring in small quantities of heroin and marijuana to distribute within Laredo. Larger quantities of drugs destined for outside markets (Houston, San Antonio, and other major cities) are smuggled through isolated crossings. The Azteca area is used by those with more limited resources, especially small-time drug pushers and users. These persons do not have the connections or experience to deal drugs at a higher level. Usually, if trust has been established with neighborhood pushers, established dealers may front them small amounts of heroin to distribute. The more extensive dealing is conducted by older IVD users.

La Ladrillera. Ladrillera is located across a series of railroad tracks by the river adjacent to the U.S.–Mexico border. This is one of the poorest communities in Laredo. The area is flat and dusty from the heavy truck and rail traffic. Many streets are unpaved with no sidewalks. Housing is predominately single-family clapboard homes on large lots set back some twenty yards from the street. Many streets dead-end on the banks of the Rio Grande or in the railyards.

To enter Ladrillera, you cross the tracks joining the National Railroad of Mexico and the Missouri Pacific, then pass acres of parked semitrailers to reach the community. Much of the legitimate U.S.– Mexico export and import trade ships through this area. Furthermore, much illegitimate trade in marijuana, cocaine, and heroin goes through Ladrillera. Authorities continually intercept semitrailers leaving this area with large loads of marijuana. The trains are also used by undocumented Mexicans and other immigrants to leave the border region.

Ladrillera is characterized by long-term residents with multigenerational family ties. Although a majority of these families are Mexican American, there is a minority of Mexican immigrant families in this community. Residents comprise close-knit exclusive networks where loyalty to extended family and neighborhood takes precedence over everything else. These characteristics, as well as the opportunities offered by the accessibility of the river, ecological isolation, and access to transportation, make it an ideal location for large-scale contrabanding.

As in communities all along the U.S.–Mexico border, several groups here are involved in high-volume alien and drug smuggling. Some of these networks are more elaborate than others, but the basic unit of organization is the family and/or neighborhood-based friendship cliques. These types of groups control a vast amount of marijuana, heroin, and cocaine, smuggled across the border. There is no large organized syndicate of drug dealers that dominates the drug trade in this region. The permeable border and the easy availability of these drugs preclude such dominance.

People involved in illicit activities are often supported by family and community networks. For those who leave their family of orientation and form their own nuclear families, marriage shifts the support system from parents to wives and the new relationships that accompany this change in status. Wives and children now must endure the many social and personal crises that are part of this subculture. For the wife, this often means being married to a person who holds no steady job, leads a life centered around illicit activities, and is incarcerated for long periods of time.

Ladrillera has a disproportionate number of IVD users. This means that their life is often centered on illicit activities essential to support their addiction. Throughout the different stages of the life cycle, these individuals find a social sanctuary within the family. Informants repeatedly referred to heroin users who return to live with their parents after long prison terms, during which time they had been divorced by their wives. Others live with brothers, uncles, or other close relatives. These families continue to support the intravenous drug user despite all the problems of living with them.

Santo Niño. Located on the southern fringes of the city along the Zapata Highway, Santo Niño is characterized as a highly exclusive and closely knit community of working-poor Mexican American families. Neighborhoods in this area have high levels of crime and drug abuse. The highway that runs through this area is lined with auto parts stores, tire shops, junkyards, automobile repair shops, and auto body shops. Several of these businesses are known as "chopshops", where stolen cars are stripped and the parts resold on the black market. Other businesses, particularly restaurants and nightclubs, are legitimate fronts for known drug dealers and other participants in the border's underground economy. Many of the tire-repair shops are known as "copping places" and "shooting galleries" for drugs. That is, heroin addicts may buy drugs and intravenously use them at these locations.

Santo Niño is dominated by owner-occupied homes. Neighborhood roads and streets are mostly unpaved and without sidewalks. Because many families are migrant farm workers who travel throughout the Midwest during the summer and only reside here during the winter, many of these homes are often boarded up. Children of the migrants often do not attend school for the full nine months and have disproportionately high drop-out rates. These children frequently become involved in illegal drugs and other unlawful activities.

Santo Niño residents are involved in a wide array of crimes, which include smuggling guns and undocumented aliens, stolen-car rings, and the distribution of marijuana, cocaine, and heroin, both locally and to areas throughout the United States. These neighborhoods have a high proportion of heroin addicts, many of them young men 17–25 years old. Being on heroin at this stage in life makes it difficult to hold steady employment, particularly since most young users have little education or marketable job skills. Most of their energy is spent getting cash to buy drugs for the day. This type of user cannot usually deal drugs successfully, and will not be able to use this means to supply his own habit. Their only access to cash is through shoplifting, breaking and entering into homes and businesses, and hustling and conning parents, family, and anyone else gullible enough to fall for their tactics.

Another type of intravenous drug user in these communities is a more mature and stable male. He usually starts shooting heroin as a young man and continues to do so throughout his life. He might have ceased using heroin intermittently, for instance, during periods of incarceration or detoxication attempts. This user might support his habit by dealing heroin himself. Maturity and extensive contacts cultivated over years of involvement in this life-style provide the discipline and knowledge to deal successfully. Others in this category might support their habit by shoplifting, often with a female partner who is a junkie herself. Shoplifting among these *veteranos*, compared to the younger *tecatos*, is more sophisticated, elaborate, and lucrative. Others within this group are involved in more organized crime activities, usually working with or for others. This includes well-organized stolen-car rings, Mexican-immigrant-smuggling operations, large-scale drug dealing, and other high-level criminal activity.

Pecos Street, typical of the many neighborhoods in Santo Niño, is located off the Zapata Highway in the southern part of this area. Pecos Street intersects with the major highway leading south from Laredo to Zapata, Texas. This neighborhood consists of single-family clapboard homes and unpaved, pot-holed streets that turn into mud during the rainy season. Fifteen years ago the Pecos Street neighborhood began to change substantially. One resident recalls:

> When we moved here about 18 years ago, we were one of the few houses in this area. The area was all monte [brush country]. You could see all the way down to the creek beds from our back yards.

Today the neighborhood has been absorbed in Laredo's metropolitan expansion and is densely populated.

For years the Pecos Street area was a small barrio where neighbors were close acquaintances and could rely on each other for favors. Families were poor, but they grew up in a community that offered sanctuary from the outside world. Residents left their homes unlocked without worrying about burglaries or vandalism. That has all drastically changed.

One resident has lived on Pecos Street for twenty years, not far from his mother, who is 70 years old and who has lived alone ever since her husband died. This person returned from military service about twelve years ago, bought a house trailer, and moved it onto his parent's lot after marrying a woman from Nuevo Laredo. The neighborhood has drastically changed during the last five years. This person has put up a six-foot-high chain link fence around his property, and he keeps two large Dobermans that viciously bark at everything that gets within thirty feet of the lot. The fence and dogs are a result of the burglaries that now characterize Pecos Street. He states:

> My mother was ripped off twice. They stole her TV, clock radio, everything that's worth anything. Then a few months later it happened to me. That's when I got the puppies.

The burglaries coincided with the appearance of heroin in the Pecos Street area. Conditions have deteriorated since two heroin dealers set up business within a block of each other. He said, "I got one heroin dealer on that side [pointing east] and another [pointing west]." The availability of heroin in the neighborhood now means that more young men are hooked.

> We never had so much crime in the area. And, you can't talk to these kids. The other day I woke up and my trailer was getting bombarded by bricks thrown by some neighborhood kids. The next day, I went to their father. He said that I shouldn't approach the kids. He would handle it. They are too dangerous.

The problems faced by families such as these are typical in these communities. They are the victims of the changing economic structure of the border economy.

Conclusion

Mexican Americans in this region traditionally have had exceedingly high levels of poverty. Laredo's recent economic prosperity did little to change the social composition of the Mexican American population in this border community. As in other Texas border regions, the economic boom of the 1970s primarily benefited the Mexican American middle class. Laredo's economic prosperity created more hardships for the lower classes. During the post-1982 period Laredo experienced an economic decline, precipitated by the Mexican peso's devaluation, which caused even greater difficulties for the poor.

This situation persists today, with a disproportionate number of families below the poverty line, female-headed households, teen-age pregnancies, and welfare dependency. A major difference between Laredo's poor communities and those associated with the underclass (Wilson 1987), however, is that these communities are more institutionally complete. Strong extended families are the major sustaining social structure in Laredo barrios. Mexican American neighborhoods are more residentially stable, and have a high proportion of home ownership. There are also greater interclass relations found in Mexican American neighborhoods. These social factors, along with a dominant ethnic culture, create a strong sense of community structure and identification missing in the black underclass.

One of the major differences between today and previous periods is that Laredo's poor are being increasingly affected by criminal activities. This study has indicated that a wide segment of the Laredo community is taking advantage of the illicit opportunities offered by the U.S.–Mexican border for their economic survival. Among the poor, crime centers around smuggling undocumented immigrants, guns, and stolen automobiles, and in particular drugs. Drug activities are carried out by exclusive networks of family and friends usually based in multigenerational neighborhoods. These networks may be small, and their operations limited to Laredo, whereas others are larger, organized drug networks with connections in Mexico and other cities throughout the United States.

These activities and conditions make drugs widely accessible in this community. The availability of heroin in particular means that many young men and women become addicts and are forced to support their habits from their local neighborhoods—by breaking and entering, shoplifting, conning relatives and friends, and other predatory behavior. Addicts in a community are socially and economically disruptive, and linked to increased crime rates in Laredo over the last ten years, primarily thefts and burglaries. This aspect of Laredo's poor closely resembles underclass conditions and may indicate a trend toward the formulation of an underclass in this community and others along the U.S.–Mexico border. The recent economic transformations and related social characteristics, however, have not at this period created an underclass in this region as it may have among groups elsewhere in the United States.

NOTES

1. The State Uniform Crime data, however, do not reflect all drug violations committed in Webb County because they exclude data from the Drug Enforcement Administration. This is very significant because the DEA administers the Webb County Multi Agency Task Force. This task force is composed of at least one officer from each law enforcement agency in Laredo and Webb counties. Serious drug violators arrested by local agencies are turned over to the DEA Task Force. The Drug Enforcement Administration does not send its Uniform Crime Reports to the Department of Public Safety as other agencies do; instead DEA sends their UCRs directly to their federal headquarters. Therefore, what is discussed in the following sections is an incomplete profile of drug violations.

2. It is unclear, for instance, whether increased apprehensions of drugs and drug traffickers might be the result of a greater concentration by the Border Patrol on this problem. During the last few years, the Border Patrol budget has been greatly increased, resulting in more manpower, equipment, and supplies directed toward drug-law enforcment, including increased use of drug-sniffing dogs. There has also been more cooperation among all federal agencies.

9

U.S. MEXICANS IN THE BORDERLANDS: BEING POOR WITHOUT THE UNDERCLASS

Carlos Vélez-Ibáñez

RECENT U.S. Government Accounting Office report stated that the term "underclass" usually refers to "people who are predominantly black [*sic*] or Hispanic."[1] It is unfortunate that such general statements strongly contribute to a mistaken application of this concept to U.S. Mexicans[2] in the U.S.–Mexico Borderlands region. The cultural and economic region of the Borderlands embraces a 2000-mile political border and 52 million persons living in ten Mexican and U.S. border states. The region includes the immediate border cities and population centers but also rural and urban centers affected by the border economy in agriculture, trade, services, manufacturing, and labor use. This chapter will concentrate on the manner in which the underclass concept is of narrow utility when applied analytically to the U.S. Mexican population living in the region and to its poverty sectors within a 400-mile-wide belt bisected by that border (Martinez 1988).[3]

The analytical focus of this work is that the concept of the underclass is of limited explanatory value and of limited applicability to the U.S. Mexican household in the region. From the point of view adopted here and the empirical evidence provided, the category of underclass, while having some useful heuristic value to describe a sector within one or more populations in Rustbelt urban centers, is largely inappropriate to describe almost all the economic and social sectors of U.S. Mexican population of the region.

Tucson, Arizona
Area

GRANT

SPEEDWAY

BROADWAY

22ND ST

AJO WAY

IRVINGTON

VALENCIA

Tucson
International
Airport

N

Spanish Speaking
Residents

☐ 0 to 24%

▨ 25% to 49%

▨ 50% to 74%

▨ 75% to 100%

Study
Neighborhoods

⌐Ⓐ┐ South Tucson

· · · · · Downtown

0   Mile   1

designed by
Cartographic
Services

This chapter will discuss the following central issues: a brief consideration of the concept of the underclass and its limited heuristic and cross-cultural value; the limitation of the concept in its application to U.S. Mexicans within the regional Southwest; the limitation of the concept in its application to U.S. Mexican households in the region, in Tucson, Arizona, and in South Tucson—a small, poor urban enclave within Tucson; and the limitation of the concept when the central features and dynamics of household clusters in poverty circumstances are understood. The conclusion discusses broader frames of analysis for U.S. Mexicans than those proposed under the underclass concept.

The Concept of the Underclass and Its Cross-Cultural Limitations

In William Julius Wilson's *The Truly Disadvantaged* (1987), the creation of a black underclass results basically from structural economic changes that shift industrial production to services and relocate manufacturing out of the central cities. For young black men this shift means that they become labor force "dropouts" and are deprived of the opportunity for suburban industrial employment. This leads to a concentration of poor persons in urban poverty areas who are unemployed, whose conditions are exacerbated by the flight of middle-class blacks and their attending religious, economic, and social institutions. Such "flattening" of the social structure results in the creation of sectors of the population that are characteristically unemployed (especially young black males), poverty-stricken, dependent upon institutional subsidies, burdened with out-of-wedlock births, having female-headed households, and short of "marriageable" males who are employed. Coupled with nonfunctional school systems and lack of support of educational achievement as a means of escape by poverty parents, a politically apathetic and passive permanent "underclass" is created largely in poor, urban contexts in which blacks suffer in disproportionate numbers.

When applied cross-culturally, the concept fails in validity and reveals its limitations, especially in discussions of urban populations outside of Chicago and the eastern U.S. Rustbelt. My own work (Vélez-Ibáñez 1983a) in large urban settlements outside Mexico City that are much poorer, with very high crime rates, in more desperate ecological conditions, with labor markets much more limited, with unemployment and underemployment at double and triple those associated in the underclass literature, and with large sets of single parents with children under age 18—all combine to form characteris-

tics like those associated with the "underclass". Yet these same urban arenas are characterized by hotbeds of political organization and
activities, of community resistance to exploitation and political control, of community self-help and communal activities without institutional support, and of familial household clusters of extended and
reciprocal relations. In spite of the structural conditions present, the
reality of most Mexican urban populations totally contradicts the
general tone and substance of the "underclass" notion.[4]

The Underclass in Regional Perspective: The U.S.–Mexico Borderlands

Similar to the limitations of the concept of the underclass when applied to urban Mexico are those that emerge when the concept is
applied within the U.S.–Mexico Borderlands. The Borderlands region has always been economically differentiated because of the economic integration of agricultural markets between borders, the simultaneous penetration of capital and labor-intensive technologies
such as mining and construction on both sides of the political border,
and the accompanying extensive movement of the Mexican population in the region to different labor markets. New capital and technologies have always transformed the regional ecology of the Borderlands, and in the present, as Moore (1988) correctly points out,
the Borderlands form part of a "border subeconomy" that is part of
the internationalization of production and the exchange of populations.

Thus "poverty" must be contextualized within the Borderlands
region as a highly fluid and dynamic characteristic, with U.S. Mexican populations periodically entering and leaving what appear to be
"underclass" sectors depending on the economic relations between
nations, the ups and downs of world markets and the manner in
which they influence labor markets of the region, and cross-border
relations between Mexican households in northern Mexico and the
southwestern United States. As well, "poverty" must be contextualized within the total labor and income characteristics of the population in order to gauge the applicability of describing entire cultural
populations under the "underclass" category, as the GAO has done.

In the present, and in contrast to the Mexico side,[5] 22.5 percent
of the U.S. Mexican labor force in the Southwest is in upper-white-
collar and upper-blue-collar occupations with the largest resulting
percentage (75 percent) concentrated in the secondary and tertiary
labor sectors such as low white-collar (21.3 percent), low blue-collar
(32.5 percent), service (15.5 percent), and a small portion as farm
workers (5.8 percent).[6] The ratio of U.S. Mexican to non-Hispanic

white per capita income is .55, and of mean household income it is .78 (Bean and Tienda 1987, p. 199). Therefore, individuals in U.S. Mexican households earn slightly more than half as much income as Anglos, and at the mean household level, Mexican households earned three-fourths as much income as did the Anglo households.

The actual distribution of U.S. Mexican households in labor sectors is that one in five households is part of the primary labor sector in income, stability, and security of employment. In such households there is a significant percentage of middle-class families for whom indebtedness rather than scarcity is the primary struggle because it is so easy to get credit. Further, three of five households have working-class income that is derived largely from employment by several household members, members having two jobs, and use of scarce resources in innovative and creative ways. Also, more households contain more adults than non-Hispanic White households, and thus there are more earners per household. This advantage, however, is offset by a larger number of children per household, greater unemployment than among the non-Hispanic White population, and, probably for the first ten years of a household cycle, intermittent employment. Finally, approximately one in five households is in poverty. Poverty is concentrated among female-headed families of the 45-year-old cohorts to be described, persons over 60, and children under 18.[7]

Poverty Characteristics in the Borderlands: The Underclass in Question

In 1980, the poverty rate for U.S. Mexicans in the five southwestern states of the border region was slightly less than 22 percent—a drop of 4.5 percent from 1970 (Stoddard and Hedderson 1987)—although recent current Census data for "Hispanic" poverty show a figure of 28 percent (U.S. Bureau of the Census, 1991).[8] However, poverty was very much concentrated in the southern border counties of the United States border region so that the probability of higher income is greatest in the western coastal counties and decreases consistently as one moves east toward the Lower Rio Grande Valley of Texas such as Starr County, where the percentage of families in poverty was 45 percent (Stoddard and Hedderson 1987) but climbed to 60 percent in 1990 (Brokaw 1993, p. 8). Yet for the most part such poverty areas are rural, not urban, centers, and the pattern of poverty is very much a consequence of the organization of industrial agriculture in those areas in which sectors of the U.S. Mexican population are relegated to poorly paid rural farm wages that are intermittent at best and nonexistent for much of the crop year.[9]

However, even in urban poverty situations underclass characteristics are counterindicated. Heavily U.S. Mexican South Texas cities like McAllen, Laredo, and Brownsville have among the lowest household incomes, highest percentage receiving public assistance, and highest poverty levels.[10] Yet in these same "poverty" areas, more than 50 percent of households are owner-occupied, indicating stable populations, with older housing stock, but residents living longer in one home.[11] This also points to the importance of low-cost home ownership to improve social stability for Mexican households in poverty circumstances. As case material will show, the prevention of the formation of "underclass" characteristics is strongly associated to low land values and the ability to develop housing in a "modular" process.

However, even poverty figures do not support the presence of a U.S.–Mexican Borderlands "underclass" in regard to household structures in which young unmarried women with children under age 18 predominate. The National Center for Health Statistics' Hispanic and Nutrition Examination Survey (HHANES) showed that most U.S. Mexican single heads of household were middle-aged (45–64 years) and that their single status resulted from divorce or separation rather than from widowhood or from never having been married (Trevino et al. 1989). This seems to be borne out by the fact that only 12.8 percent of U.S. Mexican householders were composed of single females with children under 18 and no spouse present while 37 percent of Puerto Rican householders were in the same category.[12]

As well, the statistics on U.S. Mexican women in poverty circumstances contradict expected marital behaviors of unwed single mothers in underclass situations. A study conducted in Chicago shows that it is more likely that single-parent U.S. Mexican women will marry soon after their first childbirth than will African American women in the same situation.[13] Of single U.S. Mexican women who did become pregnant, 45 percent did marry the father of the first child, whereas among young black women only 18 percent actually married.

In addition, it is highly likely that for single female U.S. Mexican parents, one of the single most important factors to prevent the development of "underclass" characteristics may lie in the ability of women to mobilize male labor and resources in times of need. There seems to be an underlying strength in U.S. Mexican household relations, as James (1988) has shown and as has my own work in the samples of households to be discussed.[14]

Thus even single-headed U.S. Mexican households do not conform to the often cited characteristics of female head of households for the "underclass". Similarly James (1988) and Moore (1988) question the behavioral, ecological, structural, and processual applicability of the underclass category to U.S. Mexicans.[15]

Educational Performance and the Underclass

In regard to the lack of formal schooling, which is one of the crucial aspects of underclass characteristics, Moore (1988) describes Hispanic (aggregate, not U.S. Mexican only) dropout rates of 40 percent before the tenth grade, with three-quarters of the students scoring in the bottom half on achievement tests and in general suffering from the highest dropout rates of all major ethnic groups. Coupled with a median educational attainment of 9.1 for adults aged 25 and over in 1980 (Bean and Tienda 1987), educational attainment seems to fit the "underclass" variety, and the educational future of U.S. Mexicans seems dismal indeed. Although other work (Rochin 1989) shows that in the Los Angeles Unified School District, 45 percent of the Chicano high school population leave school with only 5 percent academically qualified to enter the University of California, and only 7 out of 100 Chicanos from the same school cohort graduate from a university (*Final Report of the Commission on the Higher Education of Minorities 1982*), school dropout and median educational attainment figures by themselves tell us little of the dynamics of such processes nor the reasons for these dropout rates.

According to Bean and Tienda (1987), adjustments must be made to the increase of high school graduates among Mexicans from 1960 to 1980, which rose from 13 to 22 percent. Also, I would suggest that disaggregating foreign- from native-born U.S. Mexicans reveals that the median for native-born was 11.1 in 1980 and 6.1 for foreign-born in the same period. Yet the 6.1 foreign-born figure is also deceptive, because this does not indicate the fact that level of education in Mexico may be much superior to that of an equivalent grade level in the United States.

However, the native-born versus foreign-born differential is an important one to keep in mind in understanding the dynamics of educational development among Mexicans versus other Spanish-speaking groups. In fact, between 1960 and 1980, the percentage of adult native-born U.S Mexicans over 25 attaining the post-secondary school years 13–16+ has almost tripled.[16] Although these figures are somewhat encouraging, it is still, after all, a very small percent of the total U.S. Mexican population that does attain post-secondary education.

In regard to the reasons for such dropouts, it is highly probable that many such students will be already grade-delayed so most will simply go to work in low-paying service and/or relatively high-paying but intermittent construction work without much opportunity for security, protection, and wages above the minimum computed on a yearly basis. Given the dynamics of the border economy even unskilled and relatively undereducated youth will have job opportunities during periods of economic growth. However, an important intervening variable that provides relative security even in periods of economic stress is the ability of "clustered households" to mobilize sufficient resources and job contacts to stretch over difficult economic periods and limited means.

Tucson Mexican Households Clusters of the Sonora–Arizona Region[17]

Most U.S. Mexican households in the Borderlands follow a general developmental cycle of familial clustering of households or extension of families beyond the nucleated household that increase with each succeeding generation. I have termed these "clustered households" because a significant proportion organize their extended kin relations in the United States in a clustered household arrangement of dense[18] bilateral kin that basically serve as a means of rotating scarce resources and labor. In many instances such households maintain kin ties with their Mexican relatives, so that such clusters cross borders. In fact, 77.1 percent of one of our samples[19] have relatives in Mexico and maintain exchange relations of various sorts in spite of the fact that most of the sample is U.S.-born.[20]

Such clustered households have been generated as early as the eighteenth century in the Arizona–Sonora region when it was known only as Sonora during the Spanish and Mexican periods.[21] Thus "Sonorense" populations traveled and settled northward to Tucson and returned southward to Sonora as conditions in the Borderlands changed.[22] To the present time, this locational process involves individuals and groups joining already resident extended households within established class sectors in Tucson while maintaining kinship and exchange relations with households in Sonora— the totality of which may be described as "cross-border clustered" households.[23]

For Sonorenses, this has been part of a process of employment relocation through clustered household networks into Tucson without the attending cultural and social displacement experienced by European immigrants. However, such relocation has never guaranteed opportunities for rapid vertical mobility, for in fact most relocating Sonorenses join others in already resident working-class sectors, low-paid occupations, and dual wage structures.[24] In order to counteract scarcity, many Mexican households continue to rely on a variety of non-market forms of production and exchange: reciprocal exchange of tools, skills, assistance, and labor ensconced within "clustered" households, especially since Tucson is structured spatially and economically in a bimodal manner.[25]

Because spatial separation is in large measure related directly to economic separation, the area of Tucson in which 76 percent of the U.S. Mexican population is concentrated is shaded on the map (p. 196).[26] Broadly this is an area bounded to the north by Grant Road, south by the San Xavier Tohono O'odom Reservation, west by Silverbell, and east by Alvernon. The rest of the U.S. Mexican population of Tucson is distributed throughout the city. The distribution of income associated with these areas is basically bimodal. The mean Mexican household income for the area of concentration is $14,488. The mean Mexican income in the rest of Tucson is $21,994. Thus the mean income of the majority (76 percent) of the Mexican population in Tucson was $14,488, and for a small minority (24 percent), $21,994. When Anglo mean income as well as its distribution is compared, remarkable differences appear. Twenty-five percent of the Anglo population has a mean income of $17,270, and the other 75 percent a mean income of $24,245.

Per capita income is distributed with inverse characteristics. As Figure 9.1 illustrates, 76 percent of the Mexican population has a per capita income of $5,202, and 24 percent of the Mexican population a per capita income of $8,398. As the same exhibit shows, the opposite is true among the Anglo population, with 25.5 percent of the Anglo mean income at $5202 and 75 percent of the Anglo population having a per capita income of $8398 in all other districts.

Therefore, there are ample economic rationales for the appearance of clustered households in our Tucson sample. The Tucson sample was composed of 74 percent U.S.–born residents and was largely working class. Extended familial networks crossed borders and class, are dynamic in composition, and increase in following generations. Keefe, Padilla, and Carlos (1979) and others (Arce 1981; Ramirez 1980) point out that first-generation Mexicans generally have established extended family networks in the United States. Such networks become highly elaborated in the second and third generations and are actively maintained through frequent visiting and the exchange of mutual aid. Even acculturation, as measured by language scales, seems to strengthen extension. In fact, extended familism is greatest among those who are likely to be English-speakers.[27] In addition, the higher the economic and educational status of the household,

FIGURE 9.1

Per Capita Income

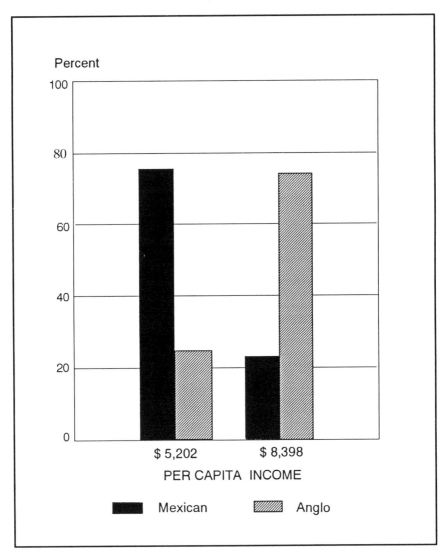

the higher the extended familial integration. These findings are supported by preliminary findings in a national study that revealed that the "clustered households" I will describe for Tucson were more common among U.S.-born Mexicans than among recently arrived Mexicans or Anglos (Ramirez 1980, p. 2).

The results from this study of Mexican households in Tucson show that though the nuclear family is not the primary locality for social life, it is in that setting that *confianza* (mutual trust) is most likely to emerge.[28] Like Keefe (1979), and Keefe and Padilla (1987), we have found that the U.S. Mexican populations operate within a cluster of kin relationships connected to other local households as well as to households across the Arizona-Sonora border. Our data in Tucson show that over 61 percent of our sample have localized kin groups made up of a number of related households involved in extended social and economic exchange relations.

Usually focused on a "core" household of active and largely employed middle-aged-to-older adults, the peripheral households carry out their life cycles very much in relation to a centrally located grandparent or parent. The core and peripheral households create social "density" not only from the fact that members of such networks are kin and in their daily lives add layers of relationships based on other contexts, but also that the person to whom one is cousin is also the person with whom one exchanges labor assistance, has a fictive kinship relation of *compadrazgo* (co-godparenthood), shares in recreational activities and visitations, participates in religious and calendric activities, and in many instances may live nearby. That cousin will either recruit or be recruited by a network member to work in the same business or occupation.

Such networks function differently depending on the situation: which one of their many functions dominates in a particular instance depends on the circumstances of the people involved. In the recruitment process mentioned above, our findings indicate that such networks function not only as a reliable defensive arrangement against the indeterminacy and uncertainty of changing circumstances but also to "penetrate" the single strands of relations between employers and employees, and to entangle them within the multiplicity of relationships within the network. In an interesting but not often understood sense, such "entanglement" is a type of social insurance against the vagaries of the employer-employee relation, which is often asymmetrical at best and exploitative at worst. Especially in the informal sector, which is marked by lack of protection, security, and wages near the minimum, the network penetration also serves as the only means of minimum insurance against sudden firings. In addition, however, such exchange does heavily involve the use of male labor for the construction of "start-up" homes of relatives. Using a type of modular design in which one or two rooms are built on relatively cheap land and then add-ons follow as income is made available, it is possible for people to obtain relatively cheap housing early in the family life cycle.

The Tucson household sample shows these networks operating in remarkable continuity despite constant disruptive pressures, with a variety of households engaged in frequent exchange relations. Most of these clustered households are continuously involved in child-care exchange, house sitting, ritual participation, visitations, and caretaking of persons outside of the household's biological unit. Very few of the clustered households rely in any appreciable degree on non-kin network members for child care, recreation, and other emotive functions.

Household Clusters in Contexts of Urban Poverty: Revitalization and Living in South Tucson

The clustering phenomenon becomes of utmost importance in the discussion of the applicability of the underclass concept in contexts of concentrated poverty and scarce resources. Within the city of Tucson its poorest households are concentrated within the incorporated city of South Tucson. Composed of 6535 residents, most of very modest means, the city of South Tucson is surrounded by Tucson's more than 400,000 residents. South Tucson is 76.5 percent U.S. Mexican, with a mean income of $10,026 and with 38 percent of the population below the poverty level.[29] In contrast, for the city of Tucson's Mexican population (22 percent of total population), the mean income was $18,241. Of over 2100 housing units in South Tucson, 43.5 percent were owner-occupied, with 3.18 persons per unit, and 56.5 percent were rented with 2.82 persons per unit. South Tucson's tax rate is based on 16 cents per $100 evaluation, while the city of Tucson's is 1.00 dollar per $100 evaluation (*Tucson Daily Citizen*, January 6, 1988), so that land values are relatively low and "start up" homes are possible. It is one square mile in area, running from 40th Street on the south to 26th Street on the north; 12th Avenue on the west to the railroad tracks—roughly Second Street—on the east. (Berry 1987).

Incorporated in 1936, South Tucson has faced periodic attempts at disincorporation, in part because of its reputation as a city of concentrated poverty and also because of operations associated with illegal activities. Its unemployment rate in 1989 was three times that of the city of Tucson, and this ratio has remained constant since 1983.[30]

In 1979, one South Tucson resident dubbed prostitution as "South Tucson's major industry" (*Tucson Daily Citizen*, April 4, 1989). For years the community had the reputation of being a haven for vagrants, and for prostitution, alcoholism, street crime, and police authorities who used speed traps as the means of ensuring revenue for city budgets. The central street—South Sixth Avenue—was noted for taverns and bars that were reputed by local wags to provide abdominal operations without anesthesia or quick appendectomies for customers without charge. In the pre-drug era of the seventies, heroin could be purchased with relative ease, and alcohol and drug addiction were not unknown. Having lived in the area for some years, the author can attest to the necessity of turning on water sprinklers to remove unwanted sleepers from Saturday night's fun.

But for South Tucson Mexican households this one-mile-square pocket of modest income was their home, and unlike the populations described in the "underclass" model who are considered apathetic, apolitical, and passive, this population revitalized its community over a space of ten years. In spite of the fact that economically and occupationally South Tucson's households were among the poorest in Arizona, they nevertheless made important political decisions that changed the face of the community in substantive ways. Thus, as the following discussion clearly shows, the applicability of the "underclass" concept even within contexts of ecological poverty seems not to be fruitful for U.S. Mexican populations.

Ten years after being anointed with the dubious honor of having prostitution as its major industry, major sting operations were conducted in which prostitution was almost wiped out by the vigorous efforts of city authorities and the community. In 1986, there were 3 homicides, 11 rapes, and 52 robberies. Crimes were reduced by providing more shelter for the homeless, but complaints against vagrancy and liquor laws violation increased (*Tucson Daily Citizen*, September 11, 1987). Further crime crackdown in 1988 reduced all crimes by 26 percent. By 1987, murder dropped by 66 percent; rape, 70 percent; robbery, 30.1 percent; aggravated assault, 54.2 percent; larceny, 13.6 percent; auto theft, 15.6 percent; and arson, 28.6 percent (*Tucson Daily Citizen*, February 12, 1988). Also in 1988, crime was reduced another 16 percent from 26 percent the year before, with reduction of larceny from 440 to 395, auto theft from 38 to 31, and aggravated assault from 60 to 49, with the rest remaining the same except for "date rape".

In 1986, more than 100 new businesses opened up, and all space was filled in the city's light industrial park. Business loans, block grants of $230,000 for twenty new or renovated businesses had been awarded since 1984, and voluntary associations like the Lion's Club provided both funds and energy to support community reform and change. The clean-up of lots and homes by absentee owners, 60 percent of whom did not reside in South Tucson, vastly improved the physical environment of the city, and in the present, schoolchildren canvass the tiny municipality for unsightly trash. South Tucson spent $1 million on street lights, and burglary dropped 30 percent in 1986 (*Tucson Daily Citizen*, December 12, 1988). Proportionally, South Tucson's burglary rate is lower than Tucson's. A new library, city park, and municipal complex were built, and together with the parish church and the two elementary schools of the municipality, citywide celebrations are held through the calendar year.

A St. Patrick's Day celebration and street march is held annually; it is a mixture of Mexican Catholicism, Mexican Independence Day, and the wearing of the green—all a Mexican adaptation to fit within the United States, with plays on "Irish-sounding" Spanish surnames like Ochoa, Otero, and Obregon. A Norteño Music Festival and Street Fair for the Benefit of the Pio Decimo neighborhood center drew 15,000 persons (*Tucson Daily Citizen*, August 11, 1989). Further, an annual Christmas Party in front of Ramon Gonzalez's house, which he began in 1970 and celebrated its nineteenth year, drew 1500 persons on Christmas, with the poor children of the area receiving two gifts each.

These various accomplishments, however, do not rest only on a sense of acquired community spirit. In fact, much of the energy stems from the ability of U.S. Mexican households to mobilize scarce resources in relatively efficient ways. Even with all the community improvements, South Tucson is still a community of poor-to-moderate-income persons. The revitalization process resulted as the aftermath of clustered householders born in South Tucson.[31] As our findings show from a recently studied sample[32] of thirty households, even the poorest household may barely survive. But as long as it has some access to familial resources, the type of underclass phenomenon described by Wilson is not as likely to become characteristic of even the most modest of U.S. Mexican households.

Central Features and Dynamics of the Household Cluster in Poverty Contexts and the Life Cycle

The central feature in the formation of household clusters in poverty contexts seems to be the ability to locate consanguineal and/or affinal members in relatively close proximity but generally not within the same home. For the most part in our sample, each associated household in a cluster either owned or was purchasing its own home. Especially in the South Tucson area, land values are relatively low, construction knowledge is rather plentiful or available within clusters, information about the lowest prices for materials is shared, and the actual labor for construction is exchanged for use. In addition, 20 percent or more of the real individual household income in our sample is derived from unreported sources such as child care within clusters and from outside sources such as income earned from housecleaning, informal labor, weekend sales, swapmeets, and barter.

A second feature that is important to note is that no household cluster is ever exclusively made up of persons in dire economic need. When poor persons are looked at from this point of view, they should be understood as *individually poor* but not part of a cluster that is necessarily impoverished. The caveat is that as long as external circumstances are held relatively constant with even minimum employment available, access to male labor in the case of single-parent female-headed households is somewhat predictable, and moderate opportunities remain for social exchange with others in slightly better economic circumstances, then even impoverished *individuals* may avoid the worst features of being poor. On the other hand, if a combination of circumstances occurs, such as a sudden immigration raid, unemployment, or illness striking portions of the cluster, then the entire network may be endangered and the already "at risk" individual forced to seek institutional remedies.

A third and crucial feature in understanding the functions of such clusters in poverty conditions is their functions within the dynamic of the life cycle in which age and generational considerations are also importantly linked to when and how individuals are impoverished. Whether poor adults are at the beginning, middle, or end of their household life cycle will in part determine the quality of poverty and its survivability. Thus poor young adults who are married with small children but are minimally employed will more than likely have access to their own parents' housing. In this case, parents provide a subsidy to poor offspring for that period of time in which income is poor, mobility limited, and shift in occupation very small.

However, adults still at a poverty or near-poverty level will be very hard-pressed to subsidize either offspring or elderly adults. It is at this point that the "clusters" appear to break down functionally and relationally and do not develop to lineal depth to include an elderly core. In fact, it is highly likely that this type of "mid-adult" household will maintain tenuous exchange relations with collateral kin of brothers and sisters and same-generation cousins.

Yet, one other dynamic is present that will finally define the quality of mid-adult poverty: that is, if collateral relations are in the same economic circumstances. As has been already stated, seldom are entire networks impoverished, even in South Tucson. However, when collateral relations are as badly off, there is a tendency toward centripetality of relations, with little social exchange expected or desired. On the other hand, the dynamic quality of the economy of the Borderlands is such that it is highly unlikely that the "underclass" economic circumstances of urban poverty ghettos described in the literature are duplicated, even in very moderate contexts like South Tucson.

In the case of the elderly, the quality of poverty is also conditioned by institutional subsidies available but by the existence of lineal relations as well. Although income may be very moderate among the South Tucson elderly, and subsidies basically only maintain minimal health and nutritional levels, for the most part such elderly will own their own homes, have paid off most debts, and have some income provided by adult offspring, usually for taking care of the children. On the other hand, there are circumstances in which the poor elderly do not have either lineal or collateral relations to take the edge off their poverty. In such cases, the elderly couple may become heavily reliant on public subsidies, especially if there is just one surviving member of the household. Yet for the most part, in all the samples of the household clusters of South Tucson and Tucson, both poverty-level and modest-income elderly were usually incorporated within a descending generation household of either daughter or son.

Lastly, a combination of social dynamics and contextual constraints determines the quality of poverty among South Tucson and most U.S. Mexican households. Households may be poor in economic terms, but household poverty is relative to the economic cycles of the region as well as to the assistance and reciprocity of other households. Single heads of households fluctuate in stability ranging from periods of despair, in which appliances are sold in order to pay rent, to periods of stability when, in combination with assistance from relatives sixty miles away, they may have enough money to refuse public assistance.

Case studies[33] demonstrate that regardless of the historical circumstance in which such household clusters emerge and the specific familial characteristics displayed by each household cluster, all seem to converge developmentally into very similarly organized and structured networks of relationships based on dense exchange. In spite of the fact that some households will be characterized by a kind of generational "hopscotching," in which one member of one generation within the same household is born in Sonora and another member of a preceding generation is born in Arizona, they all seem to "cluster" in the manner already discussed.

Each household cluster has as well accumulated and discarded "funds of knowledge" that form the basis of material survival and contain much of the previous generation's repertoire of information and skills used for subsistence.[34] Thus, at its core, each household has labor histories that reflect technological and economic changes in the region and are of crucial importance to the formation of the funds of knowledge particular to each household and cluster. Such funds also have the borderland region as an important historical and contemporary cultural reference point. What provides such funds with the potential for expression is that they are rooted in daily, useful skills and information of a very broad nature, and include mechanical, historical, creative, computational, and design mastery. Such funds are not only reposited within nuclear settings but also are part of the repertoire of information contained within the clusters of households in which younger generational cohorts learn the substance of the corpus of information and have the opportunity to experiment with it in a variety of settings.

They are in fact the currency of exchange, not only between generations but also between households, and therefore form part of the "cultural glue" that maintains exchange relations between kin.

Discussion and Commentary on the Underclass in the U.S.–Mexican Borderlands

The danger of novel ideas like the "underclass" to populations that are so described is that such concepts are applied well beyond the constraints and contexts of the original concept. In addition, such concepts are laden with unintended biases that too often create mythic causes as well as mythic characteristics of their own invention. In the first instance, the underclass idea is not a descriptor of all poor persons, nor of all poverty urban areas. Its descriptive and statistical application was intended by its author to serve specific circumstances and to identify a specific part of the African American population. The underclass category applies more to a manufacturing-dependent population of African American workers and their offspring who cannot make their living in a specific area of an urban region at a particular point in economic history. A constant, not necessarily applicable to the same degree to other populations, is that suburban and national racism underpins the inability of African American men in particular to gain employment.

In addition, as this discussion has shown, the application of the underclass notion cross-culturally to economically marginal urban areas is very limited if not inappropriate. My work in the most dismal of urban contexts does not support its major heuristic or explanatory dimensions, even though there may be aspects of the descriptors that are valid for parts of the populations studied at any one point in the life cycle of the population but cannot be reduced to a statistical percentage.

However, even within the U.S. national context, the concept cannot appropriately either describe or serve as an important analytical construct to help explain the diversity of poverty among U.S. Mexicans or other non-African American "minority" populations. Even within the same impoverished urban arena in which U.S. Mexicans and African Americans live, glaring differences distinguish each population (James 1988; Testa 1988). The overriding conclusion by James seems to be that racism as an intervening variable is one of the most important sources for the appearance of underclass characteristics, whereas the causes and consequences of poverty among U.S. Mexicans seem to "lie outside standard models of the underclass" (1988, p. 34).

As the discussion of the region has shown, the economic dynamics of change in the Borderlands have probably mitigated the appearance of the underclass characteristics among U.S. Mexicans. It is the case that poverty is an important part of the reality of the U.S. Mexican population, but as the disaggregated figures show, it is confined to specific sectors, age cohorts, and a relatively small proportion of a large working-class regional population. Even the dangerous dropout statistics seem to be associated with U.S. Mexican youth seeking and finding work rather than the type of underlying educational decay within some urban African American communities.

Of great importance in understanding U.S. Mexican poverty is the need to disaggregate immigrant from native-born in order to make sense of both economic and educational change but as well to center on important foci for policy concentration. Also, within the border region concentrated urban poverty is distributed geographically and associated with the economics of a specific area. Thus large-scale agricultural production in Texas creates labor markets for unskilled wage labor and accompanying urban areas dependent on agricultural markets and production. On the other hand, the region is so dynamic that conditions are present in which land values are still relatively low for "start-up" homes to be built, for opportunities for entrepreneurship to develop, for individuals and voluntary associations committed to community betterment to operate, for long-term residency by intact families to unfold, for important ritual and calendric activities to function, and for community celebrations to display a sense of community values. South Tucson was able to reverse conditions supporting the development of underclass phenomena by providing both the means and the opportunity for individuals and groups to join in common social endeavors and fulfill their self-interests.

Yet of prime importance is the little-known role of "household clusters" prevalent in the border region, in Tucson, and in South Tucson among U.S. Mexicans. The dynamics of such a phenomenon will not be repeated, but suffice it to suggest that as long as exchange relations are possible between households and male labor, and support is accessible to single women with children, then the dependent institutionalized type of "underclass" phenomenon cannot easily take root. Coupled with unreported income derived from cluster and non-cluster sources, then, survivability seems less problematic for individuals and individual households.

However, economic and production structures may very well have facilitated the development of a pseudo-underclass phenomenon up to the present time, in that border maquiladoras have depended on young, undereducated females as primary labor sources. There is a tendency on the part of such workers to disengage themselves from traditional conjugal and familial norms. However, the percentages of male and female workers in these plants seem to have become balanced by gender, so that an almost even percentage of men and women work in the industry and a greater feminization of poverty is not quite as likely.

An important analytical principle needs to be emphasized. As a normal phenomenon, most households undergo a developmental cycle so that when and where an analytical "snapshot" is taken will determine not only the phenomenological characteristics of the households described but also the analytical conclusions derived therefrom. It seems that the conclusions about the underclass described by the General Accounting Office (GAO) as being characteristic of "Hispanic" households were not only incorrect but obfuscate the dynamics of U.S. Mexican households of modest circumstances.

What is, however, much more disturbing about the GAO description is that it could not capture the remarkable social and cultural strengths of U.S. Mexican households even in distressing economic conditions. The long-term implication of these findings is that as long as policy makers continue to rely on misplaced categories, generalize entire populations with easily refuted ideas, and refuse to disaggregate or utilize a "distributional" approach to the impact of economic structures and racist ideology on human beings, then the more unintended destructive functions of such terms will continue with each new one invented. Not only will such terms as "minority", "disadvantaged", "culture of poverty", and "underclass" continue to haunt those relying on quick and easy categories, but also populations so described will be looked upon as objects, as beings with problems to be solved by others, and part of the market to be treated as simple commodities.

NOTES

1. Karen J. Winkler (1990). "Researcher's Examination of California's Poor Latino Population Prompts Debate Over the Traditional Definitions of the Underclass." *The Chronicle of Higher Education* 10 (October):8.

2. I use the term "Mexican" to describe those born in Mexico as well as those of Mexican parentage born in the United States. Although "Chicano" or "Mexican American" is also used for those born in the United States of Mexican heritage, "Mexican" is the generally preferred term used by the U.S.-born population. See Arce (1981); Garcia (1982); Vélez-Ibáñez (1983a).

3. The U.S.–Mexico Borderlands region includes the population of the six Mexican border states, which has increased threefold since 1950, and of the four U.S. border states, which has increased from 20 million in 1950 to 42 million in 1980. This growth has resulted from uncontrolled industrialization on both sides of the border, created by a series of symbiotic economic and technological relations in manufacturing, processing, industrial agriculture, labor exchange, and twin-plants development. Thus this discussion is not limited to the U.S.–Mexican border towns or cities but rather to the region as a whole.

4. In fact, much of urban and rural Mexico could be classified as national settings for the emergence of the "underclass" according to the descriptions provided by commentators on the subject. Nationally, 54 percent of the population receives income below the minimum wage while 84 percent live in poverty. In 1980, the minimum wage in Mexico was approximately 6390 pesos monthly when the exchange rate was 22.50 pesos to $1, and it should be noted that since 1980 the twin forces of inflation and devaluation have reduced real wages considerably. In 1980, assembly plant workers in the Northern Mexican state of Sonora, which borders Arizona, earned approximately 1400 M.N. a week, or $62. In 1989, these same workers averaged 60,000 M.N. a week, so that the real income was only $24. According to one source (*U.S.–Mexico Report* 1989b), the minimum-wage earner's purchasing power has decreased by 70 percent in the past twenty years.

     National estimates of real unemployment varied from 30 percent to 45 percent, especially if consideration is given to "disguised underemployment". According to *U.S.–Mexico Report* (1989a), 14 million unemployable persons in Mexico are part of an underground economy distributed among industrial and agricultural sectors. Therefore, the utility of the term "underclass" seems to be questionable when applied to other national urban settings or in cross-cultural perspective.

5. On the Mexican side of the Borderlands, there is a skewing of income distribution and occupational categories that has created conditions of extreme asymmetry between the Mexican and U.S. border states. As Vélez-Ibáñez and Greenberg (n.d.) indicate, for the six Mexican border states, 72 percent of the population earns the minimum wage of $284 or less monthly. At the upper end of the distribution, only 3 percent of the population earns more than $954. Approximately 25 percent of the population earns income between the minimum wage and the upper reported limit. This income distribution is also reflected in the occupational structure of the Mexican Borderlands. Seven percent are upper-white-collar occupations; 18 percent are categorized as self-employed; 69 percent are in blue-collar jobs; and 6 percent are in unpaid labor.

The category of self-employed captures two different populations. The first is composed of persons who have established their own small businesses and who are largely a part of the lower end of the formal sector. The second is composed of persons who are largely part of the informal, or "marginal", sector and include street vendors, cab drivers, scavengers, street barbers, gardeners, and countless other occupations marked by easy entry, low skills, and the need for few resources (see Eames and Goode 1973, 1980; Lloyd 1982). Finally, 1 percent are officially categorized as unemployed, but the percentage of unemployed is closer to a more realistic figure of 40 percent.

6. See Bean and Tienda (1987, p. 323) combining men and women in single occupational categories.

7. The probability of poverty in households headed by a single person is twice as great as in those headed by a married couple. Of U.S. Mexican households in poverty in 1980, only 17.1 percent were headed by couples, and close to 40 percent were headed by single persons (Stoddard and Hedderson 1987, pp. 66, 68; Bean and Tienda: 355 and 371). Similarly, the National Center for Health Statistics' Hispanic and Nutrition Examination Survey (HHANES) study showed that 63.3 percent of female-headed households were below the poverty level but only 26.1 of dual-headed households were in poverty (Treviño et al. 1989, p. 9).

8. Moore (1988, p. 2) states that the percentage of poverty among Hispanics had grown from 22 percent in 1979 to 28.2 percent in 1987. This is an aggregated figure of all Hispanics, including Puerto Ricans, which would raise the poverty percentage to that level. In disaggregating Mexican from Puerto Rican household income in 1980, the differences in income between groups becomes

clear in that for household income of $14,999 or less, Puerto Ricans are likely to have 10 percent more of their families earning between $5–9,999 than U.S. Mexicans and 12.2 percent more Puerto Rican families earning $5,000 or less than U.S. Mexicans (Spanish Origin Population, No. 46, Social and Economic Characteristics of the Spanish Origin Population 1984: 41). This illustrates the danger of using aggregate population categories to note demographic characteristics.

9. According to the 1990 U.S. Census data reported by Brokaw (1993, p. 3), Starr County's 24,150 U.S. Mexicans have an unemployment rate of 23.5 percent and only approximately two out of three families earned over $1000 a month.

10. See *The Changing Profile of Mexican America: A Sourcebook for Policy Making* (1985, pp. 40–41, 44–45).

11. Ibid., p. 48.

12. Spanish Origin Population (1984).

13. See Testa (1988), "Ethnic Variations in the Formation of Independent Households by Adolescent Welfare Mothers." Paper prepared for the Population Association of American Session on Welfare Policies, April. Appears in James 1988.

14. Other populations in the United States also have to cope with distinctive structural and substantive economic and social disparity, for example, African American populations throughout the country and Puerto Ricans on the east coast. As Kennedy (1980), Stack (1974), and Valentine (1978) have shown, such populations develop a number of creative household approaches to mitigate the effects of such conditions, including the extensive use of social networks and helping systems. Yet the regional context for Puerto Ricans and African Americans differ markedly from that of U.S. Mexicans, so careful analytical distinction should be made between each type of adaptive and coping mechanism in relation to an appropriate economic and political context.

15. James (1988, pp. 1–42) states that his analysis has found greater patterns of separation of Hispanics by class but that such separation does not have the same characteristics as for blacks because U.S. Mexicans have access to mainstream businesses and organizations. In conjunction with such separation, U.S. Mexicans do not have great rates of out-migration from their settings, and the young—males especially—are strongly motivated to work and to move among other Mexican-origin populations. Also, James states that U.S. Mexican family structure and functions differ from those of African Americans and presumably Puerto Ricans in New York. He states that, among Mexicans, family needs supersede individual ones and serve as a place of refuge in times of need. Within that context, then, the women's roles as mothers are highly valued, with attending support created for those roles to be fulfilled. He concludes from an analysis of case material in Denver, Colorado, which compares U.S. Mexicans with African Americans within the same urban poverty contexts, (1) the pace of metropoli-

tan spatial decentralization is slower in the Southwest because cities are generally newer; (2) Hispanics were not victims of economic dislocation to the same extent as African Americans; (3) there is less prevalence of underclass behavior among poor Hispanics than blacks; (4) Hispanics had high educational dropouts; (5) there was high fertility of husband-wife families not linked to underclass behavior; and (6) immigrant status was independent of underclass category. Finally, James states that "the profile of persistent poverty in Denver supports the conclusion that the main causes of persistent poverty among Hispanics lie outside standard models of the underclass" (p. 34).

In comparing U.S. Mexicans and African Americans within the same city and neighborhoods, the "underclass" concept fails to develop heuristically or as a necessary or sufficient explanation. James's (1988, p. 27) analysis of both populations in Denver's most impoverished neighborhoods clearly undermines the concept by showing that U.S. Mexicans in identical urban situations differ significantly in work and employment, support from friends, the church, family, and other community-based organizations.

Moore (1988, p. 5) states that the Sunbelt where most U.S. Mexicans live is very different from the Rustbelt, where Wilson's model might be applicable. She states that unemployment in the Southwest was 8 percent for U.S. Mexicans in 1988 compared with 12 percent for African Americans and 5 percent for Anglos. For Moore, the Borderlands is an arena in which binational economies operate and where economic processes are tied at productive, labor, and consumptive levels.

Critiquing the applicability of Wilson's neighborhood "concentration" processes of successful parts of the population engaged in "flight out" and only the poverty part of the population "staying in", Moore (pp. 6–7) states that before the 1980s U.S. Mexican communities were vertically integrated communities but that even poor barrios studied a generation ago were reasonably stable with effective neighborhood institutions, which was not the case for Puerto Ricans. She also states that there is no evidence of a middle- and working-class exodus from Mexican neighborhoods. To reinforce this assertion, Moore cites Hansen and Cardenas's (1987) data for San Antonio, Texas, which show that most (85 percent) of the businesses in Mexican neighborhoods were U.S. Mexican-owned.Other institutions such as the church, with voluntary associations and neighborhood centers, were institutionally strong.

16. As Bean and Tienda (1987, p. 235) show, nativity differentials in adult median education levels are quite persistent between 1960 and 1980, but, in fact, for Mexicans these differentials increased, so that lumping native-born and foreign-born Mexicans in the United States obfuscates the manner and process by which adult Mexicans do in fact become educated. This is no more apparent than in the comparison of post-secondary schooling among U.S.-born Mexicans and those born in Mexico. In 1960, the percentage of adult

U.S. Mexicans aged 25 and over completing 13–16+ years of schooling was 7.8 percent but only 4.0 percent for the foreign-born; in 1970, the percentage of U.S. Mexicans aged 25 and over completing 13–16+ years of schooling was 13.4 percent and 8.3 percent for foreign-born; and in 1980, almost 22 percent for U.S. Mexicans and 10 percent for the foreign-born (Bean and Tienda 1987, p. 238).

17. Portions of this section have been previously published in Vélez-Ibáñez (1988b); see especially pp. 35–36.

18. Density of relationships refers to many-stranded or multiple relations described as "the extent to which links which could possibly exist among persons do exist" (Mitchell 1969, p. 18). These relations also have a vertical and horizontal directionality (Lomnitz n.d). The vertical relations are largely unequal ones between people of different statuses or power positions, with an exchange of favors and resources tying specific persons to networks of supporting power groups. The horizontal relations are based on generalized reciprocity of basic equals. The relations with which we are concerned here are horizontal ones, which emerge as central to political coalescence in central urban Mexico, economic cooperation in Mexico and the U.S. Borderlands, clustered housing patterns in Tucson, and neonate emergence in socialization processes.

19. See Carlos G. Vélez-Ibáñez and James B. Greenberg, Multidimensional Functions of Non-Market Forms of Exchange among Mexicanos/Chicanos in Tucson, Arizona. NSF Project BNS-8418906: 1986.

20. Seventy-four percent of the sample adults were U.S.-born persons, with the rest mostly born in the state of Sonora and moving to Arizona mostly as adults between the ages of 21 and 40 in order to work.

21. The Spanish settlement periods in the Sonora region begin in the early seventeenth century; the Mexican period dates from 1821 after the Wars of Independence.

22. Conflict with Apaches was the single most important cause of population movements in the Sonoran region. Tucson was founded as a presidio in 1776 to act as an outpost against Apache raids, and not until the defeat of Apache bands in the late nineteenth century by large numbers of American cavalry troops was southern Arizona's population relatively free of the dangers of Apache raids.

23. Thus this population can hardly be described as an "immigrant" population, and in fact the establishment of the U.S.–Mexican border in the Arizona-Sonora region was established only after the Gadsden Purchase in 1857. Visas for Sonorenses were not required until 1929 in relocating to Tucson.

24. The dual wage structure organized along ethnic lines may be traced back to the establishment of a presidio by the Spanish. In the Spanish colonial and Mexican periods, the ethnic and class divisions of Tucson were between Mexican and Indian popula-

tions. The nature of these lines was fundamentally transformed with the Gadsden Purchase. While the population of Tucson remained predominantly Mexican until 1910, Tucson was soon overwhelmed by Anglo investors backed by national and international capital. Not only were Mexican ranchers progressively displaced from land, but the impact on jobs was equally dramatic. A dual labor market came into existence in which poorly paid occupations became defined as "Mexican jobs", and better-paying ones as "Anglo jobs" (Sheridan 1983, p. 15). Thus a Mexican rate was paid in railroad occupations and in copper mining until the late 1940s.

The tremendous growth of Tucson not only created jobs for both Anglo and Mexican workers but also started an integrative trend that continues today. The breakdown of segregation, however, is more superficial than substantial. Inequality still characterizes the position of Mexicans. Seventy-five percent of Mexicans have incomes that are in the lowest 25 percent of Anglo income brackets. Although upward mobility has been possible for a few Mexican families, the majority of the Mexican population works in urban, low-skilled white- and blue-collar jobs. In order to make ends meet, many Mexican households continue to rely on a variety of preexisting non-market forms of production and exchange: reciprocal exchange of skills and assistance for house building, for repairing tools and transportation, or for getting agricultural and livestock products from the neighboring Santa Cruz Valley. At the same time, however, approximately 25 percent of the Mexican households that are part of "privileged networks" (Cohen 1981) use such forms of exchange for institutional attachment.

25. As the economic gap between Mexican and Anglo communities widened with growing dependence on the world market, the combination of low-paying jobs and discrimination forced the Mexican community to adopt means of survival that were less dependent on the market. The majority of Mexican workers in the first half of this century still lived in large barrios. "In their backyards, they cultivated vegetable gardens and kept chickens, pigs, goats, and even horses and cows" (Rosales 1983, p. 63). Old timers' memories emphasize self sufficiency: "We had a few cattle, but mostly we farmed. We planted barley, chile, squash, watermelon, corn, tomatoes, beans, and even a little wheat. . . . It was an interesting life because it was rustic and we were so independent" (Antonio Cordoba in Martin 1983, p. 15). The subordinate position of the Mexican population in Tucson is not simply a local phenomenon but a reflection of the relationship between Mexico's dependent status and the international labor market.

26. These are Census Districts 10, 11, 2, and 6. In District 10, 60 percent (59.49) of the population is Mexican; in District 11, 52 percent (51.65); in District 2, 26 percent (26.11); and in District 6, 24 percent (24.41). These districts represent, to repeat, 76 percent of the Mexican/Hispanic population, and it will be in reference to this 76 percent that we will largely be concerned.

27. This finding of a relation between a preference for English and familial extension is not borne out by our study. In fact, Spanish in some combination with English is the preferred language within the Tucson sample.

28. See Vélez-Ibáñez (1983b, p. 156), in which *confianza* is defined "as the willingness to engage in generalized reciprocity".

29. This is using as a base the 1986 federal definition of "poor" as a family of four with an annual cash income of less than $11,203 (*Magnitude and Persistence of Poverty among Latinos* 1988, p. 2). For South Tucson, 34 percent of the population is under 18 and only 11 percent is over 60.

30. The percentage of unemployment in 1989 in South Tucson was 13.1 percent while 4.5 percent in the city of Tucson; in 1990 through August, 12 percent in South Tucson and 4.0 percent in Tucson city. Unemployment for South Tucson is directly tied to the economy in the city of Tucson so that variance in each is reflected in increases or decreases in the other. For 1983, the unemployment rate in the city of Tucson was 8.6 percent while in South Tucson it was 23.2 percent; and in 1984, 4.5 percent in the city of Tucson and 13.2 percent in South Tucson, respectively (*Special Unemployment Report for January through December 1989 (Final) For Arizona Local Area Statistics* 1990).

31. Third-generation South Tucsonians like Mayor Dan Eckstrom and Gilbert Mariscal, Jr., were at the core of the revitalization efforts and themselves belong to large clustered households that figure importantly in the many restaurants that operate in South Tucson (*Tucson Daily Citizen*, December 9, 1987).

32. Fifty-three household heads were selected explicitly for their place in the development life cycle. The study specifically selected households that were representative of a stage of household development in which dependent third- and fourth-grade elementary school children were present in the household, and thus adult functions were primarily focused on income mobilization. It was also likely that such a sample would encounter single- and double-parent households, persons likely to be non-U.S.-born and first generation, and given the grade level of the children, likely also to have had the opportunity to have generated household relations of the type already described.

    The mean educational level of the fifty-three household heads was 7.6, with a mean age of 40 of whom 81 percent were born in Mexico and mostly from the Sonora (70 percent). They had established a U.S. residency mean of 11 years and earned a mean income of $14,544, which differs little from a comparable community age cohort.

33. For an appreciation of the case studies, see Vélez-Ibáñez and Greenberg (1992).

34. For a complete description of "Funds of Knowledge", see Vélez-Ibáñez and Greenberg (n.d.).

BIBLIOGRAPHY

Acuña, Rodolfo 1981. *Occupied America*. New York: Harper and Row.

AFL-CIO Industrial Union Department 1986. *The Polarization of America*. Washington, DC: AFL-CIO Industrial Union Department.

Allman, T.D. 1987. *Miami, City of the Future*. New York: Atlantic Monthly Press.

Alvarez, Rodolfo 1973. "The Psycho-Historical and Socioeconomic Development of the Chicano Community in the United States." *Social Science Quarterly* 53:920–942.

Anaya, Rodolfo A. 1972. *Bless Me Ultima*. Berkeley: Quinto Sol.

——— 1976. *Heart of Aztlan*. Berkeley: Justa Publications.

——— "Atrisco Heirs Ask for Continued Connection with Petroglyphs." *Albuquerque Journal*, June 28.

Anderson, Carolyn 1991. "Factors in the Continuance of a Historical People in Los Duranes." Unpublished manuscript.

Anderson, Harry 1989. "Economic Workhorse." *Los Angeles Times*, August 21.

Aponte, Robert 1992. "Definitions of the Underclass: A Critical Analysis." In Herbert Gans, ed. *Sociology in America*, pp. 117–133. Newbury Park, CA: Sage.

Arce, Carlos 1981. "A Reconsideration of Chicano Culture and Identity." *Daedalus* 110:171–191.

——— 1982. "Dimensions of Familism." Paper delivered at the Pacific Sociological Association, San Diego, California, April 22.

Aschenbrenner, Joyce 1975. *Lifelines: Black Families in Chicago*. New York: Holt, Rinehart and Winston.

Atencio, Tomas 1985. "Social Change and Community Conflict in Old Albuquerque, New Mexico" Ph.D. dissertation, University of New Mexico.

Auletta, Ken 1981a. "A Reporter at Large (The Underclass I)." *The New Yorker* 57 (39, November 16).

——— 1981b. "A Reporter at Large (The Underclass II)." *The New Yorker* 57 (40, November 23).

——— 1981c. "A Reporter at Large (The Underclass III)." *The New Yorker* 57 (41, November 30).

——— 1982. *The Underclass*. New York: Random House.

Bailey, Thomas, and Roger Waldinger 1991. "The Changing Ethnic/Racial Division of Labor." In John Mollenkopf and Manuel Castells, eds. *Dual City: Restructuring New York*, pp. 43–78. New York: Russell Sage Foundation.

Balli, Jakim 1989. "The Development of a Drug Abuse Prevalence Estimate in Webb County, Texas." Unpublished paper. Our Lady of the Lake University, School of Social Work, San Antonio, Texas.

Banfield, Edward C. 1965. *Big City Politics.* New York: Random House.

—— 1970. *The Unheavenly City.* Boston: Little, Brown.

Barrera, Mario 1979. *Race and Class in the Southwest.* Notre Dame, IN: University of Notre Dame Press.

Bayette, Beverly 1990. "Vendors vs. the Law: Unlicensed Street Merchants: Able Entrepreneurs or Nuisances?" *Los Angeles Times,* Section E: pp. 1, 6, June 27.

Bean, Frank, and Marta Tienda 1987. *The Hispanic Population of the United States.* New York: Russell Sage Foundation.

Bernal, Guillermo 1982. "Cuban Families." In Monica McGoldrick, John Pearce, and Joseph Giordano, eds. *Ethnicity and Family Therapy,* pp. 187–207. New York: The Guilford Press.

Berry, Brian J., et al. 1976. *Chicago: Transformation of an Urban System.* Cambridge, MA: Ballinger.

Berry, J.C. 1987. "South Tucson." *Tucson Daily Citizen,* April 1.

Beyette, Beverly 1990. "Vendors vs. the Law: Unlicensed Street Merchants: Able Entrepreneurs or Nuisances?" *Los Angeles Times,* Section E: pp. 1, 6, June 27.

Bivins, Ralph 1990. "Policies Idle Real Estate Held by Thrift Bailout Agency." *Houston Chronicle,* September 15, p. 1A.

Bluestone, Barry, and Bennett Harrison 1982. *The Deindustrialization of America.* New York: Basic Books.

Bonacich, Edna 1972. "A Theory of Ethnic Antagonism: The Split Labor Market." *American Sociological Review* 37:547–549.

—— 1976. "Advanced Capitalism and Black/White Relations: A Split Labor Market Interpretation." *American Sociological Review* 41:34–51.

—— 1990. "The Garment Industry in Los Angeles." Presentation at The Conference on California Immigrants in World Perspective, UCLA.

Borjas, G.J. 1982. "The Earnings of Male Hispanic Immigrants in the United States." *Industrial and Labor Relations Review* 35:343–353.

Brokaw, C. 1993. "Incomes in Poorest U.S. Counties Hard to Believe." *Arizona Daily Star,* February 8, p. 3.

California, State of, Health and Welfare Agency, Employment Development Department 1989. *Annual Planning Information: Los Angeles–Long Beach Metropolitan Statistical Area (Los Angeles County).* Los Angeles: Employment Development Department.

Cardona, Luis Antonio 1990. *A Directory of Research on Puerto Ricans in the U.S.* Rockville, IL: Carreta Press.

Caro, Robert A. 1974. *The Power Broker: Robert Moses and the Fall of New York.* New York: Vintage.

Cassel, Virginia C. 1956. *Cultural Change among Spanish-American Aid-To-Dependent Children Clients.* Master's thesis, University of New Mexico.

Castellanos, Eulalio, Luz Echavarria, and Yvette Galindo 1989. "Educational Inequality." In Paul Ong, ed. *The Widening Divide: Income Inequality and Poverty in Los Angeles (A Student Comprehensive Project),* pp. 211–238. Los Angeles: UCLA Research Group on the Los Angeles Economy.

Castells, Manuel 1975. "Immigrant Workers and Class Struggles in Advanced Capitalism: The Western European Experience." *Politics and Society* 5:33–66.

Chambers, Campbell, Isaacson, Chaplin, Inc. 1975. *The Rio Grande in the Albuquerque Metropolis, Part 2: Data Volume.* Albuquerque: Chambers, Campbell, Isaacson, Chaplin, Inc.

The Changing Profile of Mexican America: A Sourcebook for Policy Making 1985. Claremont, CA: The Tomas Rivera Center.

Chavez, Aristides B. 1948. "The Use of the Personal Interview to Study the Subjective Impact of Culture Contacts." Master's thesis, University of New Mexico.

Chenault, Lawrence Royce 1938. *The Puerto Rican Migrant in New York.* New York: Columbia University Press.

Chicago House Hunt Book 1989. "Logan Square." Chicago: Meyers and Associates.

Chicago Tribune 1988. "Dreams, and Little Else, Go with 8th Graders." May 26, sec. 1, col. 5.

Chinchilla, Norma, and Nora Hamilton 1989. "Central American Enterprises in Los Angeles." New Directions for Latino Public Policy Research, Working Paper No. 6. Austin: IUP/SSRC Committee for Public Policy on Contemporary Hispanic Issues.

City of Albuquerque 1968. *Annexation Policies.* City Planning Department.

—— 1970. *The Downtown Plan.* City Planning.

—— 1976a. *Downtown Neighborhood Area: Sector Development Plan.* Albuquerque/Bernalillo County Planning Department.

—— 1976b. *Martineztown–Santa Barbara: Sector Development Plan.* Albuquerque/Bernalillo County Planning Department.

—— 1976c. *Los Duranes: Sector Development Plan.* Albuquerque/Bernalillo County Planning Department.

—— 1976d. *West Mesa: Sector Development Plan.* Albuquerque/Bernalillo County Planning Department.

—— 1976e. *North Barelas Sector Development Plan.* Albuquerque/Bernalillo County Planning Department.

—— 1987a. *Albuquerque Community Profile: A Source Book for Human Services Planning.* Department of Human Services.

—— 1987b. *Los Griegos Sector Development Plan: Status Report.* City Planning Department.

—— 1988. "Huning Highland Sector Development Plan." Planning Department/Redevelopment Division.

—— 1989. "Comprehensive Child Development Program Operating Grant Application." Department of Human Services.

—— 1991a. Human Services Department Housing Rehabilitation Report (Summary, revised: 43091).

—— 1991b. Hispanic Owned Certified and Non-Certified Hispanic Businesses. Purchasing Department.

City of Chicago, Department of Planning 1958. "Development Plan for the Central Area of Chicago."

—— 1984. "Population Forecast for Chicago: 1990–2000."

―――― 1989. "Life Along the Boulevards."

City of New York 1986. "New York City Community District Vital Statistics Data Book." Bureau of Health Statistics and Analysis.

Clark, Juan 1975. "The Exodus from Revolutionary Cuba (1959–1974): A Sociological Analysis." Ph.D. dissertation, University of Florida.

Clark, Margaret 1959. *Health in the Mexican American Culture*. Berkeley: University of California Press.

Clifford, Frank 1990. "Central City West: Vision of Second Downtown L.A." *Los Angeles Times*, Section A1, p. 18, May 22.

Cline, Dorothy I., and T. Phillip Wolf 1967. "Albuquerque: The End of a Reform Era." In Leonard E. Goodall, ed. *Urban Politics in the Southwest*, pp. 7–22. Tempe, AZ: Arizona State University Press.

Cobos, Ruben 1972. "Chicano History and Culture." In *Viva La Diferencia: [Proceedings of] a Chicano Cultural Awareness Conference With Emphasis on Health*. Albuquerque: Regional Medical Programs Service and the New Mexico Regional Medical Program.

Cohen, Abner 1981. *The Politics of Elite Culture: Explorations in the Dramaturgy of Power in a Modern African Society*. Berkeley: University of California Press.

Commission on the Higher Education of Minorities 1982. *Final Report*. Los Angeles: Higher Education Research Institute, Inc.

Cornelius, Wayne 1989. "The U.S. Demand for Mexican Labor." In Wayne Cornelius and Jorge Bustamante, eds. *Mexican Migration to the United States: Origins, Consequences and Policy Options*. San Diego: Center for U.S.–Mexican Studies, University of California.

Cornelius, Wayne 1990. "From Sojourners to Settlers: The Changing Profile of Mexican Migration to the United States." La Jolla, CA: University of California, San Diego, Center for U.S.–Mexican Studies. Unpublished manuscript.

County of Los Angeles, Department of Health Services, Public Health Programs and Services, Data Collection and Analysis Division 1982. "Health District Profiles." East Los Angeles and Northeast Health Districts. Unpublished.

―――― 1986. "Health District Profiles." East Los Angeles and Northeast Health Districts. Unpublished.

Crawford, Fred 1961. *The Forgotten Egg*. San Antonio, TX: Good Samaritan Center.

Cuciti, Peggy, and Franklin James 1990. "A Comparison of Black and Hispanic Poverty in Large Cities of the Southwest." *Hispanic Journal of Behavioral Sciences* 12:50–75.

Davis, Mike 1987. "Chinatown, Part Two? The 'Internationalization' of Downtown Los Angeles." *New Left Review* 164: 61–86.

―――― 1990. *City of Quartz*. London: Verso.

De Leon, Arnoldo 1989. *Ethnicity in the Sunbelt: A History of Mexican Americans in Houston*. Houston, TX: Mexican American Studies Program, University of Houston.

Dewitt, Susan 1977. "A Conversation With Felipe M. Garcia." *La Confluencia* 2:2–7.

Diaz, G.M., ed. 1980. *Evaluation and Identification of Policy Issues in the Cuban Community*. Miami: Cuban National Planning Council.

Diaz-Briquets, Sergio 1984. "Cuban-Owned Business in the United States." *Cuban Studies* 2:57–68.

────── 1986. "Cuban-Owned Businesses in the United States." *Cuban Studies* 14:57–68.

Didion, Joan 1987. *Miami*. New York: Simon and Schuster.

Diez-Canedo, Juan 1981. *Undocumented Migration to the United States: A New Perspective*. Translated from the Spanish by Dolores E. Mills. Albuquerque: Center for Latin American Studies, University of New Mexico.

Dluhy, M.J., and C.E. Krebs 1987. *Dade County, Florida: A Needs Assessment of the 60 and Over Population*. Miami: Southeast Florida Center on Aging, Florida International University.

Drennan, Matthew 1991. "The Decline and Rise of the New York Economy." In John Mollenkopf and Manuel Castells, eds. *Dual City: Restructuring New York*, pp. 25–42. New York: Russell Sage Foundation.

Duran, Tobias 1983. "Hispanics in the Union." In Robert Kern, *Building New Mexico: The Experience of a Carpenters Union in the Southwest*, pp. 189–211. Albuquerque: New Mexico Humanities Council and the District Council of the United Brotherhood of Carpenters.

Eames, E., and J. Goode 1973. *Urban Poverty in a Cross-Cultural Context*. New York: Free Press.

────── 1980. "The Culture of Poverty: Misapplication of Anthropology to Contemporary Issues." In G. Melch and W.P. Zenner, eds. *Urban Life*, pp. 273–286. New York: St. Martin's Press.

Economic Resources Associates 1979. *Feasibility of Conducting a Commercial Area Revitalization Effort (CARE) in the Pico Union Area*. Los Angeles.

The Economist (London) 1988–1989 (December 24–January 6). "America Learns to Love L.A." Reprinted in the *Los Angeles Times*, December 31, 1988.

Edmundson, Munro S. 1957. *Los Manitos: A Study of Institutional Values*. New Orleans: Tulane University, Middle American Research Institute.

Ellwood, David T. 1984. *The Impact of AFDC on Family Structure and Living Arrangements*. Washington, DC: U.S. Department of Health and Human Services, Assistant Secretary for Planning and Education.

────── 1988. *Poor Support: Poverty in the American Family*. New York: Basic Books.

Falcon, Angelo 1988. "Black and Latino Politics in New York City: Race and Ethnicity in a Changing Urban Context." In F. Chris Garcia, ed. *Latinos in the Political System*. Notre Dame, IN: University of Notre Dame Press.

Falcon, Luis, and Douglas Gurak 1991. "Features of the Hispanic Underclass: Puerto Ricans and Dominicans in New York." Unpublished manuscript.

Fagan, Jeffrey, ed. forthcoming. *The Changing Ecology of Crime and Drugs*.

Feagin, Joe R. 1988. *Free Enterprise City: Houston in Political and Economic Perspective*. New Brunswick, NJ: Rutgers University Press.

Fernandez, Raul A. 1989. *The Mexican American Border Region*. Notre Dame, IN: The University of Notre Dame Press.

Fernandez-Kelly, Patricia, and Ana Garcia 1989. "Information at the Core: Hispanic Women, Home Work and the Advanced Capitalist State." *The Informal Economy: Studies in Advanced and Less Developed Countries*, pp. 247–264. In Alejandro Portes, Manuel Castells, and Lauren Benton, eds. Baltimore: The Johns Hopkins University Press.

Fernandez-Kelly, Patricia, and Saskia Sassen 1991. "A Collaborative Study of Hispanic Women in the Garment and Electronics Industries: Executive Summary." New York: New York University, Center for Latin American and Caribbean Studies.

Ferree, Myra Marx 1979. "Employment without Liberation: Cuban Women in the United States." *Social Science Quarterly* 59:295–310.

Final Report of the Commission on the Higher Education of Minorities 1982. Los Angeles: Higher Education Research Institute.

Fisher, Irene 1976. *Bathtub and Silver Bullet*. Placitas, NM: Tumbleweed Press.

Fix, Michael 1991. *The Paper Curtain: Employer Sanctions' Implementation, Impact, and Reform*. Washington, DC: Urban Institute.

Forment, Carlos A. 1989. "Political Practice and the Rise of an Ethnic Enclave: The Cuban American Case, 1959–1979." *Theory and Society* 18:47–81.

Fujimoto, Niki, and Madeline Janis 1990. "Report of the Task Force on Street Vending in Los Angeles." Los Angeles.

Fusfeld, Daniel R., and Timothy Bates 1984. *The Political Economy of the Urban Ghetto*. Carbondale, IL: Southern Illinois University Press.

Galarza, Ernesto 1965. *Merchants of Labor*. San Jose, CA: The Rosicrucian Press, Ltd.

Garcia, John A. 1982. "Ethnicity and Chicanos: Measurement of Ethnic Identification, Identity, and Consciousness." *Hispanic Journal of Behavioral Sciences* 43:295–314.

Garcia, Philip 1985. "Immigration Issues in Urban Ecology: The Case of Los Angeles." In Lionel Maldonado and Joan Moore, eds. *Urban Ethnicity in the United States*, pp. 73–100. Beverly Hills: Sage.

Garcia y Griego, Manuel 1983. *Mexico and the United States: Migration, History, and the Idea of Sovereignty*. El Paso, TX: Center for the Interamerican and Border Studies, The University of Texas, El Paso.

Garreau, Joel 1981. *The Nine Nations of North America*. New York: Houghton Mifflin.

Garza, Estella 1989. "Two of 14 Murders Still Undecided." *Laredo Morning Times*, January 1.

Ginzberg, Eli 1976. *Labor Market: Segments and Shelters*. Washington, DC: Government Printing Office.

Glasgow, Douglas G. 1980. *The Black Underclass: Poverty, Unemployment, and the Entrapment of Ghetto Youth*. San Francisco: Jossey-Bass Publishers.

Glazer, Nathan, and Daniel P. Moynihan 1963. *Beyond the Melting Pot*. Cambridge, MA: MIT Press.

Goldschmidt, Walter 1947. *As You Sow*. New York: Harcourt, Brace.

Gonzales, Phillip B. 1985. "A Perfect Furor of Indignation: The Racial Attitude Confrontation of 1933." Ph.D. dissertation, University of California, Berkeley.

——— 1990. The City of Albuquerque's Comprehensive Child Development Program, Start-up Report.

——— 1993. "The Political Construction of Hispanic Nomenclature in Twentieth Century New Mexico." *Journal of the Southwest* 35 (in press).

Gonzalez-Archegia, B. 1987. "California-Mexico Linkages, First Annual California-Mexico Business Conference." Los Angeles, California: Unpublished manuscript.

——— 1990. The City of Albuquerque's Comprehensive Child Development Program, Start-up Report.

Gosnell, Patricia Aran 1949. *Puerto Ricans in New York City*. New York: New York University Press.

Gottschalk, P., and Sheldon Danziger 1986. "Poverty and the Underclass." Testimony before the Select Committee on Hunger, U.S. Congress. Washington, DC, August.

Grebler, Leo, Joan Moore, and Ralph Guzman 1970. *The Mexican American People*. New York: Free Press.

Greenberg, James B. 1989. "Funds of Knowledge: Historical Constitution, Social Distribution, and Transmission." Paper delivered at the Society for Applied Anthropology, Santa Fe, New Mexico.

Grenier, Guillermo 1990. "Ethnic Solidarity and the Cuban American Labor Movement in Dade County." *Cuban Studies* 20:29–48.

Griffith, Beatrice 1948. *American Me*. Boston: Houghton Mifflin.

Griswold del Castillo, Richard 1984. *La Familia: Chicano Families in the Urban Southwest, 1848 to the Present*. Notre Dame, IN: University of Notre Dame Press.

Haas, Gilda, and Alan David Heskin n.d. "Community Struggles in Los Angeles." Unpublished manuscript.

Hainer, Peter, Catherine Hines, Elizabeth Martin, and Gary Shapiro 1988. "Research on Improving Coverage in Household Surveys." Paper presented to the Bureau of the Census, Fourth Annual Research Conference, Arlington, Virginia.

Hamilton, Rabinovitz, and Alschuler, Inc. 1988. *The Size and the Demography of the Central City West Population*. Los Angeles: Central City West Transportation/Land Use Specific Plan, Work Product 7B.

——— 1989. *Baseline Estimate and Baseline Projection of the Jobs-Housing Balance in and around Central City West*. Los Angeles: Central City West Transportation/Land Use Specific Plan, Work Products 11C and 11D.

Handlin, Oscar 1959. *The Newcomers: Negroes and Puerto Ricans*. Cambridge, MA: Harvard University Press.

Hannerz, Ulf 1969. *Soulside: Inquiries into Ghetto Culture and Community*. New York: Columbia University Press.

Hanson, Niles 1981. *The Border Economy*. Austin: The University of Texas Press.

Harrell, Louis, and Dale Fischer 1985. "The 1982 Mexican Peso Devaluation and Border Area Employment." *Monthly Labor Review* 108:25–32.

Harrington, Michael 1984. *The New American Poverty*. New York: Penguin Books.

Hechter, Michael 1977. *Internal Colonialism: The Celtic Fringe in British National Development, 1536–1966*. Berkeley: University of California Press.

Heller, Celia 1966. *Mexican-American Youth*. New York: Random House.

Hernandez-Alvarez, Jose 1966. "A Demographic Profile of the Mexican Immigration to the United States, 1910–1950." *Journal of Inter-American Studies* 8:472–496.

Heyman, Joseph n.d. "The Power of the United States Border Over Mexican Lives: The Case of Cross-Border Kinship." In C. Velez-Ibanez, J. Greenberg, and R. Trotter, eds. *The U.S.–Mexico Border in Anthropological Context* (in process).

Hicklin, Charles, and Wendy Wintermute 1989. "The Employment Potential of Chicago's Service Industries." Chicago. Unpublished manuscript.

Hill, Herbert 1974. "Guardians of the Sweatshops: The Trade Unions, Racism, and the Garment Industry." In Adalberto Lopez and James Petras, eds. *Puerto Rico and Puerto Ricans: Studies in History and Society*, pp. 384–416. New York: John Wiley.

Hill, Richard Child, and Joe R. Feagin 1987. "Detroit and Houston: Two Cities in Global Perspective." In Michael Peter Smith and Joe R. Feagin, eds. In *The Capitalist City*, pp. 155–177. New York: Basil Blackwell.

Hispanic Almanac 1984. "A Report on the Numbers." Washington, DC: Hispanic Policy Development Project.

Hispanic Housing Development Corporation 1989. "Building Communities— Rebuilding Chicago." Unpublished manuscript.

Hogan, Dennis, Nan Marie Astone, and Evelyn M. Kitagawa 1985. "Social and Environmental Factors Influencing Contraceptive Use among Black Adolescents." *Family Planning Perspectives* 17:165–169.

Hudson, Berkley 1991. "Children Increasingly Fall Victim to Gang Violence." *Los Angeles Times*, Section A, pp. 1, 34–35. October 27.

Jaffe, A.J., R.M. Cullen, and T.D. Boswell 1980. *The Changing Demography of Spanish Americans*. New York: Academic Press.

James, Franklin 1988. "Persistent Urban Poverty and The Underclass: A Perspective Based on the Hispanic Experience." San Antonio, TX: Thomas Rivera Center, Trinity University.

Jencks, Christopher, and Kathryn Edin 1990. "The Real Welfare Problem." In *The American Prospect*, pp. 31–50.

Jencks, Christopher, and Paul Peterson, eds. 1991. *The Urban Underclass*. Washington, DC: Brookings.

Jorge, Antonio, and Raul Moncarz 1980. "The Cuban Entrepreneur and the Economic Development of the Miami SMSA." Unpublished manuscript, Department of Economics, Florida International University.

Katz, Michael B. 1986. *In the Shadow of the Poorhouse*. New York: Basic Books.

Keefe, Susan E. 1979. "Urbanization, Acculturation, and Extended Family Ties: Mexican Americans in Cities." *American Ethnologist* 6:349–365.

Keefe, Susan E., and Amado M. Padilla 1987. *Chicano Ethnicity*. Albuquerque: University of New Mexico Press.

Keefe, Susan E., Amado Padilla, and Manuel L. Carlos 1978. *Emotional Support Systems in Two Cultures: A Comparison of Mexican Americans and Anglo Americans*. Occasional Paper No. 7. Los Angeles: Spanish Speaking Mental Health Research Center, UCLA.

——— 1979. "The Mexican American Extended Family as an Emotional Support System." *Human Organization* 38:144–152.

Kennedy, Theodore R. 1980. *You Gotta Deal With It: Black Family Relations in a Southern Community*. New York: Oxford University Press.

Klein, David Walter 1974. *The Downtown Planning Process: An Analysis of the Albuquerque Experience*. Master's thesis, University of New Mexico.

Kluckhohn, Florence, and Fred Strodtbeck 1961. *Variations in Value Orientations*. Evanston, IL: Row, Peterson.

Kort, Michele 1990. "What Price Poverty?" *UCLA Magazine* 2:29–33.

Kurtines, William M., and Luke Miranda 1980. "Differences in Self and Family Role Perception among Acculturating Cuban-American College Students: Implications for the Etiology of Family Disruption among Migrant Groups." *International Journal of Intercultural Relations* 4:167–194.

Lamphere, Louise, Patricia Zavella, and Felipe Gonzales with Peter Evans 1993. "Working Mothers and Sunbelt Industrialization: New Patterns of Work and Family." Manuscript.

Ladner, Joyce 1971. *Tomorrow's Tomorrow: The Black Woman*. Garden City, NY: Doubleday.

Lane, Thomas 1975. "Report on Manufacturing Employment in the Los Angeles Region. Master's thesis, University of California–Los Angeles.

Laredo Police Department 1988. *Annual Report*. Laredo, TX.

Lemann, Nicholas 1986. "The Origins of the Underclass." *Atlantic Monthly* June:31–35; July:54–68.

Leonard, Olen, and Charles Loomis 1938. *Culture of a Contemporary Rural Community: El Cerito, NM*. Washington, DC: U.S. Department of Agriculture.

Lesser, Robert Charles, and Co. 1988. *Central City West Analysis of Alternative Housing Production Programs*. Los Angeles: Central City West Transportation/Land Use Specific Plan, Work Product 11E.

Levin and Associates, Architects 1988. *Architectural Resources Survey*. Los Angeles: Central City West Transportation/Land Use Specific Plan, Work Product 4.

Levine, Barry, B. 1985. "The Capital of Latin America." *Wilson Quarterly*: 46–73.

Levy, Frank 1977. "How Big Is the Underclass?" Working Paper 0090-1. Washington, DC: Urban Institute.

———— 1986. *The Logic of Welfare Reform*. Washington, DC: Urban Institute Press.

Lewis, Oscar 1966. *La Vida: A Puerto Rican Family in the Culture of Poverty*. New York: Random House.

Liebow, Elliot 1967. *Tally's Corner: A Study of Negro Street-corner Men*. Chicago: Aldine.

Litwak, Eugene 1960. "Geographic Mobility and Extended Family Cohesion." *American Sociological Review* 25:9–21.

Lloyd, Peter 1982. *A Third World Proletariat?* London: George Allen and Unwin.

Loescher, Gilbert, and John Scanian 1986. *Calculated Kindness: Refugees and the Half-Open Door. 1945 to the Present*. New York: The Free Press.

Lomnitz, Larrisa n.d. "Horizontal and Vertical Relations and the Social Structure of Urban Mexico." Unpublished manuscript.

Los Angeles Police Department 1990. "Monthly Report: A Summary of Crimes and Arrests of the City of Los Angeles for the Month of May." Los Angeles: Information Resources Division, Los Angeles Police Department.

Los Angeles Sheriffs Department 1990. "JAI Gang Code List." Photocopy.

Loucky, James, Nora Hamilton, and Norma Chinchilla 1989. *The Effects of the Immigration Reform and Control Act on the Garment, Building Maintenance and Hospitality Industries in Los Angeles*. Final Report to the Division of Immigration Policy and Research, U.S. Department of Labor.

Loya, F., P. Garcia, J. Sullivan, L. Vargas, N. Allen, and J. Mercy 1986. "Conditional Risks of Homicide among Anglo, Hispanic, Black and Asian Victims in Los Angeles, 1970–1979." In *U.S. Department of Health and Human Services,*

Report of the Secretary's Task Force on Black and Minority Health, Vol. 5: Homicide, Suicide, and Unintentional Injuries. Washington, DC: U.S. Government Printing Office.

Luckingham, Bradford 1982. *The Urban Southwest.* El Paso, TX: Texas Western Press.

Lowe, Cary 1991. "How Everybody Can Win When Reviving Inner City Neighborhoods." *Los Angeles Times,* Section M, p. 6. April 7.

Luytjes, Jan 1983. *International Banking in South Florida: Analysis and Trends.* Miami: Bureau of Business Research, Florida International University.

MacCorkle, Lyn 1984. *Cubans in the United States: A Bibliography for Research in the Social and Behavioral Sciences. 1960–1983.* Westport, CT: Greenwood Press.

Madsen, William 1964. *The Mexican Americans of South Texas.* San Francisco: Holt, Rinehart and Winston.

The Magnitude and Persistence of Poverty Among Latinos 1988. Claremont, CA: The Tomas Rivera Center.

Maldonado-Denis, Manuel 1972. *Puerto Rico: A Sociohistoric Interpretation.* New York: Random House.

——— 1976. *Puerto Riquenos en los Estados Unidos.* Mexico City: Siglo Veintiuno Editores.

Martin, Patricia P. 1983. *Images and Conversations: Mexican Americans Recall a Southwest Past.* Tucson: University of Arizona Press.

Martinez, Ruben 1992. "This Was About Something To Eat." *Los Angeles Times,* May 18.

Martinez, Oscar 1983a. "Border Cities." In Elwyn Stoddard, Richard L. Nostrand, and Jonathan P. West, eds. *Border a Source Book: A Guide to the Literature on Northern Mexico and the American Southwest,* Norman, OK: University of Oklahoma Press.

——— 1983b. "The Foreign Orientation of the Mexican Border Economy." *Border Perspectives,* No. 2. El Paso, TX: Center for Interamerican and Border Studies, The University of Texas, El Paso.

——— 1988. *Troublesome Border.* Tucson: The University of Arizona Press.

Marx, Karl, 1965[1867]. "Exploitation and the Accumulation of Misery." In Robert E. Will and Harold G. Vatter, eds. *Poverty in Affluence.* New York: Harcourt, Brace & World, Inc.

Massey, Douglas 1979. "Residential Segregation of Spanish Americans in United States Urbanized Areas." *Demography* 14:5–19.

——— 1990. "American Apartheid: Segregation and the Making of the Underclass." *American Journal of Sociology* 96:329–357.

Massey, Douglas, and Mitchell Eggers 1990. "The Ecology of Inequality: Minorities and the Concentration of Poverty." *American Journal of Sociology* 95: 1153–1188.

Masud-Piloto, Felix Roberto 1988. *With Open Arms: Cuban Migration to the United States.* Totowa, NJ: Rowman and Littlefield.

Matza, David 1966. "The Disreputable Poor." In Reinhardt Bendix and Seymour Martin Lipset, eds. *Class, Status and Power,* pp. 289–302. New York: Free Press.

McCarthy, Kevin, and R.B. Valdez 1986. *Current and Future Effects of Mexican Immigration in California.* Santa Monica, CA: Rand Corporation.

McRay, John P. 1989. "Maquiladora Sourcing Opportunities for San Antonio Businesses." Department of Economic Employment Development, City of San Antonio.

McWilliams, Carey 1949. *North From Mexico.* New York: J.B. Lippincott.

Mead, Lawrence M. 1986. *Beyond Entitlement: The Social Obligations of Citizenship.* New York, Free Press.

——— 1989. "The Logic of Workfare: The Underclass and Work Policy." *The Annals of the American Academy of Political and Social Science* 501:156–169.

——— 1992. *The New Politics of Poverty.* New York, Basic Books.

Meeker, Marcia, with J. Harris 1964. *Background for Planning.* Los Angeles: Welfare Planning Council.

Menefee, Seldon, and Orin Cassmore 1940. *The Pecan Shellers of San Antonio.* Washington: WPA, Division of Research.

Metro-Dade Planning Department, Research Division 1987. Profile of the Hispanic Population. Miami, FL: Metro-Dade County Planning Department.

Meyer, Michael 1984. *Water in the Hispanic Southwest: A Social and Legal History, 1550–1850.* Tucson: University of Arizona Press.

Meyer and Allen Associates 1988. *Urban Design Analysis.* Los Angeles: Central City West Transportation/Land Use Specific Plan, Work Product 5.

Middle Rio Grande Council of Governments of New Mexico 1991. Summary of 1990 Census. State Planning and Development, District 3.

Miller, Michael J. 1983. "Recent Growth in Texas Border Metropolitan Areas: Progress or Illusions for the Mexican-American Community." Unpublished paper.

——— 1986. "Perspective on the Social and Psychological Consequences of the 1982 Peso Devaluation in Laredo, Texas." *Border Health/Salud Fronteriza* 11: 8–15

Miller, Walter B. 1958. "Lower Class Culture as a Generating Mileu of Gang Delinquency." *Journal of Social Issues* 14:5–19.

Mills, C. Wright, Clarence Senior, and Rose K. Goldsen 1950. *The Puerto Rican Journey.* New York: Harper.

——— 1967. *The Puerto Rican Journey.* New York: Russell and Russell.

Mitchell, J. Clyde, ed. 1969. *Social Networks in Urban Situations.* Manchester: Manchester University Press for the Institute for Social Research, University of Zambia.

Mohl, Raymond 1983. "Miami: The Ethnic Cauldron." In R.M. Bernard and B.R. Rice, eds. *Sunbelt Cities: Politics and Growth Since World War II,* pp. 67–72. Austin, TX: University of Texas Press.

——— 1985. "The Origins of Miami's Liberty City." *Florida Environmental and Urban Issues* 4:9–12.

——— 1986. "The Politics of Ethnicity in Contemporary Miami." *Migration World* 14:7–11.

——— 1987a. "Ethnic Politics in Miami: 1960–86." In Randall M. Miller and George E. Pozzetta, eds. *Ethnicity in the Urban South,* pp. 143–160. Boca Raton, FL: Florida Atlantic University Press.

——— 1987b. "Trouble in Paradise: Race and Housing in Miami during the New Deal Era." *Prologue: Journal of the National Archives* 19:7–21.

——— 1988. "Immigration through the Port of Miami." In M. Mark Stolarik, ed. *Forgotten Doors: The Other Ports of Entry to the United States*, pp. 81–98. Philadelphia: Balch Institute Press.

———— 1989. "Shadows in the Sunshine: Race and Ethnicity in Miami." *Tequesta: The Journal of the Historical Association of Southern Florida* 49:39–40.

———— 1990. "On the Edge: Blacks and Hispanics in Metropolitan Miami Since 1959." *The Florida Historical Quarterly* 69: 37–56.

Montejano, David 1987. *Anglos and Mexicans in the Making of Texas 1936–1986*. Austin, TX: The University of Texas Press.

Montiel, Miguel 1970. "The Social Science Myth of the Mexican American Family." *El Grito* 3:56–63.

Montoya, Mejia, and Porfirio Noyola 1989. "The Maquiladora Program in the North Tamaulipas Region." Paper presented at the Western Social Science Association in Albuquerque, New Mexico.

Moore, Frank C. 1947. *San Jose 1946: A Study in Urbanization*. Master's thesis, University of New Mexico.

Moore, Joan 1977. "A Case Study of Collaboration: The Chicano Pinto Research Project." *Journal of Social Issues* 33:144–158.

———— 1985. "Isolation and Stigmatization in the Creation of an Underclass." *Social Problems* 33:1–12.

———— 1988. "An Assessment of Hispanic Poverty: Is There a Hispanic Underclass?" Paper prepared for a Conference on Persistent Poverty convened at Trinity University, San Antonio, Tomas Rivera Center.

———— 1989. "Is There a Hispanic Underclass?" *Social Science Quarterly* 70:265–283.

———— 1991. *Going Down to the Barrio: Homeboys and Homegirls in Change*. Philadelphia: Temple University Press.

Moore, Joan, and Ronald Edari 1989. *Final Report: Youth Initiative Needs Assessment*. Milwaukee, WI: University of Wisconsin–Milwaukee Sociology Department.

Moore, Joan, with Robert Garcia, Carlos Garcia, Luis Cerda, and Frank Valencia 1978. *Homeboys: Gangs, Drugs and Prison in the Barrios of Los Angeles*. Philadelphia: Temple University Press.

Moore, Joan, and Harry Pachon 1985. *Hispanics in the United States*. Englewood Cliffs, NJ: Prentice Hall.

Moore, Joan, and Diego Vigil 1987. "Chicano Gangs: Group Norms and Individual Factors Related to Adult Criminality." *Aztlan* 18:27–44.

Morales, Julio 1986. *Puerto Rican Poverty and Migration: We Just Had to Try Elsewhere*. New York: Praeger.

Morales, Rebecca 1985. "Transitional Labor: Undocumented Workers in the Los Angeles Automobile Industry." *International Migration Review* 17:570–96.

Morris, Michael 1989. "From the Culture of Poverty to the Underclass: An Analysis of a Shift in Public Language." *The American Sociologist* 20:123–133.

Muller, Thomas, and Thomas J. Espenshade 1986. *The Fourth Wave*. Washington, DC: Urban Institute Press.

Murray, Charles 1984. *Losing Ground*. New York: Basic Books.

Neel, Gladys 1928. *History of Albuquerque*. Master's thesis, University of New Mexico.

New Mexico Department of Labor 1989. *New Mexico Workforce 2000*. Santa Fe: New Mexico Department of Labor.

Officer, James 1981. "Arizona's Hispanic Perspective: Research Report for the 38th Town Hall." Phoenix: Arizona Academy.

O'Hare, William 1987. "Best Metros for Hispanic Businesses." *American Demographics* 9:30–33.

Ong, Paul 1988. "The Hispanization of L.A.'s Poor." UCLA, School of Planning. Photocopy.

Ong, Paul, ed. 1989. *The Widening Divide: Income Inequality and Poverty in Los Angeles (A Student Comprehensive Project)*. Los Angeles: UCLA Research Group on the Los Angeles Economy.

Orfield, Gary 1983. *Latinos in Metropolitan Chicago: A Study of Housing and Employment*. Monograph Series No. 6. Chicago: Latino Institute.

Padilla, Elena 1947. "Puerto Rican Immigrants in New York and Chicago: A Study in Comparative Assimilation." Ph.D. dissertation, University of Chicago.

——— 1958. *Up From Puerto Rico*. New York: Columbia University Press.

Padilla, Felix M. 1987. *Puerto Rican Chicago*. Notre Dame, IN: University of Notre Dame Press.

——— 1992. *The Gang as an American Enterprise*. New Brunswick, NJ: Rutgers University Press.

Pedraza-Bailey, Silvia 1985. *Political and Economic Migrants in America: Cubans and Mexicans*. Austin, TX: University of Texas Press.

Pelaez, Marta, and Max Rothman 1991. "Aging Miami." Southeast Florida Center on Aging, Florida International University. Unpublished paper.

Perez, Lisandro 1985. "The Cuban Population of the United States: The Results of the 1980 U.S. Census of Population." *Cuban Studies* 15:1–18.

——— 1986. "Immigrant Economic Adjustment and Family Organization: The Cuban Success Story Reexamined." *International Migration Review* 20:4–20.

——— 1992. "Cuban Miami." In Guillermo Grenier and Alex Stepick, eds. *Miami Now: Immigration, Ethnicity and Social Change*, pp. 83–108. Gainesville, FL: University Press of Florida.

Perez-Stable, Marfeli, and Miren Uriarte 1990. "Latinos in a Changing U.S. Economy: Cuban-Americans in Miami." SUNY–Old Westbury. Unpublished paper.

Perry, David, and Alfred Watkins 1977. *The Rise of the Sunbelt Cities*. Beverly Hills, CA: Sage.

Peterson, Jonathon 1991. "Recession Hits State with Surprising Force." *Los Angeles Times*, Section A, pp. 1, 32–33. February 18.

Peterson, Mark F., and Modesto A. Maidique 1986. "Success Patterns of the Leading Cuban-American Enterprises." WP 86-104. Research Report Series. Innovation and Entrepreneurship Institute, School of Business Administration, University of Miami.

Pico Union Neighborhood Council 1971. *Socio-Economic Survey for the Greater Pico-Union Development Area*. Los Angeles.

Porras, Armando Salas n.d. "Crisis, Maquiladoras y Estructura Sociopolitica en Chihuahua, Sonora y Baja California." Unpublished manuscript.

Porter, Bruce, and Marvin Dunn 1984. *The Miami Riot of 1980: Crossing the Bounds.* Lexington, MA: Lexington Books.

Portes, Alejandro 1969. "Dilemmas of a Golden Exile: Integration of Cuban Refugee Families in Milwaukee." *American Sociological Review* 34:505–518.

—— forthcoming. *City on the Edge: Miami and the Immigrants.* Berkeley, CA: University of California Press.

Portes, Alejandro, and Robert L. Bach 1985. *Latin Journey: Cuban and Mexican Immigrants in the United States.* Berkeley: University of California Press.

Portes, Alejandro, Manuel Castells, and Lauren A. Benton 1989. *The Informal Economy.* Baltimore: Johns Hopkins University Press.

Portes, Alejandro, and Juan Clark 1987. "Mariel Refugees: Six Years After." *Migration World Magazine* 15:14–18.

Portes, Alejandro, Juan Clark, and Robert Manning 1985. "After Mariel: A Survey of the Resettlement Experiences of 1980 Cuban Refugees in Miami." *Cuban Studies* 15:37–59.

Portes, Alejandro, and Leif Jensen 1987. "What's an Ethnic Enclave? The Case for Conceptual Clarity. Comment on Sanders and Nee." *American Sociological Review* 52:768–770.

Portes, Alejandro, and Alex Stepick 1993. *City on the Edge: The Transformation of Miami.* Berkeley: University of California Press.

Portes, Alejandro, and Alex Stepick 1985. "Unwelcome Immigrants: The Labor Market Experiences of 1980 (Mariel) Cuban and Haitian Refugees in South Florida." *American Sociological Review* 50:493–514.

Portes, Alejandro, Alex Stepick, and Cynthia Truelove 1986. "Three Years Later: The Adaptation Process of 1980 (Mariel) Cuban and Haitian Refugees in South Florida." *Population and Policy Reviews* 5:83–94.

Prieto, Yolanda 1977. "Women, Work and Change: The Case of Cuban Women in the U.S." Latin American Monograph Series. The Northwestern Pennsylvania Institute for Latin American Studies.

—— 1987. "Cuban Women in the U.S. Labor Force: Perspectives on the Nature of Change." *Cuban Studies* 17:72–91.

Prohias, R.J., and L. Casal 1973. "The Cuban Minority in the U.S.: Preliminary Report on Need Identification and Program Evaluation." Boca Raton, FL: Florida Atlantic University.

Rabinowitz, Howard N. 1983. "Albuquerque: City at a Crossroads." In Richard M. Bernard and Bradley R. Rice, eds. *Sunbelt Cities: Politics and Growth Since World War II*, pp. 255–267. Austin: University of Texas Press.

Rainwater, Lee 1970. *Behind Ghetto Walls: Black Families in a Federal Slum.* Chicago: Aldine.

Ramirez, Oscar 1980. "Extended Family Support and Mental Health Status Among Mexicans in Detroit." *La Red* 28:2.

Rand, Christopher 1958. *The Puerto Ricans.* New York: Oxford University Press.

Rich, Cynthia Jo 1974. "Pondering the Future: Miami's Cubans after 15 Years." *Race Relations Reporter* 5:49–52.

Ricketts, Erol, and Isabel V. Sawhill 1988. "Defining and Measuring the Underclass." *Journal of Policy Analysis and Management* 7:316–325.

Rieff, David 1987. *Going to Miami: Exiles, Tourists, and Refugees in the New America.* Boston: Little Brown.

——— 1991. *Los Angeles: Capital of the Third World*. New York: Simon and Schuster.

Risen, J. 1981. "Sweatshops Pervasive in Miami." *Miami Herald. Business Monday.*

Robbins, Cathy 1980. "Martineztown—Village in the City." *New Mexico Magazine* 58:74–84.

Rochin, Refugio I. 1989. *Economic Perspectives of the Hispanic Community*. San Antonio, TX: The Tomas Rivera Center.

Rodriguez, Clara 1989. *Puerto Ricans: Born in the U.S.A.* Boston: Unwin Hyman.

Rodriguez, Nestor 1987. "Undocumented Central Americans in Houston: Diverse Populations." *International Migration Review* 21:19.

——— 1989. "The Growth of Houston's Hispanic Population." In Dorothy F. Caram, Anthony G. Dworkin, and Nestor Rodriguez, eds. *Hispanics in Houston and Harris County, 1519–1986*. Houston, TX: Houston Hispanic Forum.

Rodriguez, Nestor, and Ximena Urrutia-Rojas 1990a. "Impact of Recent Refugee Migration to Texas: A Comparison of Southeast Asian and Central American Newcomers." In Wayne H. Holtzman and Thomas H. Bornemann, eds. *Mental Health of Immigrants and Refugees*. Austin, TX: The Hogg Foundation for Mental Health, The University of Texas at Austin.

——— 1990b. "Undocumented and Unaccompanied: A Mental-Health Study of Unaccompanied, Immigrant Children from Central America." Final Report, submitted to the Hogg Foundation for Mental Health, The University of Texas at Austin.

Rodriguez, Robert 1991. "Los Duranes: Neighbors All." *Albuquerque Journal*, February 16:E-1.

Rogg, E.M., and R.S. Cooney 1980. *Adaptation and Adjustment of Cubans: West New York, New Jersey*. New York Hispanic Research Center.

Romano-V, Octavio I 1968. "The Anthropology and Sociology of the Mexican Americans." *El Grito* 2:13–26.

Romo, Ricardo 1983. *East Los Angeles: History of a Barrio*. Austin, TX: University of Texas Press.

Rosales, Francisco A. 1983. "The Mexican Immigrant Experience in Chicago, Houston and Tucson: Comparison and Contrasts." In Francisco Rosales and Barry J. Kaplan, eds. *Houston: a Twentieth Century Urban Frontier*. Port Washington, NY: National University Publication Association, Faculty Press Inc.

Rubel, Arthur 1966. *Across the Tracks*. Austin, TX: University of Texas Press.

Russell, George 1977. "The American Underclass." *Time Magazine* 110 (August 28):14–27.

Sahagun, Luis 1992. "Council OKs Districts for Street Vendors." *Los Angeles Times*, January 15.

Sallee, Rad, and R.A. Dyer 1991. "Hispanics, Asians Gain Sharply in City Census as Whites Decline." *Houston Chronicle*, February 6, Section A, p. 1.

Sanchez, George 1940. *Forgotten People: A Study of New Mexicans*. Albuquerque: University of New Mexico Press.

Sanchez, Maria E., and Antonio M. Stevens Arroyo 1987. *Toward a Renaissance of Puerto Rican Studies: Ethnic and Area Studies*. New York: Columbia University Press.

Sanders, Jim M., and Victor Nee. 1987. "Limits of Ethnic Solidarity." *American Sociological Review* 52:745–767.

Sanders, Thomas G. 1986. "Maquiladoras: Mexico's In-Bond Industries." University Field Staff International, Institute of World Affairs [TGS-3-86].

Sargeant, Kathryn, and Mary Davis. 1986. *Shining River, Precious Land: An Oral History of the North Valley.* Albuquerque: Albuquerque Museum.

Sassen, Saskia 1988. *The Mobility of Labor and Capital: A Study in International Investment and Labor Flows.* Cambridge: Cambridge University Press.

——— 1989. "New Trends in the Sociospatial Organization of the New York City Economy." In Robert Beauregard, ed. *Economic Restructuring and Political Response.* Newbury Park, CA.

Sassen-Koob, Saskia 1984. "The New Labor Demand in Global Cities." In Michael Smith, ed. *Cities in Transformation.* Beverly Hills, CA: Sage.

Saunders, Lyle 1954. *Cultural Differences and Medical Care.* New York: Russell Sage Foundation.

Schick, Frank L., and Renee Schick 1991. *Statistical Handbook on U.S. Hispanics.* Phoenix: The Oryx Press.

Secretaria de Programacion y Presupuesto 1984. *X Censo General de Poblacion y Vivienda, 1980.* Resumen General Abreviado. Vol. III. Mexico, D.F.: Instituto Nacional de Estadistica, Geografia y Informatica.

Sena-Rivera, Jaime 1980. "La Familia Hispana as a Natural Support System: Strategies for Prevention." In R. Valled and W. Vega, eds. *Hispanic Natural Support Systems,* pp. 75–81. State of California: Department of Mental Health, Office of Prevention.

Senior, Clarence Ollson 1965. *Our Citizens from the Caribbean.* New York: McGraw Hill.

Sheets, Robert, Stephen Nord, and John Phelps 1987. *The Impact of Service Industries on Underemployment in Metropolitan Economies.* Lexington, MA: Lexington Books.

Shelton, Beth Anne, Nestor P. Rodriguez, Joe R. Feagin, Robert D. Bullard, and Robert D. Thomas 1989. *Houston: Growth and Decline in a Sunbelt Boomtown City.* Philadelphia: Temple University Press.

Sheridan, T. 1983. "Del Rancho al Barrio." Tucson: Arizona Heritage Center.

Simmons, Marc 1982. *Albuquerque: A Narrative History.* Albuquerque: University of New Mexico Press.

Sjoberg, Gideon 1947. *Culture Change as Revealed by a Study of Relief Clients of a Suburban New Mexico Community.* Master's thesis, University of New Mexico.

Smith, Barton 1989. *Handbook on the Houston Economy.* Houston: Center for Public Policy, University of Houston.

Smith, Michael P., and Joe R. Feagin, eds. 1987. *The Capitalist City: Global Restructuring and Community Politics.* Oxford: Basil Blackwell.

Smith, C. 1984. "Local History in Global Context: Social and Economic Transitions in Western Guatemala." *Comparative Studies in Society and History* 26:193–228.

Soja, Edward 1987. "Economic Restructuring and the Internationalization of the Los Angeles Region." In Michael Peter Smith and Joe R. Feagin, eds. *The Capitalist City,* pp. 178–198. New York: Basil Blackwell.

Soja, Edward W., Rebecca Morales, and G. Wolff 1983. "Urban Restructuring:

An Analysis of Social and Spatial Change in Los Angeles." *Economic Geography* 59:195–230.

Southwest Land Research, Inc. 1989. *Supply and Demand Estimates for Low and Moderate Income Housing in the Albuquerque Area.* Prepared for the City of Albuquerque Department of Human Services. Albuquerque: Southwest Land Research, Inc.

Spanish Origin Population, 1984. United States Summary. *Statistical Abstract of the U.S. 10th Edition.* Washington, DC: U.S. Bureau of the Census.

Special Unemployment Report for January through December 1989 (Final) for Arizona Local Area Statistics 1990. Pima County, Department of Economic Security, State of Arizona.

Stack, Carol 1974. *All Our Kin.* New York: Harper and Row.

Stack, John F., and Christopher L. Warren 1992. "The Reform Tradition and Ethnic Politics: Metropolitan Miami Confronts the 1990s." In Guillermo Grenier and Alex Stepick, eds. *Miami Now: Immigration, Ethnicity and Social Change,* pp. 160–185. Gainesville, FL: University Press of Florida.

Stegman, Michael A. 1988. "Housing and Vacancy Report: New York City, 1987." New York: City of New York, Department of Housing Preservation and Development.

Steinberg, Stephen. 1989. *The Ethnic Myth: Race, Ethnicity and Class in America.* Boston: Beacon Press.

Stepick, Alex 1989. "Miami's Two Informal Sectors." In A. Portes, M. Castells, and L. Benton, eds. *The Informal Economy: Studies in Advanced and Less Developed Countries,* pp. 111–131. Baltimore: The Johns Hopkins University Press.

——— 1990. "Community Growth versus Simply Surviving: The Informal Sectors of Cubans and Haitians in Miami." In M. E. Smith, ed. *Perspectives on the Informal Economy,* pp. 183–205. Washington, DC: University Press of America.

Stepick, Alex, Max Castro, Marvin Dunn, and Guillermo Grenier 1990. "Changing Relations among Newcomers and Established Residents: The Case of Miami." Miami: Center for Labor Research and Studies, Florida International University.

Stevens Arroyo, Antonio M. 1974. *The Political Philosophy of Pedro Abizu Campos: Its Theory and Practice.* Ibero American Language and Area Center. New York: New York University Press.

Stevenson, J.M. 1973. "Cuban-Americans: New Urban Class." Ph.D. dissertation, Wayne State University.

Stevenson, Richard W. 1989. "California, Star of U.S. Economy, Sees Short-Term Prospects Dim." *Los Angeles Times,* January 11, pp. 1, 4.

Steward, Julian H. 1956. *The People of Puerto Rico.* Urbana, IL: University of Illinois Press.

Stoddard, Elwyn R., and J. Hedderson 1987. *Trends and Patterns of Poverty Along the U.S.–Mexico Border.* Las Cruces, NM: Borderlands Research Monograph Series, No. 3.

Sullivan, Mercer L. 1989a. *Getting Paid: Youth Crime and Work in the Inner City.* Ithaca: Cornell University Press.

——— 1989b. "Absent Fathers in the Inner City." *The Annals of the American Academy of Political and Social Science* 501:48–58.

———1990. "An Ethnographic Study of the Number of Persons in Households in Selected New York City Neighborhoods." Washington, DC: U.S. Bureau of the Census, Center for Survey Methods Research.

Szapocznik, Jose, and Roberto Hernandez 1988. "The Cuban American Family." In Charles H. Mindel, Robert W. Habenstein, and Roosevelt Wright, Jr., eds. *Ethnic Families in America*, pp. 160–172. New York: Elsevier.

Szapocznik, Jose, Mercedes A. Scopetta, and Wayne Tillman 1978. "What Changes, What Remains the Same, and What Affects Acculturative Change in Cuban Immigrant Families." In Jose Szapocznik and Maria Cristina Herrera, eds. *Cuban Americans: Acculturation, Adjustment and the Family*, pp. 35–49. Washington, DC: National Coalition of Hispanic Mental Health and Human Services Organization.

Taylor, Paul 1928. *Mexican Labor in the U.S.: Imperial Valley*. Berkeley: University of California Publications in Economics.

——— 1930. *Mexican Labor in the U.S.: Dimit County, Winter Garden District, South Texas*. Berkeley: University of California Publications in Economics

——— 1934. *An American-Mexican Frontier*. Chapel Hill, NC: University of North Carolina Press.

TELACU 1978. "TELACU: A Framework for Greater East Los Angeles Community Union." Los Angeles: TELACU.

Testa, M. 1988. "Ethnic Variations in the Formation of Independent Households by Adolescent Welfare Mothers." Paper prepared for the Population Association of America.

Texas Department of Human Resources 1989. Foodstamp Applications and Caseloads. San Antonio, Texas.

Texas Department of Public Safety 1988. "Crime in Texas." Austin, Texas.

Texas Employment Commission 1990. "South Texas Source Delivery Area." Planning Information PY 1991. Austin, TX: ERA Department.

Texas Labor Market Review 1989. Texas Employment Commission, Austin, Texas. May.

Tiano, Susan B. 1985. *Export Processing, Women's Work, and the Employment Problem in Developing Countries: The Case of the Maquiladora Program in Northern Mexico*. El Paso, Texas: Center for Interamerican and Border Studies, University of Texas, El Paso.

Tienda, Marta, and Jennifer Glass 1984. "Household Structure and Labor Force Participation of Black, Hispanic, and White Mothers." *Demography* 22:381–394.

Tobar, Hector 1990. "Operation MacArthur: Police Announce Strategy to Retake Crime-Plagued Park." *Los Angeles Times*, Section B, pp. 3, 8 June 22.

Tobier, Emanuel 1984. *The Changing Face of Poverty: Trends in New York City's Population in Poverty*. New York: Community Service Society.

Treviño, F., D.B. Trevino, C.A. Stroup, and L. Ray 1989. *The Feminization of Poverty among Hispanic Households*. San Antonio, TX: The Tomas Rivera Center.

Tuck, Ruth 1956. *Not with the Fist*. New York: Harcourt, Brace and Co.

Tucson Daily Citizen 1987. September 11.

——— 1987. December 9.

——— 1988. January 6.

——— 1988. Feburary 12.

——— 1989. April 15.

——— 1989. August 11.

U.S. Border Patrol, Laredo Sector 1988 and 1987. Fiscal Year Report. Laredo, Texas.

U.S. Border Patrol, Laredo Sector 1989. "End of the Month News Releases." Laredo, Texas. June.

U.S. Bureau of the Census 1962. *1960 Census of Population and Housing: Census Tracts.* Final Report PHC(1), 26. Washington, DC: U.S. Government Printing Office.

———— 1963. *1960 Census of Population.* Vol. 1: *Characteristics of the Population, Part 11, Florida.* Washington, DC: U.S. Government Printing Office.

———— 1970. *1970 Census of Population and Housing: Census Tracts. Houston, Texas SMSA.* Washington, DC: U.S. Government Printing Office.

———— 1973. *1970 Census of Population, General Social and Economic Characteristics, Florida.* Final Report PC. Washington, DC: U.S. Government Printing Office.

———— 1983a. *1980 Census of Population, General Social and Economic Characteristics, Florida.* PC 80. Washington, DC: U.S. Government Printing Office.

———— 1983b. *1980 Census of Population and Housing: Census Tracts, Houston, Texas SMSA,* PHC80-2-184. Washington, DC: U.S. Government Printing Office.

———— 1983c. *1980 Census of Population and Housing, Census Tracts, New York, N.Y.–N.J. Standard Metropolitan Statistical Area.* Washington, DC: U.S. Government Printing Office.

———— 1983d. *1980 Census of Population and Housing.*

———— 1983e. "Condition of Hispanics in America Today." Prepared for Subcommittee Hearings on Census and Population (9/13/83), U.S. House of Representatives Committee on Post Office and Civil Service. Washington, DC: Superintendent of Documents.

———— 1991a. "The 1990 Census, Redistricting Data for New Mexico; First Release." Public Law Tape 94-171.

———— 1991b. *The Hispanic Population in the United States: March 1991.* Current Population Reports, Series P-20, No. 455. Washington, DC: U.S. Government Printing Office.

U.S. Commission on Civil Rights 1982. "Confronting Racial Isolation in Miami." Washington, DC: Government Printing Office.

U.S.–Mexico Report 1989a. 8:16–17.

U.S.–Mexico Report 1989b. 8:11.

U.S.–Mexico Report 1989c. 8:18–19.

United Way, Planning and Resource Development Division 1988. *State of the County: Los Angeles 1987.* Los Angeles, CA: United Way, Inc.

Vaca, Nick 1970. "The Mexican American in the Social Sciences." *El Grito* 3:17–52.

Valentine, Betty Lou 1978. *Hustling and Other Hard Work.* New York: John Wiley & Sons.

Van Haitsma, Martha 1991. "Attitudes, Social Context and Labor Force Attachment: Blacks and Immigrant Mexicans in Chicago Poverty Areas." Unpublished manuscript presented at the University of Chicago Urban Poverty and Family Structure Conference.

Vélez-Ibáñez, Carlos G. 1980. "Los Movimientos Chicanos: Problemas y Perspectivas." In David Barkin, ed. *Las Relaciones Mexico/Estados Unidos,* pp. 217–235. Mexico D.F.: Editorial Nueva Imagen.

———— 1983a. *Bonds of Mutual Trust: The Cultural Systems of Rotating Credit Associations among Urban Mexicans the Chicanos.* New Brunswick, NJ: Rutgers University Press.

———— 1983b. *Rituals of Marginality: Politics, Process, and Culture Change in Central Urban Mexico, 1969–1974.* Berkeley and Los Angeles: University of California Press.

———— 1988a. "Forms and Functions among Mexicans in the Southwest: Implications for Classroom Use." Paper delivered at the American Anthropological Association.

———— 1988b. "Networks of Exchange Among Mexicans in the U.S. and Mexico: Local Level Mediating Responses to National and International Transformation." *Urban Anthropology and Studies of Cultural Systems and World Economic Development* 17:27–51.

———— 1989. "Transmission and Patterning of Funds of Knowledge: Shaping and Emergence of Confianza in U.S. Mexican Children." Paper delivered to the Society for Applied Anthropology, Santa Fe, New Mexico.

———— forthcoming. "Plural Strategies of Survival and Cultural Formation in U.S. Mexican Households in a Region of Dynamic Transformation: The U.S.–Mexico Borderlands." In Shep Foreman, ed. *Diagnosing America.* Ann Arbor: University of Michigan Press.

Vélez-Ibáñez, Carlos G., and J.B. Greenberg 1984. "Multidimensional Functions of Non-Market Forms of Exchange among Mexicans/Chicanos in Tucson, Arizona." Unpublished manuscript.

———— 1992. "Formation and Transformation of Funds of Knowledge Among U.S. Mexican Households: Contexts for Educational Reformation in the Southwest Region." *Anthropology and Education Quarterly* 23:313–335.

Vélez-Ibáñez, Carlos G., J.B. Greenberg, and B. Johnstone 1984. "The Ethnic, Economic, and Educational Structure of Tucson, Arizona: The Limits of Possibility for Mexican Americans in 1982." In *Proceedings of the 1984 Meeting of the Rocky Mountain Council on Latin American Studies,* pp. 154–164. Las Cruces, NM: Center for Latin American Studies, New Mexico State University.

Ventura, S.J. 1984. "Births of Hispanic Parentage: 1983–84." *Monthly Vital Statistics Report,* National Center for Health Statistics, Department of Health and Human Services, 36(4), Table 8.

Vergara, Camilo Jose 1991. "Lessons Learned: Lessons Forgotten: Rebuilding New York City's Poor Communities." *The Livable City* 15:3–9.

Vigil, James Diego 1982. "Human Revitalization: The Six Tasks of Victory Outreach." *Drew Gateway* 52:49–59.

———— 1988. *Barrio Gangs.* Austin, TX: University of Texas Press.

Vincent, Maria Girard 1966. "Ritual Kinship in an Urban Setting: Martineztown, New Mexico." Master's thesis, University of New Mexico.

Vogel, Albert W. 1967. *Barelas-Arenal and Los Lunas. A Photographic Essay on Poverty in New Mexico.* Albuquerque: University of New Mexico.

Wagenheim, Kal 1975. *A Survey of Puerto Ricans on the U.S. Mainland.* New York: Praeger.

Waggoner, Laura 1941. *San Jose: A Study in Urbanization.* Master's thesis, University of New Mexico.

Wakefield, Dan 1959. *Island in the City.* New York: Corinth Books.

Waldinger, Roger 1990. "Ethnic Business in Sunset Park." In Louis Winnick, *New People in Old Neighborhoods: The Role of New Immigrants in Rejuvenating New York'sNeighborhoods,* pp. 249–271. New York: Russell Sage Foundation.

Walter, Paul A., Jr. 1939. "The Spanish-Speaking Community in New Mexico." *Sociology and Social Research* 24:150–157.

Warren, Christopher L., John Stack, and John Corbett 1986. "Minority Mobilization in an International City: Rivalry and Conflict in Miami." *PS* 19:626–634.

Webb County Sheriff's Department 1988. Uniform Crime Reports, Laredo, Texas.

Weicher, John 1990. "How Poverty Neighborhoods are Changing." In Laurence Lynn and Michael McGeary, eds. *Inner-City Poverty in the United States,* pp. 69–110. Washington, DC: National Academy Press.

White, Michael J. 1988. "The Segregation and Residential Assimilation of Immigrants." Washington, DC: The Urban Institute.

Wilbanks, William 1984. *Murder in Miami.* Lanham, MD: University Press of America.

Wilson, Kenneth, and Alejandro Portes 1980. "Immigrant Enclaves: An Analysis of the Labor Market Experiences of Cubans in Miami." *American Journal of Sociology* 86:295–319.

Wilson, William Julius 1985. "Cycles of Deprivation and the Underclass Debate." *Social Service Review* 59:541–591.

——— 1987. *The Truly Disadvantaged: The Inner City, the Underclass, and Public Policy.* Chicago: The University of Chicago Press.

——— 1990. "Social Theory and Public Agenda Research: The Challenge of Studying Inner-city Social Dislocations." Paper presented at Annual Meeting of the American Sociological Association.

Winkler, K.J. 1990. "Researcher's Examination of California's Poor Latino Population Prompts Debate Over the Traditional Definitions of the Underclass." *The Chronicle of Higher Education,* October 10, p. 8.

Winnick, Louis 1990. *New People in Old Neighborhoods: The Role of New Immigrants in Rejuvenating New York's Neighborhoods.* New York: Russell Sage Foundation.

Wolf, Eric R. 1966 *Peasants.* Englewood Cliffs, NJ: Prentice Hall.

Woo, Elaine 1988. " '60s 'Blowouts' Leaders of Latino School Protest See Little Change." *Los Angeles Times,* Part II, pp. 1–2, March 7.

Zavella, Patricia 1987. "The Impact of Sunbelt Industrialization on Chicanas." *Frontiers* 8:21–27.

Zinn, Maxine Baca 1976. *The Power Structure of an Urban Barrio.* Master's thesis, University of New Mexico.

Zucker, Norman L., and Naomi F. 1987. *The Guarded Gate: The Reality of American Refugee Policy.* San Diego, CA: Harcourt Brace Jovanovich.

INDEX

Boldface numbers refer to tables and figures.